CIVIL RIGHTS
AND
LIBERTIES
IN THE
1970s

CIVIL RIGHTS
AND
LIBERTIES
IN THE
1970s

Edited by Richard M. Pious
York University

Random House New York

First Edition

987654321

Library of Congress Cataloging in Publication Data

Pious, Richard M   1944–   comp.
  Civil rights and liberties in the 1970's.

  Bibliography: p. 233
  1. Civil rights—United States. I. Title.
KF4749.P5   342'.73'085   72-10897
ISBN 0-394-31707-6

Manufactured in the United States of America. Composed by Cherry Hill
Composition, Pennsauken, N.J. Printed and bound by The Kingsport Press, Inc.,
Kingsport, Tenn.

Designed by James McGuire

In Memory of My Father

Acknowledgments

I should like to thank David Adamany, Larry Jackson, Carol Sanders, Morty Manford, Carl Aron, John Prados, and Arlene Schnier for their help in preparing materials for this edition. I should also like to thank Nancy Nahra, Jane Cullen, and Barry Rossinoff of the editorial staff at Random House.

Contents

CIVIL RIGHTS
AND
LIBERTIES
IN THE
1970s

1 INTRODUCTION

Every nation has its winners and losers. In America the losers are the blacks, the Latins, the American Indians, the poor, uneducated whites, and others locked into inner-city ghettos or dispersed in depressed rural areas. Even in the affluent America of the downtown office building and the suburban development there are losers: women, who are expected to remember that their place is at home or in male-dominated institutions; homosexuals, who know that failure to maintain a "straight" image will subject them to penalties; students, who are "tracked" from high school through college by well-meaning educators intent on placing them in "plastics."

Losers in America are cared for by institutions that kill them with "kindness": a welfare system for the poor that provides less than the minimum income needed to meet nutritional standards; an educational system in ghettos that ends the possibility of college education for most of its students; a correctional system that makes hardened criminals out of juvenile delinquents and recidivists out of adult offenders; and job training programs and employment services that do little more than provide an unskilled proletariat with dead-end jobs.

This book deals with the demands of various demographic and clientele groups, demands that involve a redefinition of the social identity of the members of these groups. (A demographic group is one whose members share racial, social, religious, sexual, and ethnic traits: blacks, black Jews under twenty, etc. A clientele group is one whose members are served by the same bureaucracy: public housing tenants served by the housing project management, clients served by the Legal Services Program, etc.) The articles and judicial decisions contained in this volume describe struggles occurring today. Common to all these struggles is the breakdown of a traditional institution, a set of demands made by a demographic or clientele group contributing to the breakdown.

THE STRUGGLE FOR IDENTITY

Demographic and clientele groups that attempt to gain benefits for their members must press their demands through the political system. At least five kinds of demands may be made:

Procedural Due Process

Procedural due process involves fair and impartial treatment of clientele by officials, so that arbitrary administrative fiat is replaced by the

3

rule of law. Before an action is taken by officials, the agency involved must justify it through reference to statutory or case law or to agency directives. The client must receive adequate advance notice that an action affecting him will be taken, and he may request an administrative hearing prior to its implementation. Welfare procedures often entail special hearings (see *Goldberg* v. *Kelley*), as do juvenile proceedings (see *In re Gault*), housing eviction notices, and school suspension hearings.

At the hearing the client may be represented by competent counsel, has the right to hear charges and evidence against him, and may cross-examine witnesses testifying against him. He must be given the opportunity to present evidence and witnesses in his favor. He may appeal the decision to higher review boards within the agency, and after exhausting his options within the administration, he may appeal to the judiciary. For these purposes there is a written transcript of all proceedings.

Procedural due process preserves the dignity of the individual client. It enables him to challenge arbitrary actions of agency personnel and to demand to be treated as a *person* rather than as a problem. Also, procedural due process can be demanded by a lawyer in order to create a negotiating position for his client. Since the procedures cost the agency time and money, it will in most cases prefer an informal disposition of the matter. If enough clients demand due process rights, the agency may be willing to change its behavior and deal with clients differently.

Finally, the assertion of due process rights may place such a burden on the agency that it is forced to consider drastic changes in its operations. The "fair hearing" (observance of due process) procedures instituted in welfare agencies, for example, led to a massive increase in welfare rolls after organized welfare groups and poverty lawyers combined to aid eligible people in applying for benefits. The increase in the rolls in turn placed such a fiscal burden on many states that the national government was forced to consider major changes in its welfare system. Besides welfare hearings, similar practices are now being followed in agencies dealing with housing grievances and eligibility for unemployment compensation.

The Right to Mandated Services

A second struggle waged by clientele groups is for the right to receive services to which they are entitled by law. If a state establishes a correctional facility to rehabilitate prisoners, it can be argued that officials have an obligation to provide facilities for rehabilitation. The public school system should be expected to educate, rather than simply store, children enrolled in it. Hospitals, mental institutions, homes for the mentally retarded, and homes for the elderly should be required to have an adequate number of supervisors and nurses for each ward. It is not uncommon for wards to be left unattended in these institutions because of financial crises; neither is it uncommon for fatalities or serious accidents to occur in such situations.

The normal condition in American public service institutions is that only a fraction of the universe of needs can be met by the agency and only minimal services provided. For example, the Legal Services Program of the Office of Economic Opportunity serves only one-fourteenth of the eligible population. The struggle to obtain mandated services is based on the notions that all persons in need should be aided and that such aid should be a serious attempt to deal with the problems, rather than a means of institutionalizing, incarcerating, or "storing" people (in public housing or the welfare system or the public schools).

The Right to Equal or Equitable Treatment

Demographic groups, such as blacks, Latins, American Indians, and women, struggle to end discrimination as practiced by public and private organizations against their members. The minimal goal is to see that no invidious discrimination is practiced against members of the group because of race, creed, religion, color, ethnic origin, sex, or sexual orientation. This goal may involve the struggle for *equal* treatment under law.

Demands for *equitable* treatment under law involve a more controversial struggle; groups may ask for additional goods and services to compensate for past deprivation. The use of "benign" quotas in college admission policies or in the government service and preference shown by private businesses in the hiring and promotion of minority group members are attempts to redress past unfairness. The principle of remedial equity is followed by federal courts in dismantling school systems that practice racial segregation. When courts end such de jure segregation, they consciously consider the racial composition in the district in order to end imbalance, and they may provide for busing of students. Remedial equity is also applied by state legislatures and Congress when legislation providing aid to local school districts allows extra funds for poorer school districts.

The question of remedial equity has also arisen in connection with public services. Federal courts are now deciding cases involving the provision of municipal services in ghettos. In some small towns the poorer sections (often inhabited by members of minority groups) do not receive street lights, sewers, paved roads, or other municipal facilities or services. To offer equal treatment would mean that all areas must in the future receive similar treatment; equitable treatment might mean that poor areas would receive additional services and capital expenditures in order to "catch up" with other parts of town.

The Right to Privacy

Government officials often attempt to control the private lives of those to whom they distribute goods and services. Welfare caseworkers may make "midnight raids" and unannounced home visits in attempts to catch recipients with a "man in the house"—a situation that can lead to suspension of benefits. Housing project managers sometimes conduct searches of tenants' apartments, and school officials search students' lockers. Law enforcement agencies invade constitutional rights when, in the absence of probable cause that a crime has been committed, they conduct searches without warrants.

Besides harassment by officials who overstep their authority, there remains the problem of laws that violate the right to privacy. Laws against abortion, contraception, and the dissemination of birth control information, for example, regulate intimate details of heterosexual behavior. Laws against consensual sodomy interfere with the privacy of consenting sexual behavior.

The Rights of Political Expression

First Amendment rights of freedom of speech, press, assembly, and petition for redress of grievances are among the most important constitutional rights, for without them people could not form groups, or protest the effect of bureaucratic behavior. In order to operate effectively, such groups must be free from surveillance, infiltration by agents, harassment, and interception of private communications. Their phones must not be tapped, offices bugged, or activities taped or filmed.

Groups that are harassed must spend time combatting the activities of agents rather than furthering their causes. The general public may assume that the group is subversive if the government is conducting surveillance, and potential members may not join the group. To protect their First Amendment rights, clientele and demographic groups must struggle for adequate judicial and legislative supervision of the activities of law enforcement agencies.

AUTHORITY MAINTENANCE

When organized groups press their demands on public officials, they are likely to receive any of the following responses:

1. The validity of the demands will be denied. The officials will claim that the group speaks only for a disaffected minority.

2. Officials may argue that to accede to the demands would mean giving in to a militant group, raising the specter of a takeover of the agency by an outside group.

3. The officials will characterize those making the demands as "outside agitators" or "hardcore militants" or "troublemakers." Sometimes officials will claim that the membership is disturbed or even mentally ill, and group leaders may be redbaited.

4. Officials will create a clientele advisory group. In many cases members will be handpicked by officials in order to counter the demands of an autonomous clientele group.

5. Officials may implement some demands with much publicity. With public opinion on their side, they can then refuse to implement more meaningful reforms, claiming budget shortages. Or the costly demands may be satisfied temporarily, and when public attention turns elsewhere, the situation will be allowed to deteriorate again. Overcrowding and other inhumane conditions in detention facilities and prisons periodically lead to investigations and alleviation of conditions; yet months later overcrowding is again a problem.

6. "Progressive" officials (i.e., those concerned with their own images and career advancement) will implement their own reforms. These will often involve research and demonstration programs that will affect a tiny fraction of the clientele. These programs serve to improve the professional career prospects of agency personnel who conduct them; they are also "showpiece" programs for the benefit of the mass media, serving to pacify the general public and a naïve clientele. They are bureaucratic ploys and public relations gimmicks, which enable agencies to divert attention from the ineffectiveness of their routine activities.

7. Officials will take the position that they are acting out of charity and giving privileges to clients, rather than performing duties which are required of them. They attempt to suspend services to clients who question their decisions, and this may involve the violation of the clients' constitutional rights. Thus when tenants in housing projects protest the lack of heat, hot water, guards, and windowpanes, they may be expelled from the project for holding a "disruptive" mass protest meeting. In the welfare system the charity view leads caseworkers to use the threat of grant cutoffs to control the private lives of recipients and repress protest.

8. Officials will attempt to professionalize agency personnel by either hiring persons who are college graduates or by upgrading personnel—as many police departments do—by requiring a college degree for advance-

ment. Although this seems like a progressive idea, it carries the danger that the professional code of ethics will be substituted for the rule of law in the agency. The professional will assume that he knows what is best for the client and will consider the point of view of the client irrelevant. Professionalization increases the danger that clients will be treated in a dehumanizing and arbitrary fashion by officials hiding behind professional roles. The agency may also reject claims made by clientele interest groups, legislatures, and political officials, arguing that only the professionals understand the problem.

THE FEDERALISM PROBLEM

At the local and state levels officials must resort to such defenses against clientele groups because their agencies do not receive sufficient funding. Caseloads are too high, staff personnel too poorly paid, and agencies understaffed and poorly supervised. These defects are partly due to public apathy, but they are also due to structural flaws in the American political system.

The traditional theory of federalism views states as laboratories for the solution of social problems. In as large a country as the United States, with its diversity of regional interests and heterogeneous population, local initiative is often effective in dealing with problems. Successful experimentation at the local and state levels can point the way to solution of national problems.

Whatever merit the traditional theory has, it must also be pointed out that localities and states are competitors for industrial and commercial development. They offer investors the advantages of their geographical area (climate, transportation) as well as a certain tax structure and set of labor laws. Obviously the investors will prefer a light tax burden, and if the tax rates rise too high, they may move their facilities elsewhere. A state that spends a great deal on the "losers" (the poor, blacks, and other minorities) must increase its tax rates. It then finds that people enter the state to take advantage of the social benefits and industry and workers leave the area to avoid the tax burden. Also, to the extent that the choice of how to spend tax revenues is left to competing localities and states, expenditures will be directed toward maintaining industry and increasing the attraction for the working and middle classes, rather than toward providing aid for people in need of social services. Therefore, the political strategy of clientele groups must be to press demands on the national political system for funds to support social services.

CIVIL RIGHTS AND LIBERTIES

Demographic groups also find it difficult to win their demands for equal or equitable treatment from state and local officials because of federalism and bureaucratic disfunctions. These groups also turn to national political institutions and the federal judiciary.

The petition for redress of grievances to the national government, guaranteed by the First Amendment of the Bill of Rights, is at the heart of the workings of the federal system, which anticipates that the tyranny of local majorities can be ended by the federal government. The Bill of Rights provides certain due process and other substantive rights to citizens as protection against the actions of the *national* government, as explained above; the Fourteenth Amendment provides that the states and localities within them must provide due process and equal protection under the laws. In several cases, the Supreme Court has interpreted the "due process" clause of the Fourteenth Amendment to "incorporate" many of the protections in the Bill of Rights—that is, to guarantee these protections for the citizen against *state* action.

In a few progressive states in the North, demographic groups often win some symbolic protection of their rights at the local or state level. But often such concessions are designed to pacify the members of the group and induce them to continue to support the political party that sponsored the protective legislation. Because the coverage is limited to only a few states and the provisions of the laws are often weak, the groups attempt to precipitate action by the national government, particularly in such areas as fair housing legislation and equal employment opportunities.

Many demographic groups begin by formulating their goals, often in the form of a "Bill of Rights." The next step is to publicize the asserted rights as a national convention or caucus modeled after those held by the political parties. Prominent politicians are asked to endorse the goals of the group.

Favorable governmental responses include the establishment of study commissions, the convening of conferences on the problems of the group, and the drafting of a legislative proposal. If the legislature is serious about remedying the situation, hearings will be scheduled by committees and a bill will be reported to the floor for a vote.

If a law is passed, the struggle for civil rights and liberties has just begun. The group may find that it has achieved a symbolic victory rather than substantive gains. Laws and executive orders to protect rights begin with ringing declarations and slogans, but the specific provisions sometimes make a mockery of the act:

1. Enforcement provisions may not be included. Instead, the agency charged with administering the law may be given only the power to mediate or conciliate complaints. No criminal penalties for violation of the law will be included. Or the penalties will be very weak, and the agency personnel too few in number to make more than minimal enforcement efforts.

2. The agency may lack the power to take affirmative action to ensure compliance with the laws. It will not be permitted to "test" for violations by using its own personnel to impersonate group members who may suffer discrimination. Instead, the agency must wait for complaints.

3. The agency will be permitted to dispose of cases on an individual basis, but forbidden to issue orders affecting the policies behind such discrimination. With resources limited, the time needed to dispose of each case may run to years.

4. The law may provide that the agency cannot litigate in the courts to secure compliance with the law by private individuals. The burden of prosecuting the offender rests with the individual.

5. The law may provide that state courts must decide cases brought by the agency before they can be taken to a federal court. But the congestion of the state court system may delay resolution of the issues. Also, state courts are often less sympathetic to civil rights claims than are federal courts, especially in the South.

Civil rights laws and executive orders are of little value unless they provide for aggressive and massive administrative enforcement, stiff penalties for violators, and immediate litigation in the federal courts. Most civil rights legislation at both the state and national levels does not meet these standards.

JUDICIAL PROTECTION FOR GROUPS

Some of the great symbolic victories for groups have come about through litigation before the Supreme Court. These landmark decisions may declare unconstitutional (and hence null and void) laws of Congress, state laws, and actions of federal and state agencies. As a result of these decisions, the elected officials are often forced to develop new policies and provide new rights for demographic groups and new services for clientele groups. Such litigation, advanced deliberately by lawyers representing the groups, is part of a conscious strategy for social change.

Because the Supreme Court is the final arbiter of the constitutionality of government action, our Constitution embodies the principle of *judicial supremacy*. Yet nowhere in the Constitution itself is that power specifically mentioned; rather, it was asserted by the Supreme Court itself in cases it decided early in the nineteenth century. Today, that power is conceded to the Supreme Court by the other branches of government and the states. In good measure the Supreme Court retains the power of judicial supremacy because it is not really the final arbiter of public policy; its decisions can be nullified by the actions of other branches of the national government or by state governments through the operation of *checks and balances* provided for in the Constitution.

Judicial decisions are not self-executing. The Supreme Court is considered the least dangerous branch of government, because its decisions depend for their effect on implementation by the other branches of government. For example, after the Court ordered an end to racial segregation in public schools "with all deliberate speed," state and local officials in the South adopted a policy of "massive resistance." But the President made no attempt to lead the nation in following the Court, and Congress took no action. The result was that only token desegregation occurred until Congress passed the Civil Rights Act of 1964 and the Elementary and Secondary Education Act of 1965 and the Department of Health, Education, and Welfare began to attack school segregation, with strong support from President Lyndon Johnson.

The Supreme Court has placed restrictions on the interrogation practices of local police departments. In *Miranda* v. *Arizona*, decided in 1966, Chief Justice Earl Warren propounded the now famous "Miranda rule." This stipulated that no statement obtained from a criminal suspect during custodial interrogation could be introduced as evidence against him in a trial unless he had been clearly warned prior to the interrogation that he had the right to remain silent, that anything he said could later be used against him in a court of law, that he had the right to have counsel present during questioning, and that if he lacked funds to obtain a lawyer, he would be provided with one by the state. If, however, a suspect who had been warned of these rights knowingly and intelligently waived them prior to his questioning, then any statement he made could be used against him in court.

Yet because compliance by local officials is with the letter rather than the spirit of the law, abuses still occur. The police can either develop new procedures or continue to use their present interrogation techniques so that the intent of the Supreme Court decision is nullified. Unless a federal judge is placed in every squad car or precinct interrogation room, the implementation of the decision will depend on the good faith of local officials. The attitude of the local police, not the protection offered by the Supreme Court, is the most important factor in determining how interrogations will proceed.

The selection of members of the Supreme Court is subject to political pressures. The President appoints justices with the advice and consent of the Senate. He can nominate members likely to reverse certain decisions. Since a vacancy occurs on the Court approximately every eighteen months, no Court can defy a president for two terms (barring unexpected longevity). A patient president is bound to create his own majority on the Court, provided the Senate confirms his nominees.

The number of justices on the Court is subject to change. By law the number of justices can be increased; the president and Congress can "pack" the Court with additional justices who would overturn a decision that is unpopular with their respective constituents.

Much of the jurisdiction of the Supreme Court can be limited. The Congress (under Article III, Section 2 of the Constitution) may make "exceptions" to the appellate jurisdiction of the Supreme Court. It may take away the jurisdiction of the Court in certain areas and create new courts or regulatory agencies to decide the cases. There is even a proposal that Congress create a "Court of the Union," composed of the chief justices of the fifty state high courts, to hear certain kinds of cases, thus removing them from the jurisdiction of the Supreme Court.

Decisions can be overturned by the passage of a constitutional amendment. Two-thirds of the members of each house of Congress can propose an amendment, or two-thirds of the state legislatures can tell a convention to draft a constitutional amendment. If three-fourths of these legislatures or conventions called in three-fourths of the states ratify the proposal, it becomes a part of the Constitution and overturns any contrary decision of the Supreme Court. The amendment providing for an income tax, for example, was passed as a response to a Supreme Court decision finding such a tax unconstitutional. More recently, amendments have been proposed to reverse Supreme Court decisions prohibiting religious prayers in public schools, mandating reapportionment of state legislature districts, and desegregating public school systems.

Thus, judicial supremacy does not prevent other political institutions from overturning the decisions of the Supreme Court. Even if the Court were to usurp power (which it does not) in making controversial decisions, there is no danger of government by judiciary under the checks and balance system.

Only rarely do federal courts or the Supreme Court impose sweeping changes when they decide cases. Most often the judiciary follows a policy of self-imposed restraint, rather than the contrary policy of "judicial activism." For example, courts attempt, if possible, to follow precedents (cases previously decided). Rarely will the Supreme Court overturn a previous decision directly; it prefers to modify the decision or limit its reach. This restraint provides for incremental changes in case law rather than sweeping revision; it means that if a series of prior cases have legitimized certain bureaucratic practices, the Courts will modify these practices slowly. The Supreme Court took almost thirty years to reach the "Miranda Warning," which affected police interrogation of suspects; and hundreds of federal court cases chipped away at police practices prior to that landmark decision.

When dealing with bureaucracies, the lower courts prefer to guarantee due process rights and leave benefits and services to the determination of the legislature. The Supreme Court takes a more active role in guaranteeing procedural due process in bureaucracies than in providing for substantive economic benefits.

The Equal Protection Clause is generally interpreted to mean that any rational standard adopted by the legislature will be upheld by the Court. This interpretation of the clause provides great flexibility for legislatures and bureaucrats in establishing classifications of clientele or demographic groups. Only rarely will the Court take a more active role, and it does so only when it considers a particular policy area to be of "fundamental interest" and the classification made by the legislature to be "suspect." Racial classifications are now considered suspect, but classifications based on wealth usually have not been held suspect by the Supreme Court. Moreover, few areas of public policy are considered "fundamental." So even though the Supreme Court has a means for using the equal protection clause to strike down many forms of discrimination, it prefers—under the doctrine of "judicial restraint"—to take the approach that gives maximum latitude to elected and appointed political officials. The tendency toward restraint can be expected to increase in the next few years as the majority fashioned by President Richard Nixon refuses to follow the Warren Court's approach of being a catalyst for fundamental social reform.

2 RACISM

American society has always been racist. Almost two hundred years ago the Constitution provided, *sub silentio,* for the perpetuation of slavery and explicitly noted that "other persons" not citizens of the United States were to be counted as three-fifths of a person in the enumeration of the population. Today, descendants of the slaves earn approximately three-fifths of the average income earned by whites.

The Thirteenth Amendment (1865) freed the slaves and gave them citizenship, the Fourteenth Amendment (1868) provided that all citizens were to be treated equally and granted due process of law, and the Fifteenth Amendment (1870) specifically provided that suffrage could not be denied male inhabitants of a state on the grounds of race, color, or previous condition of servitude. The Civil Rights Act of 1875 provided for nondiscriminatory treatment in many other areas of life.

But these were limited victories. By the end of Reconstruction the former slaves were in economic bondage. By the 1890s their vote had been taken away through the use of literacy tests and other devices and segregation had been established in most American institutions. The Civil Rights Act of 1875 was declared unconstitutional by the Supreme Court in 1883, and the Fourteenth Amendment provision reducing the congressional representation of states that discriminated in suffrage was not enforced against the South. It was as if part of the Constitution had been put to sleep.

The South embraced Segregation through positive use of state law and local ordinances. The North created a segregated society through private discriminatory action as well as through manipulation of federal policies. The Supreme Court, for example, struck down ordinances requiring segregated housing as early as 1917 in *Buchanan* v. *Warley,* yet it was not until 1948 in *Shelley* v. *Kraemer* that it prohibited lower courts from honoring racially restrictive covenants in property deeds. Thus, the transfer of most real estate involved racial discrimination untouched by the courts until the 1950s. After World War II, federal highway programs, GI loans, and federal mortgage programs created opportunities for suburban development. Federal guidelines for bankers regarding FHA-insured mortgages and the codes of local real estate brokers combined to segregate people by income and race. The inner cities contained ghettos and reservations for the blacks, Latins, ethnic immigrants, and the elderly, while the urban fringes and suburbs filled up with middle-class and working-class whites.

School systems in most parts of the country were also segregated by race (and sometimes by income). Blacks, Indians, Orientals, and

Mexican-Americans have been at one time or another segregated by state law in separate school systems in the South, while in the North housing patterns have segregated schools by race, and the private school systems have enabled the urban upper-middle classes to avoid confronting the failure of the public school system.

In the 1950s, as a result of litigation before the Supreme Court sponsored by the National Association for the Advancement of Colored People, the segregated school systems of the South were declared unconstitutional. In *Sweatt* v. *Painter* the Supreme Court held that separate law schools for blacks and whites in a state was prohibited by the Equal Protection Clause of the Fourteenth Amendment when the white school could be demonstrated to be superior in both physical facilities and the intangible qualities making for greatness in a law school. *McLaurin* v. *Oklahoma State Regents* struck down rules which segregated a black student from white classmates in a graduate school. Finally, *Brown* v. *Board of Education* ruled unconstitutional the maintenance of segregated public school systems.

These decisions did not solve the problem of de facto segregation in the North. While no state may maintain either a segregated school system or dual school systems, does it have any obligation under the Constitution to take affirmative action to achieve racial balance in any particular school or school system? When federal courts and the Supreme Court began ruling that racial imbalance should be ended, school busing exploded as the major domestic political issue of the 1970s. On one side was the Supreme Court and some lower federal courts, and on the other side was President Richard Nixon, who opposed anything more than the end of de jure segregation. Proposals for legislation and a constitutional amendment banning busing were defeated in Congress in 1972.

The segregated school systems of the South derived their constitutional legitimacy from the landmark case of Plessy v. Ferguson, **decided by the Supreme Court in 1896. That case, involving segregated railroad facilities, upheld segregation of the races as a reasonable exercise of state power not forbidden by the Constitution. Lower federal courts then interpreted the decision to mean that segregated facilities must be "separate but equal" in order to comply with the Equal Protection Clause of the Fourteenth Amendment (the phrase does not appear in the decision of the Supreme Court).**

Even the "separate but equal" doctrine was not followed in practice: Educational expenditures for white students far exceeded those for blacks; the funds given to the state college systems for blacks were far less than those the

university and graduate school systems for whites received; public accommodations for blacks (drinking fountains, toilets, etc.) were inferior to those
provided for whites; and some municipal services provided to whites were
often not provided to blacks (street lights, garbage collection, paved roads).
Yet it took fifty years for the judicial system to strike down segregated school
systems, an example of the slow pace of litigation that involves social justice.

Plessy v. Ferguson

Mr. Justice Brown . . . delivered the opinion of the court. . . .

The constitutionality of this act is attacked upon the ground that it
conflicts both with the Thirteenth Amendment of the Constitution,
abolishing slavery, and the Fourteenth Amendment, which prohibits
certain restrictive legislation on the part of the states.

1. That it does not conflict with the Thirteenth Amendment, which
abolished slavery and involuntary servitude, except as a punishment for
crime, is too clear for argument. . . .

A statute which implies merely a legal distinction between the white
and colored races—a distinction which is founded in the color of the
two races, and which must always exist so long as white men are distinguished from the other race by color—has no tendency to destroy
the legal equality of the two races, or reestablish a state of involuntary
servitude. Indeed, we do not understand that the Thirteenth Amendment
is strenuously relied upon by the plaintiff in error in this connection.

2. By the Fourteenth Amendment, all persons born or naturalized in
the United States, and subject to the jurisdiction thereof, are made
citizens of the United States and of the state wherein they reside; and
the states are forbidden from making or enforcing any law which shall

From *Plessy* v. *Ferguson,* 163 U.S. Reports 537. (An explanation of notations
identifying court cases and other legal materials appears in the Research Guide
—Ed.)

abridge the privileges or immunities of citizens of the United States, or shall deprive any person of life, liberty, or property without due process of law, or deny to any person within their jurisdiction the equal protection of the laws. . . .

The object of the amendment was undoubtedly to enforce the absolute equality of the two races before the law, but in the nature of things it could not have been intended to abolish distinctions based upon color, or to enforce social, as distinguished from political equality, or a commingling of the two races upon terms unsatisfactory to either. Laws permitting, and even requiring, their separation in places where they are liable to be brought into contact do not necessarily imply the inferiority of either race to the other, and have been generally, if not universally, recognized as within the competency of the state legislatures in the exercise of their police power. The most common instance of this is connected with the establishment of separate schools for white and colored children, which has been held to be a valid exercise of the legislative power even by courts of states where the political rights of the colored race have been longest and most earnestly enforced. . . .

It is claimed by the plaintiff in error that, in any mixed community, the reputation of belonging to the dominant race, in this instance the white race, is property, in the same sense that a right of action, or of inheritance, is property. Conceding this to be so, for the purposes of this case, we are unable to see how this statute deprives him of, or in any way affects his right to, such property. If he be a white man and assigned to a colored coach, he may have his action for damages against the company for being deprived of his so called property. Upon the other hand, if he be a colored man and be so assigned, he has been deprived of no property, since he is not lawfully entitled to the reputation of being a white man.

In this connection, it is also suggested by the learned counsel for the plaintiff in error that the same argument that will justify the state legislature in requiring railways to provide separate accommodations for the two races will also authorize them to require separate cars to be provided for people whose hair is of a certain color, or who are aliens, or who belong to certain nationalities, or to enact laws requiring colored people to walk upon one side of the street, and white people upon the other, or requiring white men's houses to be painted white, and colored men's black, or their vehicles or business signs to be of different colors, upon the theory that one side of the street is as good as the other, or that a house or vehicle of one color is as good as one of another color. The reply to all this is that every exercise of the police power must be reasonable, and extend only to such laws as are enacted in good faith for the promotion of the public good, and not for the annoyance or oppression of a particular class. . . .

So far, then, as a conflict with the Fourteenth Amendment is concerned, the case reduces itself to the question whether the statute of Louisiana is a reasonable regulation, and with respect to this there must necessarily be a large discretion on the part of the legislature. In determining the question of reasonableness it is at liberty to act with reference to the established usages, customs, and traditions of the people, and with a view to the promotion of their comfort, and the preservation of the public peace and good order. Gauged by this standard, we cannot say that a law which authorizes or even requires the separation of the two races in public conveyances is unreasonable, or more obnoxious to the Fourteenth Amendment than the acts of Congress requiring separate schools for colored children in the District of Columbia, the constitutionality of which does not seem to have been questioned, or the corresponding acts of state legislatures.

We consider the underlying fallacy of the plaintiff's argument to consist in the assumption that the enforced separation of the two races stamps the colored race with a badge of inferiority. If this be so, it is not by reason of anything found in the act, but solely because the colored race chooses to put that construction upon it. The argument necessarily assumes that if, as has been more than once the case, and is not unlikely to be so again, the colored race should become the dominant power in the state legislature, and should enact a law in precisely similar terms, it would thereby relegate the white race to an inferior position. We imagine that the white race, at least, would not acquiesce in this assumption. The argument also assumes that social prejudices may be overcome by legislation, and that equal rights cannot be secured to the Negro except by an enforced commingling of the two races. We cannot accept this proposition. If the two races are to meet upon terms of social equality, it must be the result of natural affinities, a mutual appreciation of each other's merits, and a voluntary consent of individuals. . . .

The judgment of the court below is, therefore, affirmed.

Mr. Justice Harlan, dissenting . . .

The white race deems itself to be the dominant race in this country. And so it is, in prestige, in achievements, in education, in wealth, and in power. So, I doubt not, it will continue to be for all time, if it remains true to its great heritage and holds fast to the principles of constitutional liberty. But in view of the Constitution, in the eye of the law, there is in this country no superior, dominant ruling class of citizens. There is no caste here. Our Constitution is color-blind, and neither knows nor tolerates classes among citizens. In respect of civil rights, all citizens are equal before the law. The humblest is the peer of the most powerful. The law regards man as man, and takes no account of his surroundings or of his color when his civil rights as guaranteed by the supreme law of the land are involved. It is, therefore, to be regretted that this high tribunal, the final expositor of the fundamental law of the land, has reached the conclusion that it is competent for a state to regulate the enjoyment by citizens of their civil rights solely on the basis of race. . . .

The sure guarantee of the peace and security of each race is the clear, distinct, unconditional recognition by our governments, national and state, of every right that inheres in civil freedom, and of the equality before the law of all citizens of the United States without regard to race. State enactments, regulating the enjoyment of civil rights, upon the basis of race, and cunningly devised to defeat legitimate results of the war, under the pretence of recognizing equality of rights, can have no other result than to render permanent peace impossible, and to keep alive a conflict of races, the continuance of which must do harm to all concerned. . . .

The arbitrary separation of citizens, on the basis of race, while they are on a public highway, is a badge of servitude wholly inconsistent with the civil freedom and the equality before the law established by the Constitution. It cannot be justified upon any legal grounds. . . .

Until 1954 the laws of seventeen states, and the District of Columbia, required maintenance of racially segregated schools. In 1954, the Supreme Court in Brown v. Board of Education determined such racial segregation unconstitutional. The following year the Court rejected arguments of the National Association for the Advancement of Colored People that desegregation should be ordered within two years and, instead, adopted the guideline "with all deliberate speed." It was not immediately clear what the Court meant by that phrase, but many areas of the South adopted the strategy of "massive resistance" in an attempt to find out.

Brown v. Board of Education (I)

Mr. Chief Justice Warren delivered the opinion of the Court.

In each of the cases, minors of the Negro race, through their legal representatives, seek the aid of the courts in obtaining admission to the public schools of their community on a nonsegregated basis. In each instance, they had been denied admission to schools attended by white children under laws requiring or permitting segregation according to race.

This segregation was alleged to deprive the plaintiffs of the equal protection of the laws under the Fourteenth Amendment. In each of the cases other than the Delaware case, a three-judge federal district court denied relief to the plaintiffs on the so-called "separate but equal" doctrine announced by this court in *Plessy* v. *Ferguson.* . . .

Under that doctrine, equality of treatment is accorded when the races are provided substantially equal facilities, even though these facilities be separate. In the Delaware case, the Supreme Court of Delaware adhered to that doctrine, but ordered that the plaintiffs be admitted to the white schools because of their superiority to the Negro schools.

The plaintiffs contend that segregated public schools are not "equal" and cannot be made "equal," and that, hence, they are deprived of the equal protection of the laws. Because of the obvious importance of the question presented, the Court took jurisdiction. Argument was heard in the 1952 term on certain questions propounded by the Court.

Reargument was largely devoted to the circumstances surrounding the adoption of the Fourteenth Amendment in 1868. It covered, exhaustively, consideration of the amendment in Congress, ratification by the states, then existing practices in racial segregation, and the views of proponents and opponents of the amendment.

This discussion and our own investigation convince us that, although these sources cast some light, it is not enough to resolve the problem with which we are faced.

At best, they are inconclusive. The most avid proponents of the post-war amendments undoubtedly intended them to remove all legal distinctions among "all persons born or naturalized in the United States."

Their opponents, just as certainly, were antagonistic to both the letter and the spirit of the amendments and wished them to have the

From *Brown* v. *Board of Education*, U.S. Reports 98 Lawyers' Edition 873.

most limited effect. What others in Congress and the state legislatures had in mind cannot be determined with any degree of certainty.

An additional reason for the illusive nature of the amendment's history, with respect to segregated schools, is the status of public education at that time. In the. South, the movement toward free common schools, supported by general taxation, had not yet taken hold. Education of white children was largely in the hands of private groups. Education of Negroes was almost nonexistent, and practically all of the race was illiterate. In fact, any education of Negroes was forbidden by law in some states.

Today, in contrast, many Negroes have achieved outstanding success in the arts and sciences as well as in the business and professional world. It is true that public education has already advanced further in the North, but the effect of the amendment on Northern states was generally ignored in the Congressional debates.

Even in the North, the conditions of public education did not approximate those existing today. The curriculum was usually rudimentary; ungraded schools were common in rural areas; the school term was but three months a year in many states; and compulsory school attendance was virtually unknown.

As a consequence, it is not surprising that there should be so little in the history of the Fourteenth Amendment relating to its intended effect on public education. . . .

Our decision, therefore, cannot turn on merely a comparison of these tangible factors in the Negro and white schools involved in each of the cases. We must look instead to the effect of segregation itself on public education.

In approaching this problem, we cannot turn the clock back to 1868, when the amendment was adopted, or even to 1896, when *Plessy* v. *Ferguson* was written. We must consider public education in the light of its full development and its present place in American life throughout the nation. Only in this way can it be determined if segregation in public schools deprives these plaintiffs of the equal protection of the laws.

Today, education is perhaps the most important function of state and local governments. Compulsory school attendance laws and the great expenditures for education both demonstrate our recognition of the importance of education to our democratic society. It is required in the performance of our most basic public responsibilities, even service in the armed forces. It is the very foundation of good citizenship.

Today, it is a principal instrument in awakening the child to cultural values, in preparing him for later professional training, and in helping him to adjust normally to his environment.

In these days, it is doubtful that any child may reasonably be expected to succeed in life if he is denied the opportunity of an education. Such an opportunity, where the state has undertaken to provide it, is a right which must be made available to all on equal terms.

We come then to the question presented: Does segregation of children in public schools solely on the basis of race, even though the physical facilities and other "tangible" factors may be equal, deprive the children of the minority group of equal educational opportunities? We believe that it does.

In *Sweatt* v. *Painter* . . . in finding that a segregated law school for Negroes could not provide them equal educational opportunities, this court relied in large part on "those qualities which are incapable of objective measurement but which make for greatness in a law school."

In *McLaurin* v. *Oklahoma State Regents* . . . the court, in requiring that a Negro admitted to a white graduate school be treated like all other students, again resorted to intangible considerations: ". . . his ability to study, engage in discussions and exchange views with other students, and, in general, to learn his profession.

Such considerations apply with added force to children in grade and high schools. To separate them from others of similar age and qualifications solely because of their race generates a feeling of inferiority as to their status in the community that may affect their hearts and minds in a way unlikely ever to be undone.

The effect of this separation on their educational opportunities was well stated by a finding in the Kansas case by a court which nevertheless felt compelled to rule against the Negro plaintiffs:

> Segregation of white and colored children in public schools has a detrimental effect upon the colored children. The impact is greater when it has the sanction of the law; for the policy of separating the races is usually interpreted as denoting the inferiority of the Negro group.
> A sense of inferiority affects the motivation of a child to learn. Segregation with the sanction of the law, therefore, has a tendency to retard the educational and mental development of Negro children and to deprive them of some of the benefits they would receive in a racially integrated school system.

Whatever may have been the extent of psychological knowledge at the time of *Plessy* v. *Ferguson*, this finding is amply supported by modern authority.

. . . Any language in *Plessy* v. *Ferguson* contrary to this finding is rejected.

We conclude that in the field of public education the doctrine of "separate but equal" has no place. Separate educational facilities are inherently unequal. Therefore, we hold that the plaintiffs and others similarly situated for whom the actions have been brought are, by reasons of the segregation complained of, deprived of the equal protection of the laws guaranteed by the Fourteenth Amendment. This disposition makes unnecessary any discussion whether such segregation also violates the Due Process Clause of the Fourteenth Amendment.

Brown v. Board of Education (II)

Mr. Chief Justice Warren delivered the opinion of the Court.

Full implementation of these constitutional principles may require solution of varied local school problems. School authorities have the primary responsibility for elucidating, assessing, and solving these problems: courts will have to consider whether the action of school authorities constitutes good faith implementation of the governing constitutional principles. Because of their proximity to local conditions and the possible need for further hearings, the courts which originally heard these cases can best perform this judicial appraisal. Accordingly, we believe it appropriate to remand the cases to those courts.

In fashioning and effectuating the decrees, the courts will be guided by equitable principles. Traditionally, equity has been characterized by a practical flexibility in shaping its remedies and by a facility for adjusting and reconciling public and private needs. These cases call for the exercise of these traditional attributes of equity power. At stake is the personal interest of the plaintiffs in admission to public schools as soon as practicable on a nondiscriminatory basis. To effectuate this interest may call for elimination of a variety of obstacles in making the transition to school systems operated in accordance with the constitutional principles set forth in our May 17, 1954, decision. Courts of equity may properly take into account the public interest in the elimination of such

From *Brown v. Board of Education*, 99 Lawyers' Edition 1083.

obstacles in a systematic and effective manner. But it should go without saying that the vitality of these constitutional principles cannot be allowed to yield simply because of disagreement with them.

While giving weight to these public and private considerations, the courts will require that the defendants make a prompt and reasonable start toward full compliance with our May 17, 1954, ruling. Once such a start has been made, the courts may find that additional time is necessary to carry out the ruling in an effective manner. The burden rests upon the defendants to establish that such time is necessary in the public interest and is consistent with good faith compliance at the earliest practicable date. To that end, the courts may consider problems related to administration, arising from the physical condition of the school plant, the school transportation system, personnel, revision of school districts and attendance areas into compact units to achieve a system of determining admission to the public schools on a nonracial basis, and revision of local laws and regulations which may be necessary in solving the foregoing problems. They will also consider the adequacy of any plans the defendants may propose to meet these problems and to effectuate a transition to a racially nondiscriminatory school system. . . .

It is so ordered.

After the second Brown decision the struggle over school desegregation in the South began. State officials vowed "massive resistance" and refused to desegregate except under federal court order. State legislatures passed "freedom of choice" laws that would prevent school authorities from assigning students to neighborhood schools on an integrated basis. State legislatures provided tuition grant programs for parents wishing to send children to private schools in areas affected by desegregation orders. Only in the border states, such as West Virginia, Kentucky, Missouri, and Oklahoma, and in the District of Columbia was there more than token compliance in the 1950s.

In 1964 Congress passed Title VI of the Civil Rights Act of 1964, and the Department of Health, Education, and Welfare was thereupon empowered to end federal aid to school systems practicing racial discrimination. The Justice Department was authorized to intervene in federal court proceedings to obtain desegregation orders against local school systems. By the late 1960s substantial numbers of black children were attending schools with whites, and in the early 1970s the last of the dual school systems were finally being dismantled.

Yet the end of de jure segregation did not end the problems of de facto segregation based on housing patterns in the North or the South. Most schools would still remain segregated in the North, and "freedom of choice" and private academies in the South kept most black children in segregated schools. Within integrated schools, officials still segregated pupils in classes on the basis of race, or "placement tests" would put all black children into one classroom and all white children into different classrooms.

In the late 1960s federal courts and the Supreme Court began requiring busing in order to achieve racial balance in Southern schools which had previously been segregated. The most important of these decisions was Swann v. Charlotte-Mecklenburg, Board of Education, **delivered by a unanimous court headed by Chief Justice Warren E. Burger. Since that 1971 decision, lower federal courts have broadened the ruling to require busing across city lines. The suburbs and more affluent whites are now facing the prospect of school busing affecting their children.**

Swann v. Charlotte-Mecklenburg

Mr. Chief Justice Burger delivered the opinion of the Court.

We granted certiorari in this case to review important issues as to the duties of school authorities and the scope of powers of federal courts under this Court's mandates to eliminate racially separate public schools established and maintained by state action (*Brown* v. *Board of Education*). . . .

This case and those argued with it arose in states having a long history of maintaining two sets of schools in a single school system deliberately operated to carry out a governmental policy to separate pupils in schools solely on the basis of race. That was what *Brown* v. *Board of Education* was all about. These cases present us with the problem of defining in more precise terms than heretofore the scope of the duty of school authorities and district courts in implementing *Brown I* and the mandate to eliminate dual systems and establish unitary systems at once. . . . This Court, in *Brown I*, appropriately dealt with the large constitutional principles; other federal courts had to grapple with the flinty, intractable realities of day-to-day implementation of those consti-

From *Swann* v. *Charlotte-Mecklenburg*, 28 Lawyers' Edition 2nd 554.

tutional commands. Their efforts, of necessity, embraced a process of "trial and error," and our effort to formulate guidelines must take into account their experience. . . .

The Charlotte-Mecklenburg school system, the forty-third largest in the nation, encompasses the city of Charlotte and surrounding Mecklenburg County, North Carolina. The area is large—550 square miles—spanning roughly 22 miles east-west and 36 miles north-south. During the 1968–1969 school year the system served more than 84,000 pupils in 107 schools. Approximately 71 per cent of the pupils were found to be white and 29 per cent Negro. As of June 1969 there were approximately 24,000 Negro students in the system, of whom 21,000 attended schools within the city of Charlotte. Two-thirds of those 21,000—approximately 14,000 Negro students—attended 21 schools which were either totally Negro or more than 99 per cent Negro.

This situation came about under a desegregation plan approved by the district court at the commencement of the present litigation in 1965, . . . based upon geographic zoning with a free transfer provision. The present proceedings were initiated in September 1968 by Petitioner Swann's motion. . . . All parties now agree that in 1969 the system fell short of achieving the unitary school system that those cases require.

The district court held numerous hearings and received voluminous evidence. In addition to finding certain actions of the school board to be discriminatory, the court also found that residential patterns in the city and county resulted in part from federal, state, and local government action other than school board decisions. School board action based on these patterns, for example, by locating schools in Negro residential areas and fixing the size of the schools to accommodate the needs of immediate neighborhoods, resulted in segregated education. These findings were subsequently accepted by the court of appeals.

In April 1969 the district court ordered the school board to come forward with a plan for both faculty and student desegregation. . . . In December 1969 the district court held that the board's submission was unacceptable and appointed an expert in education administration, Dr. John Finger, to prepare a desegregation plan. Thereafter in February 1970, the district court was presented with two alternative pupil assignment plans—the finalized "board plan" and the "Finger plan."

The Board Plan

As finally submitted, the school board plan closed seven schools and reassigned their pupils. It restructured school attendance zones to achieve greater racial balance but maintained existing grade structures and rejected techniques such as pairing and clustering as part of a desegregation effort. The plan created a single athletic league, eliminated the previously racial basis of the school bus system, provided racially mixed faculties and administrative staffs, and modified its free transfer plan into an optional majority-to-minority transfer system.

The board plan proposed substantial assignment of Negroes to nine of the system's ten high schools, producing 17 per cent to 36 per cent Negro population in each. The projected Negro attendance at the tenth school, Independence, was 2 per cent. The proposed attendance zones for the high schools were typically shaped like wedges of a pie, extending outward from the center of the city to the suburban and rural areas of the county in order to afford residents of the center city area access to outlying schools.

As for junior high schools, the board plan rezoned the twenty-one school areas so that in twenty the Negro attendance would range from 0 per cent to 38 per cent. The other school, located in the heart of the Negro residential area, was left with an enrollment of 90 per cent Negro.

The board plan with respect to elementary schools relied entirely upon gerrymandering of geographic zones. More than half of the Negro elementary pupils were left in nine schools that were 86 per cent to 100 per cent Negro; approximately half of the white elementary pupils were assigned to schools 86 per cent to 100 per cent white.

The Finger Plan

The plan submitted by the court-appointed expert, Dr. Finger, adopted the school board zoning plan for senior high schools with one modification: it required that an additional 300 Negro students be transported from the Negro residential area of the city to the nearly all-white Independence High School.

The Finger plan for the junior high schools employed much of the rezoning plan of the board, combined with the creation of nine "satellite" zones. Under the satellite plan, inner-city Negro students were assigned by attendance zones to nine outlying predominantly white junior high schools, thereby substantially desegregating every junior high school in the system.

The Finger plan departed from the board plan chiefly in its handling of the system's seventy-six elementary schools. Rather than relying solely upon geographic zoning, Dr. Finger proposed use of zoning, pairing, and grouping techniques, with the result that student bodies throughout the system would range from 9 per cent to 38 per cent Negro.

. . .

Nearly seventeen years ago this Court held, in explicit terms, that state-imposed segregation by race in public schools denies equal protection of the laws. At no time has the Court deviated in the slightest degree from that holding or its constitutional underpinnings. None of the parties before us challenges the Court's decision of May 17, 1954, that "in the field of public education the doctrine of 'separate but equal' has no place. Separate educational facilities are inherently unequal. Therefore, we hold that the plaintiffs and others similarly situated . . . are, by reason of the segregation complained of, deprived of the equal protection of the laws guaranteed by the Fourteenth Amendment. . . ."

. . .

Over the fifteen years since *Brown II,* many difficulties were encountered in implementation of the basic constitutional requirement that the state not discriminate between public school children on the basis of their race. Nothing in our national experience prior to 1955 prepared anyone for dealing with changes and adjustments of the magnitude and complexity encountered since then. Deliberate resistance of some to the Court's mandates has impeded the good-faith efforts of others to bring school systems into compliance. The detail and nature of these dilatory tactics have been noted frequently by this Court and other courts.

By the time the Court considered *Green* v. *County School Board,* . . . very little progress had been made in many areas where dual school systems had historically been maintained by operation of state laws. In *Green,* the Court was confronted with a record of a freedom-of-choice program that the district court had found to operate in fact to preserve a dual system more than a decade after *Brown II.* While acknowledging that a freedom-of-choice concept could be a valid remedial measure in some circumstances, its failure to be effective in *Green* required that

> The burden on a school board today is to come forward with a plan that promises realistically to work . . . *now* . . . until it is clear that state-imposed segregation has been completely removed. . . .

This was plain language, yet the 1969 Term of Court brought fresh evidence of the dilatory tactics of many school authorities. *Alexander* v. *Holmes County Board of Education* . . . restated the basic obligation asserted in *Griffin* v. *School Board* . . . and *Green* . . . that the remedy must be implemented *forthwith.*

The problems encountered by the district courts and courts of appeals make plain that we should now try to amplify guidelines, however incomplete and imperfect, for the assistance of school authorities and courts. The failure of local authorities to meet their constitutional obligations aggravated the massive problem of converting from the state-enforced discrimination of racially separate school systems. This process has been rendered more difficult by changes since 1954 in the structure and patterns of communities, the growth of student population, movement of families, and other changes, some of which had marked impact on school planning, sometimes neutralizing or negating remedial action before it was fully implemented. Rural areas accustomed for half a century to the consolidated school systems implemented by bus transportation could make adjustments more readily than metropolitan areas with dense and shifting population, numerous schools, congested and complex traffic patterns.

. . .

If school authorities fail in their affirmative obligations under these holdings, judicial authority may be invoked. Once a right and a violation have been shown, the scope of a district court's equitable powers to remedy past wrongs is broad, for breadth and flexibility are inherent in equitable remedies.

. . .

School authorities are traditionally charged with broad power to formulate and implement educational policy and might well conclude, for example, that in order to prepare students to live in a pluralistic society each school should have a prescribed ratio of Negro to white students reflecting the proportion for the district as a whole. To do this as an educational policy is within the broad discretionary powers of school authorities; absent a finding of a constitutional violation, however, that would not be within the authority of a federal court. As with any equity case, the nature of the violation determines the scope of the remedy. In default by the school authorities of their obligation to proffer acceptable remedies, a district court has broad power to fashion a remedy that will assure a unitary school system.

The school authorities argue that the equity powers of federal district courts have been limited by Title IV of the Civil Rights Act of 1964, 42 USC § 2000c. The language and the history of Title IV shows that it was not enacted to limit but to define the role of the federal government in the implementation of the *Brown I* decision. It authorizes the commissioner of education to provide technical assistance to local boards in the preparation of desegregation plans, to arrange "training institutes" for school personnel involved in desegregation efforts, and to make grants directly to schools to ease the transition to unitary systems. It also authorizes the attorney general, in specified circumstances, to initiate federal desegregation suits. Section 2000c(b) defines "desegregation" as it is used in Title IV:

> "Desegregation" means the assignment of students to public schools and within such schools without regard to their race, color, religion, or national origin, but "desegregation" shall not mean the assignment of students to public schools in order to overcome racial imbalance.

Section 2000c–6, authorizing the attorney general to institute federal suits, contains the following proviso:

> nothing herein shall empower any official or court of the United States to issue any order seeking to achieve a racial balance in any school by requiring the transportation of pupils or students from one school to another or one school district to another in order to achieve such racial balance, or otherwise enlarge the existing power of the court to insure compliance with constitutional standards.

On their face, the sections quoted purport only to insure that the provisions of Title IV of the Civil Rights Act of 1964 will not be read as granting new powers. The proviso in § 2000c–6 is in terms designed to foreclose any interpretation of the act as expanding the *existing* powers of federal courts to enforce the Equal Protection Clause. There is no suggestion of an intention to restrict those powers or withdraw from courts their historic equitable remedial powers. The legislative history of Title IV indicates that Congress was concerned that the act might be read as creating a right of action under the Fourteenth Amendment in the situation of so-called "de facto segregation," where racial imbalance exists in the schools but with no showing that this was brought about by discriminatory action of state authorities. In short, there is nothing in the act which provides us material assistance in answering the question of remedy for state-imposed segregation in violation of *Brown I.* The basis of our decision must be the prohibition of the Fourteenth Amendment that no state shall "deny to any person within its jurisdiction the equal protection of the laws."

. . .

The central issue in this case is that of student assignment, and there are essentially four problem areas:

1. to what extent racial balance or racial quotas may be used as an implement in a remedial order to correct a previously segregated system;
2. whether every all-Negro and all-white school must be eliminated as an indispensable part of a remedial process of desegregation;
3. what are the limits, if any, on the rearrangement of school districts and attendance zones, as a remedial measure; and
4. what are the limits, if any, on the use of transportation facilities to correct state-enforced racial school segregation. . . .

The constant theme and thrust of every holding from *Brown I* to date is that state-enforced separation of races in public schools is discrimination that violates the Equal Protection Clause. The remedy commanded was to dismantle dual school systems.

We are concerned in these cases with the elimination of the discrimination inherent in the dual school systems, not with myriad factors of human existence which can cause discrimination in a multitude of ways on racial, religious, or ethnic grounds. . . .

Our objective in dealing with the issues presented by these cases is to see that school authorities exclude no pupil of a racial minority from any school, directly or indirectly, on account of race; it does not and cannot embrace all the problems of racial prejudice, even when those problems contribute to disproportionate racial concentrations in some schools.

.   .   .

The record in this case reveals the familiar phenomenon that in metropolitan areas minority groups are often found concentrated in one part of the city. In some circumstances certain schools may remain all or largely of one race until new schools can be provided or neighborhood patterns change. Schools all or predominantly of one race in a district of mixed population will require close scrutiny to determine that school assignments are not part of state-enforced segregation.

In light of the above, it should be clear that the existence of some small number of one-race, or virtually one-race, schools within a district is not in and of itself the mark of a system which still practices segregation by law. The district judge or school authorities should make every effort to achieve the greatest possible degree of actual desegregation and will thus necessarily be concerned with the elimination of one-race schools. No per se rule can adequately embrace all the difficulties of reconciling the competing interests involved; but in a system with a history of segregation the need for remedial criteria of sufficient specificity to assure a school authority's compliance with its constitutional duty warrants a presumption against schools that are substantially disproportionate in their racial composition. Where the school authority's proposed plan for conversion from a dual to a unitary system contemplates the continued existence of some schools that are all or predominately of one race, they have the burden of showing that such school assignments are genuinely nondiscriminatory. The court should scrutinize such schools, and the burden upon the school authorities will be to satisfy the court that their racial composition is not the result of present or past discriminatory action on their part.

.   .   .

The maps submitted in these cases graphically demonstrate that one of the principal tools employed by school planners and by courts to break up the dual school system has been a frank—and sometimes drastic—gerrymandering of school districts and attendance zones. An additional step was pairing, "clustering," or "grouping" of schools with attendance assignments made deliberately to accomplish the transfer of Negro students out of formerly segregated Negro schools and transfer of white students to formerly all-Negro schools. More often than not, these zones are neither compact nor contiguous; indeed they may be on opposite ends of the city. As an interim corrective measure, this cannot be said to be beyond the broad remedial powers of a court.

Absent a constitutional violation there would be no basis for judicially ordering assignment of students on a racial basis. All things being equal, with no history of discrimination, it might well be desirable to assign pupils to schools nearest their homes. But all things are not equal in a system that has been deliberately constructed and maintained to enforce racial segregation. The remedy for such segregation may be administratively awkward, inconvenient, and even bizarre in some situations and may impose burdens on some; but all awkwardness and inconvenience cannot be avoided in the interim period when remedial adjustments are being made to eliminate the dual school systems.

. . .

The scope of permissible transportation of students as an implement of a remedial decree has never been defined by this Court and by the very nature of the problem it cannot be defined with precision. No rigid guidelines as to student transportation can be given for application to the infinite variety of problems presented in thousands of situations. Bus transportation has been an integral part of the public education system for years, and was perhaps the single most important factor in the transition from the one-room schoolhouse to the consolidated school. Eighteen million of the nation's public school children, approximately 39 per cent, were transported to their schools by bus in 1969–1970 in all parts of the country.

The importance of bus transportation as a normal and accepted tool of educational policy is readily discernible in this and the companion case. The Charlotte school authorities did not purport to assign students on the basis of geographically drawn zones until 1965 and then they allowed almost unlimited transfer privileges. The district court's conclusion that assignment of children to the school nearest their home serving their grade would not produce an effective dismantling of the dual system is supported by the record.

Thus the remedial techniques used in the district court's order were within that court's power to provide equitable relief; implementation of the decree is well within the capacity of the school authority.

. . . we find no basis for holding that the local school authorities may not be required to employ bus transportation as one tool of school desegregation. Desegregation plans cannot be limited to the walk-in school.

An objection to transportation of students may have validity when the time or distance of travel is so great as to risk either the health of the children or significantly impinge on the educational process. . . .

The court of appeals, searching for a term to define the equitable remedial power of the district courts, used the term "reasonableness." In *Green,* . . . this Court used the term "feasible" and by implication, "workable," "effective," and "realistic" in the mandate to develop "a plan that promises realistically to work, and . . . to work *now."* On the facts of this case, we are unable to conclude that the order of the district court is not reasonable, feasible, and workable. However, in seeking to define the scope of remedial power or the limits on remedial power of courts in an area as sensitive as we deal with here, words are poor instruments to convey the sense of basic fairness inherent in equity. Substance, not semantics, must govern, and we have sought to suggest the nature of limitations without frustrating the appropriate scope of equity.

At some point, these school authorities and others like them should have achieved full compliance with this Court's decision in *Brown I.* . . .

The federal court orders requiring busing in order to achieve racial balance threatened to provoke a constitutional crisis between Congress and the judiciary. In 1968 Congress passed an appropriations measure that prevented the Department of Health, Education, and Welfare from using funds to end racial imbalance. Funds could only be used to end the de jure segregated school systems. In 1970 the "Whitten amendment" blocked HEW from cutting off federal school funds from Southern school districts that maintained "freedom of choice" plans, and the "Stennis amendment" to the Elementary and Secondary Education Act provided that HEW must apply school desegregation plans equally to the North and to the South. If busing were to be used to end de jure racial segregation in the South, it would also be required to end de facto racial segregation in the North.

In the fall of 1971 the situation became more acute: A federal district judge in Virginia ordered the busing of children across political boundaries separating Richmond from the suburbs. Public opinion was clearly opposed to such busing: In February 1972 a Gallup poll revealed that while 66 per cent of Americans favored integrated schools, 69 per cent opposed busing of children in order to overcome racial imbalance.

Some Northern Congressmen proposed a constitutional amendment, which read:

No public school student shall, because of his race, creed, or color, be assigned to or required to attend a particular school.

The amendment would have restored the "freedom of choice" plan used to perpetuate segregation and would have rolled back the clock to the era of "token desegregation." Still another version of the amendment added a provision for "equal educational opportunity," which would have meant equalizing expenditures for pupils under a system of de facto segregation.

In February 1972 Congress began considering various legislative proposals designed to end court-ordered busing. On February 29 the Senate approved an amendment, offered by the majority and minority leaders, which provided that federal funds could not be used to bus children except at the request of local officials, that federal authorities would refrain from ordering busing if it would impair the health of a child or take him to a school inferior to the one in his neighborhood, and that would delay enforcement of any court decision ordering busing across school district lines until June 30, 1973. If this amendment had passed, it would have delayed the enforcement of busing orders until the Supreme Court had ruled. But as drafted, it was actually a "breather" designed to permit politicians to escape the wrath of the electorate in the fall elections.

Later, the senate refused to approve a much tougher amendment, which would have provided that

> No court of the United States shall have jurisdiction to make any decision, enter any judgment, or issue any order, the effect of which would be to require that pupils be transported to or from school on the basis of their race, color, religion, or national origin.

In 1970 a similar amendment had received thirty-five votes in the Senate; early in 1972 it received forty-seven votes. Neither these amendments, nor the legislative proposals, were voted into law in 1972.

If the Congress passed such an amendment, limiting the jurisdiction of the federal courts, it would create a constitutional crisis. Congress can provide for the jurisdiction of the lower federal courts, but the Supreme Court can invalidate laws of Congress if they are unconstitutional. It is possible that such an amendment might be declared unconstitutional by the Supreme Court.

The crisis that would then ensue is explored by Congressman John Rarick, who in the speech reprinted here attacks the doctrine of judicial supremacy and judicial review and invokes the powers of Congress to justify maintenance of de facto segregation—a traditional Southern viewpoint.

———————————————

What Is the Law of the Land?

John Rarick

Mr. Chairman, the Supreme Court continues to behave as if it is above and beyond obedience to the supreme law of the land; that is, the U.S. Constitution and the laws of Congress enacted pursuant thereto.

The court decisions handed down on busing are in contravention of the Constitution itself, are contrary to the statutes enacted by this Congress and constitute clear usurpation. Certainly the Court's continued role of tyranny cannot go unchallenged. Our people must be reminded of the proper perspective of the respective roles of government to prevent chaos and further distrust of our federal system.

Tragically, truth has become all but a stranger in our land and those who control the vehicle and means of communication to inform our people either are not doing so or they are distorting the truth.

The average American has been told from his TV set and has read in his newspaper that the Supreme Court has now "legalized" busing of schoolchildren and that the Supreme Court's order is the law of the land. Now we hear the same old line being parroted in this Chamber. Nothing could be further from the truth. In fact, disregarding the constitutional questions presented, the latest decisions, if they do anything, leave the question of busing in a more confused state than before.

But what is the law of the land?

We start with the Constitution of the United States, where the law of the land is defined in no uncertain terms in what is called the supremacy clause, found in article VI.

> This Constitution and the Laws of the United States which shall be made in pursuance thereof; and all Treaties made, or which shall be made, under the Authority of the United States, shall be the supreme Law of the Land; and the Judges in every State shall be bound thereby . . .

The crucial provision of our Constitution is:

> This Constitution and the Laws of the United States which shall be made in pursuance thereof . . . shall be the supreme Law of the Land . . .

Nothing is provided about Supreme Court decisions being the law of

From *Congressional Record*, November 4, 1971, H10455-56. John Rarick is a Democratic Representative from Louisiana.

the land. On the other hand, judges are bound by acts of Congress.

Now Congress has enacted laws pursuant to the Constitution which are the law of the land. One of these laws goes right to the heart of our school problems today and points out the usurpation by the Supreme Court's ruling on busing.

Title 42 of the United States Code, section 2000c–B reads:

> . . . provided that nothing herein shall empower any official or court of the United States to issue any order seeking to achieve a racial balance in any school by requiring the transportation of pupils or students from one school to another or the school district to another in order to achieve racial balance or otherwise enlarge the existing power of the court to insure compliance with Constitutional Standards.

42 USC 2000c definition (b) reads:

> Desegregation means the assignment of students to public schools and within such schools without regard to their race . . . but desegregation shall not mean the assignment of students to public schools in order to overcome racial imbalance.

And then to make sure that the intent of Congress was not misunderstood, when we appropriated money to operate the Department of Health, Education, and Welfare, we wrote into that law—in English so plain no one can misunderstand—a provision forbidding HEW to misuse taxpayers' moneys in busing to achieve racial balance.

The language of the HEW Appropriations Act reads:

> No part of the funds contained in this Act may be used to force busing of students, abolishment of any school, or to force any student attending any elementary or secondary school to attend a particular school against the choice of his or her parents or parent in order to overcome racial imbalance.

These laws are the law of the land.

And the courts are in direct disobedience of the very law which they are sworn to uphold.

Supreme Court decisions are not—I repeat "not"—the law of the land. All they are is the decision in a certain lawsuit between certain parties.

Of course, they may mean that the same judges, on the same facts, dealing with the same law, will decide a new case in the same way. But again, they may not.

The law of the land is the Constitution—and the laws enacted pursuant thereto.

The word of the Constitution repeatedly establishes the supremacy of Congress over the Supreme Court. It grants Congress general powers to regulate all the federal courts. It takes up the question of the courts' honoring the Constitution, and instructs the state courts to do so. While on the subject it omits any mention of either a right or responsibility of the Supreme Court in the matter.

It gives the Supreme Court original jurisdiction in certain federal matters, such as cases arising out of treaties. But in allowing the Supreme Court to hear appeals—which is where it has raised the most ruckus—it was made inferior to Congress, for the Constitution explicitly gives Congress the right to regulate the Court's hearing of appeals. The Constitution, in naming three things that will be the "supreme law of the land," limits them to three—thus excluding all pretentions of the modern Court that *it* is the author of "supreme law" too, unless it is conceded that the Court is free to rewrite the Constitution.

The "independence of the judiciary" is applauded on all sides, but what is meant by it is not settled. As some see it, it means that the Congress shall not tamper with the functioning of the courts. There shall be trial by jury. On the High Court the justices shall be appointed for life "during good behavior" and Congress shall not meddle with this. Congress does have power to impeach judges for "bad behavior," and it has been exercised a few times on federal jurists, though not at the Supreme Court level. In this view, any right of courts to [annul] laws is not part of the "independence of the judiciary." It is rather a trampling on the "independence of the legislature."

But this dilemma has often been voiced: Suppose that the states and Congress defy the Constitution? Who, then, if not the Supreme Court, will defend it? As Jefferson implied in his "Bunker Hill" analogy, the people will. They can get at legislators who defy the basic law on each election day and replace them. But there is no election day for the Supreme Court, so the more serious dilemma is "Who will defend the Constitution if the Court abuses it?"

Our responsibility under that Constitution is plain. The American people have no redress but in this House. The power of impeachment rests with us. The power of the purse rests with us. The very existence and jurisdiction of every district court and court of appeals in the federal system rests with us. The appellate and supervisory jurisdiction of the Supreme Court is entirely ours to bestow, limit, or abolish.

We behold judges ignore the positive statute law which we have enacted and the Constitution which they have sworn to uphold.

Freedom of choice is not an empty slogan. Freedom of choice is the heart and soul of American liberty. The American people still understand this and we must understand that there is a point beyond which the great law-abiding majority cannot be pushed. We are perilously near that point.

Mr. Chairman, I state plainly and simply that this busing by the Supreme Court of the United States is founded neither in any possible construction of the Constitution nor in any possible understanding of the law.

It is a classic example of the arbitrary and unfettered exercise of naked power.

Long years ago Thomas Jefferson warned free men of this very possibility, when he dramatically pointed out that of all tyranny, judicial tyranny is the most fearful.

If the Constitution of the United States forbids a state to assign pupils to a school solely because of their race, it makes no difference whether the object of such assignment is segregation or forced integration under the newly invented "doctrine of racial proportion." If government has no power to forcefully segregate, it has no power to forcefully integrate.

It does not take genius to understand that the state either has that power or does not. Until 1954, it had such power. The Constitution did not change, but in 1954 the Warren court decided the power had vanished. The Warren-Burger court has now decided that although the state has no such power, the court has.

What this preposterous decision amounts to is that racial school assignments are unconstitutional if they are made by the states, but constitutional if made by the courts.

These decisions are a gross distortion of any possible interpretation of the Constitution.

There is yet another problem.

The Constitution of the United States places the legislative power in the Congress. It requires that the President execute the laws. Congress has stated plainly that desegregation does not mean integration, and has prohibited the use of federal moneys for busing to further the "doctrine of racial proportions."

Mr. Chairman, this is judicial tyranny in its worst form. Federal judges—not one of whom was elected by or [is] responsible to the people—have combined to promulgate and attempt to enforce by judicial fiat compliance with rules contrary to the laws enacted by the Congress which are the law of the land.

The people whose children are endangered by this usurpation of power cannot be expected meekly to submit—nor should they.

In the guise of controlling public education, the judiciary has now destroyed it. The people are not deceived. They understand the total lawlessness of this attempt. As free Americans, they will do what is necessary to protect their children, and what they can to educate them. People across the nation are awakening. They are asking questions, and they are demanding answers. They are not satisfied with the explanations they are receiving.

We must be strong and patient. These are dark times for those of us who love our children. But we have had other dark times in our history, and the courage to face them and win out.

Valley Forge was dark—so was Reconstruction.

To condone tyranny which we have the power to end, makes us responsible parties with the initial perpetrators.

———————————————

Presidents have rarely given strong backing to efforts to end racial segregation. President Eisenhower never affirmed support for the principles of Brown v. Board of Education, and did not respond in a number of cases when federal court judges issued desegregation orders and were ignored by state or local officials. President Kennedy acted vigorously after state officials refused to permit black students to enroll in colleges in Alabama and Mississippi and after mobs attacked "Freedom Riders" attempting to integrate facilities in interstate commerce. Yet he delayed for two years issuing an executive order providing for integration of federally assisted and financed public housing. And once the order was issued, it was carefully worded to exclude almost all housing built with federal funds.

Lyndon Johnson was the first president to identify openly with the black cause. He supported the Civil Rights Act of 1964, the Voting Rights Act of 1965, and the Open Housing Act of 1968. Moreover, he gave support to efforts of the Department of Health, Education, and Welfare to prevent federal funds from being used to maintain segregated school systems in the South.

President Nixon began his term of office by continuing the enforcement efforts of the Johnson administration. However, in July 1969 Attorney General Mitchell and HEW Secretary Robert Finch announced a new set of procedures for desegregating school districts. These procedures involved primary emphasis on litigation rather than on cutoffs of federal funds. They also permitted additional delays for some Southern school districts and the use of token "freedom of choice" plans, which would prevent real integration of student bodies. In 1969, in Holmes v. Alexander, the Supreme Court overruled HEW and ordered immediate desegregation of dual systems.

The Nixon administration does not favor any affirmative action to end de facto school desegregation through busing. The President established a White House Committee to study the problem, and after consulting with legislative leaders of his party, he sent the following message, together with proposed legislation, to the Congress on March 17, 1972.

———————————————

Busing

Richard M. Nixon

The maze of differing and sometimes inconsistent orders by the various lower courts has led to contradiction and uncertainty, and often to vastly unequal treatment among regions, states, and local school districts. In the absence of statutory guidelines, many lower court decisions have gone far beyond what most people would consider reasonable, and beyond what the Supreme Court has said is necessary in the requirements they have imposed for the reorganization of school districts and the transportation of school pupils.

All too often, the result has been a classic case of the remedy for one evil creating another evil. In this case, a remedy for the historic evil of racial discrimination has often created a new evil of disrupting communities and imposing hardships on children—both black and white—who are themselves wholly innocent of the wrongs that the plan seeks to set right.

The Fourteenth Amendment to the Constitution—under which the school desegregation cases have arisen—provides that "the Congress shall have power to enforce, by appropriate legislation, the provisions of this article."

Until now, enforcement has been left largely to the courts which have operated within a limited range of available remedies, and in the limited context of case law rather than of statutory law. I propose that the Congress now accept the responsibility and use the authority given to it under the Fourteenth Amendment to clear up the confusion which contradictory court orders have created, and to establish reasonable national standards.

The legislation I propose today would accomplish this.

It would put an immediate stop to further new busing orders by the federal courts.

It would enlist the wisdom, the resources, and the experience of the Congress in the solution of the vexing problems involved in fashioning school desegregation policies that are true to the constitutional requirements and fair to the people and communities concerned.

It would establish uniform national criteria, to ensure that the federal courts in all sections and all states would have a common set of standards to guide them.

These measures would protect the right of a community to maintain neighborhood schools—while also establishing a shared local and federal responsibility to raise the level of education in the neediest neighborhoods, with special programs for those disadvantaged children who need special attention.

At the same time, these measures would not roll back the Constitution, or undo the great advances that have been made in ending school segregation, or undermine the continuing drive for equal rights.

There are some people who fear any curbs on busing because they fear that it would break the momentum of the drive for equal rights for blacks and other minorities. Some fear it would go further, and that it would set in motion a chain of reversals that would undo all the advances so painfully achieved in the past generation.

It is essential that whatever we do to curb busing be done in a way that plainly will not have these other consequences. It is vitally important that the nation's continued commitment to equal rights and equal opportunities be clear and concrete.

On the other hand, it is equally important that we not allow emotionalism to crowd out reason, or get so lost in symbols that words lose their meaning.

One emotional undercurrent that has done much to make this so difficult an issue, is the feeling some people have that to oppose busing is to be antiblack. This is closely related to the arguments often put forward that resistance to any move, no matter what, that may be advanced in the name of desegregation is "racist." This is dangerous nonsense.

For most Americans, the school bus used to be a symbol of hope—of better education. In too many communities today, it has become a symbol of helplessness, frustration, and outrage—of a wrenching of children away from their families, and from the schools their families may have moved to be near, and sending them arbitrarily to others far distant.

Busing for the purpose of desegregation was begun—mostly on a modest scale—as one of a mix of remedies to meet the requirements laid down by various lower federal courts for achieving the difficult transition from the old dual school system to a new, unitary system.

But in the past three years, progress toward eliminating the vestiges of the dual system has been phenomenal—and so too has been the shift in public attitudes in areas where dual systems were formerly operated. In state after state and community after community, local civic, business, and educational leaders of all races have come forward to help make the transition peacefully and successfully. Few voices are now raised urging a return to the old patterns of enforced segregation.

At the same time, there has been a marked shift in the focus of concerns by blacks and members of other minorities. Minority parents have long had a deep and special concern with improving the quality of their children's education. For a number of years, the principal emphasis of this concern—and of the nation's attention—was on desegregating the schools. Now that the dismantling of the old dual system has been substantially completed there is once again a far greater balance of emphasis on improving schools, on convenience, on the chance for parental involvement—in short, on the same concerns that motivate white parents—and, in many communities, on securing a greater measure of control over schools that serve primarily minority-group communities.

Moving forward on desegregation is still important—but the principal concern is with preserving the principle, and with ensuring that the great gains made since *Brown,* and particularly in recent years, are not rolled back in a reaction against excessive busing. Many black leaders now express private concern, moreover, that a reckless extension of busing requirements could bring about precisely the results they fear most: a reaction that would undo those gains, and that would begin the unraveling of advances in other areas that also are based on newly expanded interpretations of basic constitutional rights.

Also, it has not escaped their notice that those who insist on system-wide racial balance insist on a condition in which, in most communities, every school would be run by whites and dominated by whites, with blacks in a permanent minority—and without escape from that minority status. The result would be to deny blacks the right to have schools in which they are the majority.

As we cut through the clouds of emotionalism that surround the busing question, we can begin to identify the legitimate issues.

Concern for the quality of education a child gets is legitimate.

Concern that there be no retreat from the principle of ending racial discrimination is legitimate.

Concern for the distance a child has to travel to get to school is legitimate.

Concern over requiring that a child attend a more distant school when one is available near his home is legitimate.

Concern for the obligation of government to assure, as nearly as possible, that all the children of a given district have equal educational opportunity is legitimate.

Concern for the way educational resources are allocated among the schools of a district is legitimate.

Concern for the degree of control parents and local school boards should have over their schools is legitimate.

Against this background, the objectives of the reforms I propose are:

To give practical meaning to the concept of equal educational opportunity.

To apply the experience gained in the process of desegregation, and
also in efforts to give special help to the educationally disadvantaged.

To ensure the continuing vitality of the principles laid down in *Brown* v.
Board of Education.

To downgrade busing as a tool for achieving equal educational opportunity.

To sustain the rights and responsibilities vested by the states in local
school boards.

In times of rapid and even headlong change, there occasionally is an
urgent need for reflection and reassessment. This is especially true
when powerful, historic forces are moving the nation toward a conflict
of fundamental principles—a conflict that can be avoided if each of us
does his share, and if all branches of government will join in helping
to redefine the questions before us.

The Congress has both the constitutional authority and a special
capability to debate and define new methods for implementing constitutional principles. And the education, financial, and social complexities
of this issue are not, and are not properly, susceptible of solution by
individual courts alone or even by the Supreme Court alone.

I propose, therefore, that the Congress act to impose a temporary
freeze on new busing orders by the Federal courts to establish a waiting
period while the Congress considers alternative means of enforcing
Fourteenth Amendment rights. I propose that this freeze be effective
immediately on enactment, and that it remain in effect until July 1, 1973,
or until passage of the appropriate legislation, whichever is sooner.

This freeze would not put a stop to desegregation cases; it would only
bar new orders during its effective period, to the extent that they
ordered new busing.

This, I recognize, is an unusual procedure. But I am persuaded that
the Congress has the constitutional power to enact such a stay, and I
believe the unusual nature of the conflicts and pressures that confront
both the courts and the country at this particular time requires it.

It has become abundantly clear, from the debates in the Congress and
from the upwelling of sentiment throughout the country, that some
action will be taken to limit the scope of busing orders. It is in the
interest of everyone—black and white, children and parents, school
administrators and local officials, the courts, the Congress, and the
executive branch, that while this matter is being considered by the Congress we not speed further along a course that is likely to be changed.

The legislation I have proposed would provide the courts with a new set of standards and criteria that would enable them to enforce the basic constitutional guarantees in different ways.

A stay would relieve the pressure on the Congress to act on the long-range legislation without full and adequate consideration. By providing immediate relief from a course that increasing millions of Americans are finding intolerable, it would allow the debate on permanent solutions to proceed with less emotion and more reason.

There are now a number of proposals before the Congress, with strong support, to amend the Constitution in ways designed to abolish busing or to bar the courts from ordering it.

These proposals should continue to receive the particularly thoughtful and careful consideration by the Congress that any proposal to amend the constitution merits.

It is important to recognize, however, that a constitutional amendment—even if it could secure the necessary two-thirds support in both houses of the Congress—has a serious flaw: it would have no impact this year; it would not come into effect until after the long process of ratification by three-fourths of the state legislatures. What is needed is action now; a constitutional amendment fails to meet this immediate need.

Legislation meets the problem now. Therefore, I recommend that as its first priority the Congress go forward immediately on the legislative route. Legislation can also treat the question with far greater precision and detail than could the necessarily generalized language of a constitutional amendment, while making possible a balanced comprehensive approach to equal educational opportunity.

The following selection makes it clear that the real issue is not busing—it is racism. Americans have long bused children to schools without complaint. In fact, maintenance of a segregated school system depended on busing children to schools away from the "neighborhood schools." Now, when busing will be used to provide educational opportunity for black children rather than separate and unequal schools, the nation rediscovers the "neighborhood school" and extols its virtues. Yet some political leaders are willing to wage the fight against de facto segregation, as the following two selections demonstrate.

Busing in Perspective

Walter F. Mondale

School desegregation is a fact of American educational life. The law of the land is clear, and it will not change. Officially imposed school segregation—whether the result of state law or covert policy—must be overcome. A unanimous Supreme Court resolved any lingering doubts last April with Chief Justice Burger's decision in *Swann* v. *Charlotte-Mecklenburg.* A racial balance is not required. All-white or all-black schools may remain after all reasonable steps have been taken. But every reasonable effort must be made to overcome the results of officially approved school segregation: "School authorities should make every effort to achieve the greatest possible degree of actual desegregation. . . ." And reasonable transportation will be required where necessary to defeat the results of racially discriminatory student assignment policies. ". . . We find no basis for holding that the local school authorities may not be required to employ bus transportation as one tool of school desegregation. Desegregation plans cannot be limited to the walk-in school."

There has been legitimate criticism of the process of school desegregation: court orders have at times been arbitrary; student transportation has in a few cases worked unnecessary hardships; some federal administrators have been overbearing and rigid. There are other equally legitimate criticisms which we have heard less often: thousands of qualified black teachers and administrators have been demoted or dismissed; black children have been subjected to abuse by fellow students, by teachers and by school administrators; the wealthy have fled to suburbs or placed their children in private schools, so that desegregation has affected only the poor.

But we will not answer these criticisms by refusing the federal support needed to make school desegregation educationally successful, or by withdrawing the federal government from enforcement of the Fourteenth Amendment. The choice is not between blind acceptance of "massive busing for racial balance" or total rejection of support for any transportation to achieve school desegregation. Busing is one means— and at times the only means—by which segregation in public education can be reduced. In itself, busing can be either helpful or harmful. It can

From *The New Republic*, 166 (March 4, 1972), pp. 16–19. Reprinted by permission of *The New Republic*, © 1972, Harrison-Blaine of New Jersey, Inc. Walter F. Mondale is a Democratic senator from Minnesota.

be the safest, most reasonable way for children to reach integrated schools of high quality. Or it can be used to uproot stable communities and destroy the one chance that parents have to provide the best for their children.

Like the President, I do not support "unnecessary transportation to achieve an arbitrary racial balance," and none of the hundreds of educators with whom I have talked in the past two years supports this kind of effort. The Supreme Court has made it very clear that busing will be required only where it is reasonable and does not place undue burdens on school children: "Busing will not be allowed to significantly impinge on the educational process." Thus, educationally advantaged students should not be bused to schools where they will be overwhelmed by a majority of students from the poorest and most disadvantaged backgrounds. All the evidence we have collected indicates that this kind of "desegregation" helps no one at all.

But if we bar the use of reasonable transportation as one tool for achieving desegregation, we will set in concrete much school segregation which is the clear and direct product of intentional government policy—segregation which would not exist if racially neutral policies had been followed.

In South Holland, Illinois, for instance, a U.S. district court found public agencies deeply involved in fostering school segregation. The schools were located in the center rather than at the boundaries of segregated residential areas in order to achieve school segregation. School assignment policies were adopted under which black children living nearer to white schools attended black schools, and white children living nearer to black schools attended white schools. School buses were used to transport students out of their "neighborhoods" in order to achieve segregation. Finally, teachers were assigned on a racial basis. If transportation to achieve desegregation is prohibited, public school segregation in South Holland will continue.

The courts have found virtually identical conditions in Norfolk, Virginia; Pasadena, California; Charlotte, North Carolina; Denver, Colorado; and countless other communities.

Contrary to popular impression, courts have not generally ordered excessive busing or engaged in indiscriminate "racial balancing." The proportion of children riding buses to school in the Deep South is less than three per cent above the national average, and barely seven per cent above the average for the northern and western states. Recent HEW studies show that aggregate busing has not increased as a result of desegregation. In Louisiana and Florida, although the total number of students bused has increased, the average distance traveled has increased substantially. And in the South's twenty-five largest school districts this year, 33 per cent of the total black enrollment attend virtually all-black schools. This hardly indicates overzealous "racial balancing."

For nearly two years, I have served as Chairman of the Select Committee on Equal Educational Opportunity in the Senate. It has been a painful two years, and I am left with a deep conviction that American education is failing children who are born black, brown, or simply poor. In Hartford, Connecticut, the median IQ level of black elementary school students is perilously close to eligibility for special schools for the mentally retarded; in rural Appalachia, fewer than 50 of every 100 fifth graders graduate from high school; in New York City, the dropout rate of Puerto Rican children between grades ten and twelve is 56.7 per cent; 50 per cent of American Indian students never complete high school.

What are we to do? Those who want us to abandon school integration . . . say all our energies should be devoted to improving the quality of education in racially and economically isolated schools. They rightly point out that thousands of children attend schools that will not be integrated—racially or economically—in the next decade, and that ways must be found to provide better education in schools serving only the disadvantaged. But we have not found those ways! With few exceptions, an annual federal investment of $1.5 billion in "compensatory" education has little perceptible impact on mounting educational disadvantage. We must increase our efforts, but success is far from certain. At the same time, we cannot afford to abandon other hopeful approaches. *And it has been demonstrated that integrated education—sensitively conducted and with community support—can be better education for all children, white as well as black, rich as well as poor.* It has been tried and is working.

Nearly 1000 minority group students, selected on a random basis, are bused each day from the Hartford, Connecticut ghetto to suburban schools, as part of Project Concern. Extensive testing of these children since the inception of the project in 1966 shows that time spent in the suburban schools has a dramatic impact on achievement. Fifth graders who have been in the program two years are five months ahead of those who have been in the project only one year. Those who have spent three years in the project in turn scored another four months ahead of the two-year group or a full academic year ahead of the first group. The chances for a significant gain in basic reading and arithmetic skills have been increased threefold. In Berkeley, California, where a major effort has been made to record the educational impact of integration, average achievement of black students increased by 60 per cent while the achievement rate for white students also rose. Similar results emerge from less comprehensive testing programs in Sacramento, California, and White Plains and Rochester, New York.

Hoke County is a small rural community of 18,000 in eastern North Carolina. Its schools serve 4,850 children: 50 per cent black, 35 per cent white and 15 per cent Lumbee Indian. The county had separate schools and classes for each group and a triple transportation system. Then in 1968 and 1969, Hoke County established a unitary system under which each school reflected the county-wide population distribution. They didn't just mix the children together and forget them once they entered the schoolhouse door. They tested every child to determine his level of achievement and took account of the low achieving students' special needs. They made sure that no teachers or principals were displaced or demoted—in fact, Indian and black personnel were promoted. They talked with fearful parents and counseled apprehensive students; they integrated all extracurricular activities so that every school-sponsored organization had representatives of all races in both its membership and its leadership.

Here's a school system which is 65 per cent minority and it's making integration work. How? By being human about it and by focusing on what happens at the end of the bus ride. Before integration, white sixth graders were a year ahead of their Indian and black counterparts. By twelfth grade the gap was two full years. At the end of the first year of integration, white students continued to progress as before. Black students gained a year and a half; their rate of achievement was more than 50 per cent better than before. Could this have happened without integration? The superintendent thought not: "I don't think it would ever happen," he said, "if we kept the schools segregated and kept pouring in money for compensatory education in segregated schools. But I believe in an integrated system that we will eventually work it out."

The Hoke County children ride to school on buses fifteen fewer minutes each day to integrated schools than they did under the segregated school system. The five-member local school board provided the kind of positive leadership necessary to make integration successful. It never reneged, publicly or privately, on its commitment to integration and it was reelected. The candidate who thought the system moved too fast toward integration finished last in a field of nine candidates.

Hoke County is not unique. Nor is Berkeley, California, the largest city in the nation to integrate its entire school system voluntarily. Berkeley is 45 per cent white, 44 per cent black and 11 per cent Asian and Spanish-surnamed. Its schools were integrated more than three years ago, and they are building a quality, integrated system, because everyone is involved. Anglo youngsters' achievement rates are accelerating and those that are growing the fastest are those of students who have been in integrated classes longest. White third graders who have been in integrated classes for two years gained four months over those third graders who have been in integrated classes for one year. At the same time, black student achievement has increased from half to eight-tenths of a year's growth per year.

Berkeley is a university town with a high tax base, well above average in per pupil expenditure. Baldwin, Michigan on the other hand has a low tax base, a low per pupil expenditure, a school operating budget deficit of $100,000 a year and dismally low achievement levels. Its schools are the second worst academically in Michigan. Twelve per cent of Baldwin's working force is unemployed; 40 per cent of its families have incomes under $3000 per year; 53 per cent of its people have less than nine years of formal education. Baldwin has its problems. But "busing" and "racial balance" are not among them. Every child is in an integrated class. More than 80 per cent of its 1041 students are bused. Some students board their buses as early as 7 a.m. and travel sixty miles to arrive at school at 8:20. The shortest one-way bus ride in this 370 square mile school district is twenty miles. The superintendent told our select committee: "We are proud of the fact that we are an integrated school system. In fact this year during our football season we came up with a little pin that really exemplifies what we are talking about. I would like to leave this with you. It says, 'Baldwin has Soul.' "

I asked him whether there was any opposition to busing. He said: "Our neighbors in Cadillac, Luddington, Big Rapids, etc., are pretty shook up over there. They think we are going to bus some of our black children over to their schools. So busing is an issue in Baldwin only as far as our neighbors are concerned."

Let's be candid: busing is the way the overwhelming majority of school children outside our central cities get to school. Twenty million elementary and secondary school children are bused. They rode 256,000 yellow buses 2.2 billion miles last year, at a cost of $1.5 billion. Forty per cent of our school children—65 per cent when those riding public transportation are included—ride to school every day for reasons that have nothing at all to do with school desegregation. So the issue is not to bus or not to bus; it is whether we will build on successful examples to make school desegregation work; whether we will help the courts to avoid educational mistakes—or leave them to face the complexities of school desegregation alone.

And there are complexities. Court-ordered desegregation is costing Pontiac, Michigan $700,000 and Pontiac has had to cut educational programs to meet these costs. The superintendent and chairman of the school board in Dade County, Florida testified last June that, "The financial impact of desegregation is placing severe demands and burdens on the affected school systems." School desegregation in Dade County, which has a $250-million school budget, cost an additional $1.5 million in just six months. Additional transportation is costing $670,000 a year. Pasadena, California is spending $300,000 in Federal Aid for Impacted Areas which would otherwise be used for instructional programs. Pasadena is implementing a federal desegregation court order. In Harrisburg, Pennsylvania, which is desegregating under state administrative procedures, additional transportation expenses are more than $500,000 a year. Harrisburg has had to cut additional programs to pay for busing. In Nashville, Tennessee, because of an inadequate number of school buses, opening times for schools have been staggered so that some children start school as early as 7:00 a.m., and others arrive home after dark. The inconvenience this has caused threatens public support for education in Nashville.

And yet ... the Department of Health, Education, and Welfare has refused to allow expenditures of any of the $65 million in emergency desegregation funds appropriated by Congress this year to support transportation.

No one has suggested that every school can—or should—be integrated tomorrow. No one is requiring that. Segregated schools remain in Atlanta under federal court order; segregated schools will continue in the great urban centers of the North despite our best efforts. But if we abandon support for school integration where it can be accomplished, if we refuse to support the essential remedy, which busing so often is, and if we destroy the public goodwill necessary to make desegregation successful once it has taken place—we will work tragic harm. We're at a crossroads. School desegregation in the South is largely completed. But we from the North are now beginning to feel the pressure to abandon the course set by the Fourteenth Amendment. If we do, in the name of antibusing, we will deal a blow to public education in the North and in the South from which it may never recover.

3 POVERTY

Does anyone have a *right* to a guaranteed minimum income? The Constitution did not embody any provisions making it the responsibility either of the federal or the state governments to provide income for poor people. In fact, the practice in the eighteenth century was to imprison debtors, place them in workhouses, or banish them.

Today federal and state governments operate a welfare system that provides caseworker supervision and money income for some of the poor. States determine eligibility for the various programs, administer payments, and supervise clients, subject only to certain congressional statutes and administrative regulations of the Department of Health, Education, and Welfare. Until recently, most state administrative actions regarding the poor were taken without allowing clients the right to due process of law. In most states the grant levels provide for bare subsistence, if even that.

The welfare system is under attack, both from conservatives opposed to the concept of welfare and from client groups that want a complete change in the system. The latter groups want an end to caseworker supervision, due process in the administration of grants, and some form of cash payment plan (either a negative income tax, a guaranteed minimum income, or family assistance payments) that would increase the level of payments. The state and local officials who call for welfare reform intend to institute "workfare." This is the requirement that all able-bodied recipients of aid, including mothers with school-age children, be required to register and accept work in return for their welfare payments (which means that recipients would work for less than federal and most state minimum wages).

New York and California, for example, have been reducing benefits and imposing stricter eligibility requirements, including some form of "workfare." These requirements are being litigated in federal and state courts.

Drastic changes in the welfare system have been proposed by both the Nixon Administration and the National Welfare Rights Organization, a client group. Some form of minimum income, paid for by federal funds, seems likely in the 1970s. The real issue is whether such a plan is a means to raise incomes for the poor to adequate levels or simply a fiscal device to transfer the welfare burden to the federal government so that state governments can use their funds to provide other services.

What is wrong with the welfare system? It doesn't help enough people. In August 1972 15 million people were receiving public assistance, yet in that same month there were approximately 24 million people with incomes below the poverty level. States and localities cannot even provide adequate income for those already on the rolls, and faced with mounting costs, they cut back assistance levels and tighten eligibility rules.

The article below points out that under the present intergovernmental system, the fiscal plight of the states—and the human plight of recipients—can only become worse.

The Mounting and Insurmountable Welfare Problem

Sar A. Levitan and David Marwick

A total of 14.4 million persons received public assistance in March 1971, at an annual cost of $10 billion in cash. Aid to the aged, the blind, and dependent children was established by the 1935 [Social Security] Act. The permanently and totally disabled were added in 1950. Under these programs, the federal government contributes more than half of the total cost, but delegates administration to the states within broad federal guidelines. There is, in addition, a network of completely state-administered and financed programs of general income assistance.

. . .

Aid to Families with Dependent Children (AFDC) accounts for 6 of every 10 public assistance dollars and is virtually synonymous with the term "welfare".... Between 1960 and 1969, the number of Americans living in poverty dropped steadily from 40 million to 24 million (or from 22 per cent of the population to 12 per cent); the unemployment rate fell below 4 per cent in 1965 and stayed at that level until the end of

From *Current History*, 61 (November 1971), pp. 261–265. Reprinted by permission of the authors and Current History, Inc. Sar A. Levitan and David Marwick are affiliated with the Center for Manpower Studies, The George Washington University.

the decade. But the AFDC rolls rose from 2.9 million at the beginning of 1960 to 7.3 million at the end of 1969, and public assistance payments grew from $1.0 billion to $3.2 billion.

Although the "causes" of the rise of AFDC during the post-World War II era cannot be pinpointed, some important contributory factors can be identified. Population growth and changing family patterns have resulted in a rise of female-headed families as out of wedlock births, desertions, and divorces have increased substantially in the past three decades. (Charges that AFDC actually fosters illegitimacy are unsubstantiated; but the structure of benefits can encourage the parents of an unborn child not to marry and can ease the breakup of an existing family.)

Liberalized federal and state laws have helped to increase the number of persons qualifying for AFDC. The 1961 amendments to the Social Security Act extended benefits to children of unemployed but employable males. About half the states have since adopted this provision, which covered a total of 870,000 persons in March 1971. Federal regulations governing maximum income ceilings and earnings exemptions have also allowed more people to qualify for AFDC, and local welfare agencies have been accepting a markedly high proportion of all applications. Supreme Court decisions have also swelled relief rolls. In 1961, the Court ruled against provisions which allowed states to disqualify families from assistance unless they maintained a "suitable home," a necessarily subjective criterion. The "man in the house" rule which had barred women living with a man other than the father of her children from receiving assistance was voided in 1968. In 1969, the Court struck down states' residency requirements. Mobility has always been a characteristic of the American population and many who migrated from rural areas to urban centers after World War II ended up on welfare, although this was rarely their goal. Residency requirements were enacted in large part to discourage such migration.

Perhaps the most fundamental basis of the increase has been the broader attractiveness of AFDC relative to other sources of income. Between 1947 and 1962, average AFDC payments kept pace with spendable average weekly earnings of all private employees, each rising by about two-thirds. During the following eight years, AFDC payments increased by 60 per cent while earnings rose 37 per cent. Substantial expansion of in-kind benefits of AFDC clients—not reflected in the cash payments—have tilted the balance even more in favor of welfare. The faster rise of AFDC payments is especially significant to female-headed families—who are the heart of the current welfare "problem"—because they did not share fully in the unprecedented economic expansion of the 1960s. Poverty became increasingly concentrated in these families;

in 1969, they contained only 12 per cent of all children, but 45 per cent of those living in poverty. Even for those who want to be self-supporting, a considerable work effort is required to equal available public assistance, and in some instances public assistance payments surpass the earnings capacity of recipients even when they gain full-time employment.

. . .

THE WELFARE "PROBLEM"

Those who foot the bill have never liked public assistance programs. But antagonism to AFDC is unusually fierce. The changing characteristics of its recipients during the past quarter-century would probably have given rise to much opposition even if the financial costs had not become so considerable. Perhaps the most salient change has been in the reasons for lack of parental support. Widows and fatherless children have traditionally been accepted as public charges when their status was due to a catastrophe, such as the death or incapacity of the father. Unmarried mothers or mothers whose husbands desert after marriage have been considered less "deserving" because their circumstances are, at least in part, the result of their own actions. The proportion of AFDC families whose fathers are dead or disabled has plummeted steadily from nearly three of every five in 1948 to fewer than one in five two decades later. Meanwhile, the incidence of living but absent fathers has increased during the same period from nearly half to fully three-quarters of all AFDC cases and the proportion of unmarried mothers has doubled to two in seven. Opposition to AFDC has also been intensified because of the rise in the proportion of nonwhites among recipients, from about three in ten in 1948 to nearly five in ten, a proportion that remained constant during the 1960s.

Other objections are based on charges of inequity. The increase of AFDC relative to wages, mentioned above as a factor in AFDC's growth, has nourished opposition because millions of workers do not earn enough to escape poverty. The unfairness is obvious when welfare mothers, most of whom do not work, receive incomes which compare favorably with the earnings of full-time workers, and while the number of working mothers in the population has grown constantly since the early days of AFDC. . . . But the image that AFDC mothers shun work is distorted. Leonard Goodwin of The Brookings Institution has found, for example, that the "work ethic" in welfare mothers is actually similar to that of suburbanites.

Not only have the recipients changed in their personal characteristics but in their geographic distribution as well, with profound results. Over time the welfare population generally, and especially the AFDC population, has become concentrated in a few states. By early 1971, the two most populous states, California and New York, contained 19 per cent of the total population, but 29 per cent of all AFDC recipients. The top six states (including California and New York) contained 38 per cent of the total population and 48 per cent of all AFDC recipients. . . .

Dissatisfaction with welfare has been exacerbated by steadily mounting costs. On a national basis, the proportion of the gross national product (the value of all goods and services produced) distributed through public assistance programs had climbed from 0.6 per cent in 1945 to 0.8 per cent in 1960 to 1.2 per cent in early 1971. Nor is this increasingly heavy burden borne evenly by states and cities. Costs depend on the size of the welfare caseload and the level of benefits and are largely the result of state actions. Although the federal government pays more than half the cost, states have substantial latitude in establishing qualifications for aid, including aid to unemployed but employable fathers, aid to children over eighteen while attending school, and limitations on ownership of property and other assets. Each state also sets its own benefit level; payments vary widely. Average grant per AFDC recipient in March, 1971, ranged from $14 in Mississippi to $78 in New York, averaging $50 for the country. The variation in welfare utilization is also great. In 1968, the proportion of poor persons who were AFDC recipients was twice as high in Chicago and Philadelphia as in Atlanta, and four times as high in New York City.

. . .

All the variability of benefit levels and of state-local cost-sharing leads to great diversity in the distribution of costs among governmental levels. In 1970, the federal government paid 54 per cent of the total national AFDC bill; states, 35 per cent; and localities, 11 per cent. . . .

For hard-pressed state and local governments, growing welfare outlays are cause for grave concern. In early 1971, Governor Ronald Reagan of California, noting that welfare costs were increasing more than three times as fast as revenues, contended that "welfare has proliferated and grown into a leviathan of unsupportable proportions." Mayor John Lindsay of New York City, where welfare costs absorb one-quarter of the budget, filed suit against the federal and state governments, claiming that welfare regulations would bankrupt the city. Governor Nelson Rockefeller of New York complained that the welfare "emergency is so serious and so great that we cannot continue," while Governor Richard Ogilvie of Illinois projected that the rise of welfare costs would absorb fully 85 per cent of the growth in state revenues during the next year.

The mounting welfare burden is bringing forth reaction from all levels of government. Federal efforts initiated in 1962 to "rehabilitate" relief recipients have been expanded and recast to substitute "workfare for welfare," to use President Richard Nixon's slogan. A freeze on AFDC rolls was passed by Congress in 1967, but rejected a year later, the day before it was to become effective. In considering an overhaul of the welfare system, Congress is becoming increasingly hard-nosed.

After consistently increasing allotments during the 1960s, many states, too, are now attempting to tighten eligibility and reduce payments. A survey by the Department of Health, Education, and Welfare in July 1971 disclosed that nine states had acted to reduce AFDC benefits within the previous year; eleven others expected action on a reduction; twenty-four expected no change; and ten had acted, or were expected to act, to increase benefits. The most famous actions occurred in California and New York, which have the largest AFDC rolls. In hopes of "excising the cancer eating at our vitals," Governor Reagan began to pare the welfare rolls by administrative action, and pushed for legislation to place a ceiling on state spending for welfare. Governor Rockefeller led the fight to cut by 10 per cent money payments; reduce by 10 per cent the ceiling for Medicaid eligibility; and require that welfare recipients pick up their checks at a state employment office. In each state, a small decline in caseloads has been hailed as evidence of the effectiveness of tougher measures. Other states which have enacted, or expect to enact, cuts include Illinois, New Jersey, Pennsylvania, and Texas.

Lawyers representing welfare recipients have challenged the administration of the system. They have won the right to represent clients at administrative hearings to determine eligibility for welfare. The Supreme Court has struck down laws requiring residency in a state as unconstitutional in Shapiro v. Thompson (1969). It has also ruled that the "man in the house" rule (providing for cutoff of payments if a recipient was found with a man in her domicile) cannot be enforced.

In Goldberg v. Kelly (1970) the Supreme Court determined that due process requirements apply to hearings prior to any termination of welfare benefits. The decision is typical of the incremental changes which have been brought about in the administration of the system through litigation.

Goldberg v. Kelly

Mr. Justice Brennan delivered the opinion of the Court.

The question for decision is whether a state that terminates public assistance payments to a particular recipient without affording him the opportunity for an evidentiary hearing prior to termination denies the recipient procedural due process in violation of the Due Process Clause of the Fourteenth Amendment.

This action was brought in the District Court for the Southern District of New York by residents of New York City receiving financial aid under the federally assisted program of Aid to Families with Dependent Children (AFDC) or under New York State's general Home Relief program. Their complaint alleged that the New York State and New York City officials administering these programs terminated, or were about to terminate, such aid without prior notice and hearing, thereby denying them due process of law. . . .

The constitutional issue to be decided, therefore, is the narrow one whether the Due Process Clause requires that the recipient be afforded an evidentiary hearing *before* the termination of benefits. The district court held that only a pretermination evidentiary hearing would satisfy the constitutional command, and rejected the argument of the state and city officials that the combination of the posttermination "fair hearing" with the informal pretermination review disposed of all due process claims.

. . .

It is true, of course, that some governmental benefits may be administratively terminated without affording the recipient a pretermination evidentiary hearing. But we agree with the district court that when welfare is discontinued, only a pretermination evidentiary hearing provides the recipient with procedural due process. . . . Thus the crucial factor in this context—a factor not present in the case of the blacklisted government contractor, the discharged government employee, the taxpayer denied a tax exemption, or virtually anyone else whose governmental entitlements are ended—is that termination of aid pending resolution of a controversy over eligibility may deprive an *eligible* recipient of the very means by which to live while he waits. Since he lacks independent resources, his situation becomes immediately desperate. His need to

From *Goldberg* v. *Kelly*, 25 Lawyers' Edition 2nd 287.

concentrate upon finding the means for daily subsistence, in turn, adversely affects his ability to seek redress from the welfare bureaucracy.

Moreover, important governmental interests are promoted by affording recipients a pretermination evidentiary hearing. From its founding the nation's basic commitment has been to foster the dignity and well-being of all persons within its borders. We have come to recognize that forces not within the control of the poor contribute to their poverty. This perception, against the background of our traditions, has significantly influenced the development of the contemporary public assistance system. Welfare, by meeting the basic demands of subsistence, can help bring within the reach of the poor the same opportunities that are available to others to participate meaningfully in the life of the community. At the same time, welfare guards against the societal malaise that may flow from a widespread sense of unjustified frustration and insecurity. Public assistance, then, is not mere charity, but a means to "promote the general Welfare, and secure the Blessings of Liberty to ourselves and our Posterity." The same governmental interests that counsel the provision of welfare, counsel as well its uninterrupted provision to those eligible to receive it; pretermination evidentiary hearings are indispensable to that end.

. . .

... The requirement of a prior hearing doubtless involves some greater expense, and the benefits paid to ineligible recipients pending decision at the hearing probably cannot be recouped, since these recipients are likely to be judgment-proof. But the state is not without weapons to minimize these increased costs. Much of the drain on fiscal and administrative resources can be reduced by developing procedures for prompt pretermination hearings and by skillful use of personnel and facilities.... Thus, the interest of the eligible recipient in uninterrupted receipt of public assistance, coupled with the state's interest that his payments not be erroneously terminated, clearly outweighs the state's competing concern to prevent any increase in its fiscal and administrative burdens. As the district court correctly concluded,

> the stakes are simply too high for the welfare recipient, and the possibility for honest error or irritable misjudgment too great, to allow termination of aid without giving the recipient a chance, if he so desires, to be fully informed of the case against him so that he may contest its basis and produce evidence in rebuttal. . . .

We also agree with the district court, however, that the pretermination hearing need not take the form of a judicial or quasi-judicial trial.

... Thus, a complete record and a comprehensive opinion, which would serve primarily to facilitate judicial review and to guide future decisions, need not be provided at the pretermination stage. We recognize, too, that both welfare authorities and recipients have an interest in relatively speedy resolution of questions of eligibility, that they are used to dealing with one another informally, and that some welfare departments have very burdensome caseloads. These considerations justify the limitation of the pretermination hearing to minimum procedural safeguards, adapted to the particular characteristics of welfare recipients, and to the limited nature of the controversies to be resolved. . . .

. . .

... a recipient must be allowed to state his position orally. Informal procedures will suffice; in this context due process does not require a particular order of proof or mode of offering evidence. . . .

In almost every setting where important decisions turn on questions of fact, due process requires an opportunity to confront and cross-examine adverse witnesses. . . . What we said in *Greene* v. *McElroy* . . . is particularly pertinent here:

> . . . We have formalized these protections in the requirements of confrontation and cross-examination. They have ancient roots. They find expression in the Sixth Amendment. . . . This Court has been zealous to protect these rights from erosion. It has spoken out not only in criminal cases, . . . but also in all types of cases where administrative . . . actions were under scrutiny.

Welfare recipients must therefore be given an opportunity to confront and cross-examine the witnesses relied on by the department.

... We do not say that counsel must be provided at the pretermination hearing, but only that the recipient must be allowed to retain an attorney if he so desires. Counsel can help delineate the issues, present the factual contentions in an orderly manner, conduct cross-examination, and generally safeguard the interests of the recipient. We do not anticipate that this assistance will unduly prolong or otherwise encumber the hearing. . . .

Finally, the decision maker's conclusion as to a recipient's eligibility must rest solely on the legal rules and evidence adduced at the hearing. . . . To demonstrate compliance with this elementary requirement, the decision maker should state the reasons for his determination and indicate the evidence he relied on, . . . though his statement need not amount to a full opinion or even formal findings of fact and conclusions of law. And, of course, an impartial decision maker is essential. . . . We agree with the district court that prior involvement in some aspects of a case will not necessarily bar a welfare official from acting as a decision maker. He should not, however, have participated in making the determination under review.

Affirmed.

$\mathbf{F}$aced with increased welfare rolls due to economic conditions and the stricter application of due process standards, state legislatures have adopted a number of statutory and administrative devices to limit the resources available to recipients. Some states appropriate a fixed sum for welfare payments, and if the rolls increase, the welfare offices begin to cut the payment levels. In many states caseworkers determine the level of need for families, but only a specified percentage of that amount is then granted.

Maryland has a law that sets a maximum limit on the amount that any family may receive in public assistance. If members are added to the family (through birth or migration), they must share in the original grant level. If not all members of the family can be supported on the grant, some may have to be placed with relatives, since under no circumstances will additional funds be provided.

In Dandridge v. Williams (1970) the Supreme Court upheld the Maryland regulation as a reasonable exercise of state power. Poverty lawyers may be successful in gaining due process rights for recipients, but when it comes to money, the Supreme Court takes an entirely different attitude toward the rights of welfare recipients.

Dandridge v. Williams

Mr. Justice Stewart delivered the opinion of the Court.

This case involves the validity of a method used by Maryland, in the administration of an aspect of its public welfare program, to reconcile

From *Dandridge* v. *Williams,* 25 Lawyers' Edition 2nd 491.

the demands of its needy citizens with the finite resources available to meet those demands. . . . Some states provide that every family shall receive grants sufficient to meet fully the determined standard of need. Other states provide that each family unit shall receive a percentage of the determined need. Still others provide grants to most families in full accord with the ascertained standard of need, but impose an upper limit on the total amount of money any one family unit may receive. Maryland, through administrative adoption of a "maximum grant regulation," has followed this last course. This suit was brought by several AFDC recipients to enjoin the application of the Maryland maximum grant regulation on the ground that it is in conflict with the Social Security Act of 1935 and with the Equal Protection Clause of the Fourteenth Amendment. . . .

. . . The regulation here in issue imposes upon the grant that any single family may receive an upper limit of $250 per month in certain counties and Baltimore City, and of $240 per month elsewhere in the state. The appellees all have large families, so that their standards of need as computed by the state substantially exceed the maximum grants that they actually receive under the regulation. The appellees urged in the district court that the maximum grant limitation operates to discriminate against them merely because of the size of their families, in violation of the Equal Protection Clause of the Fourteenth Amendment. They claimed further that the regulation is incompatible with the purpose of the Social Security Act of 1935, as well as in conflict with its explicit provisions.

. . . For the reasons that follow, we have concluded that the Maryland regulation is permissible under the federal law.

In *King* v. *Smith,* . . . we stressed the states' "undisputed power," under these provisions of the Social Security Act, "to set the level of benefits and the standard of need". . . . We described the AFDC enterprise as "a scheme of cooperative federalism," . . . and noted carefully that

> there is no question that states have considerable latitude in allocating their AFDC resources, since each state is free to set its own standard of need and to determine the level of benefits by the amount of funds it devotes to the program. . . .

Congress was itself cognizant of the limitations on state resources from the very outset of the federal welfare program. The first section of the act . . . provides that the act is

> For the purpose of encouraging the care of dependent children in their own homes or in the homes of relatives by enabling each state to furnish financial assistance and rehabilitation and other services, *as far as practicable under*

the conditions in such state, to needy dependent children and the parents or relatives with whom they are living to help maintain and strengthen family life and to help such parents or relatives to attain or retain capability for the maximum self-support and personal independence consistent with the maintenance of continuing parental care and protection. . . . (Emphasis added.)

Thus the starting point of the statutory analysis must be a recognition that the federal law gives each state great latitude in dispensing its available funds.

. . .

The states must respond to this federal statutory concern for pre-serving children in a family environment. Given Maryland's finite resources, its choice is either to support some families adequately and others less adequately, or not to give sufficient support to any family. We see nothing in the federal statute that forbids a state to balance the stresses that uniform insufficiency of payments would impose on all families against the greater ability of large families—because of the inherent economies of scale—to accommodate their needs to dimin-ished per capita payments. The strong policy of the statute in favor of preserving family units does not prevent a state from sustaining as many families as it can, and providing the largest families somewhat less than their ascertained per capita standard of need. Nor does the maximum grant system necessitate the dissolution of family bonds. For even if a parent should be inclined to increase his per capita family in-come by sending a child away, the federal law requires that the child, to be eligible for AFDC payments, must live with one of several enumerated relatives. The kinship tie may be attenuated but it can not be destroyed.

. . . So long as some aid is provided to all eligible families and all eligible children, the statute itself is not violated.

This is the view that has been taken by the Secretary of Health, Education, and Welfare (HEW) who is charged with the administration of the Social Security Act and the approval of state welfare plans. The parties have stipulated that the secretary has, on numerous occasions, approved the Maryland welfare scheme, including its provision of max-imum payments to any one family, a provision that has been in force in various forms since 1947. Moreover, a majority of the states pay less than their determined standard of need, and twenty of these states impose maximums on family grants of the kind here in issue. The secretary has not disapproved any state plan because of its maximum grant provision. On the contrary, the secretary has explicitly recognized state maximum grant systems.

Finally, Congress itself has acknowledged a full awareness of state maximum grant limitations. In the amendments of 1967 Congress added to § 402(a) a subsection, 23:

> [The state shall] provide that by July 1, 1969, the amount used by the state to determine the needs of individuals will have been adjusted to reflect fully changes in living costs since such amounts were established, and *any maximums that the state imposes on the amount of aid paid to families will have been proportionately adjusted. . . .* (Emphasis added.)

This specific Congressional recognition of the state maximum grant provisions is not, of course, an approval of any specific maximum. The structure of specific maximums Congress left to the states, and the validity of any such structure must meet constitutional tests. However, the above amendment does make clear that Congress fully recognized that the act permits maximum grant regulations.

For all of these reasons, we conclude that the Maryland regulation is not prohibited by the Social Security Act. . . .

Although a state may adopt a maximum grant system in allocating its funds available for AFDC payments without violating the act, it may not, of course, impose a regime of invidious discrimination in violation of the Equal Protection Clause of the Fourteenth Amendment. Maryland says that its maximum grant regulation is wholly free of any invidiously discriminatory purpose or effect, and that the regulation is rationally supportable on at least four entirely valid grounds. The regulation can be clearly justified, Maryland argues, in terms of legitimate state interests in encouraging gainful employment, in maintaining an equitable balance in economic status as between welfare families and those supported by a wage-earner, in providing incentives for family planning, and in allocating available public funds in such a way as fully to meet the needs of the largest possible number of families. . . .

. . .

In the area of economics and social welfare, a state does not violate the Equal Protection Clause merely because the classifications made by its laws are imperfect. If the classification has some "reasonable basis," it does not offend the Constitution simply because the classification "is not made with mathematical nicety or because in practice it results in some inequality". . . .

. . . And it is a standard that is true to the principle that the Fourteenth Amendment gives the federal courts no power to impose upon the states their views of what constitutes wise economic or social policy.

Under this long-established meaning of the Equal Protection Clause, it is clear that the Maryland maximum grant regulation is constitutionally valid. We need not explore all the reasons that the state advances in justification of the regulation. It is enough that a solid foundation for the regulation can be found in the state's legitimate interest in encouraging employment and in avoiding discrimination between welfare families and the families of the working poor. By combining a limit on the recipient's grant with permission to retain money earned, without reduction in the amount of the grant, Maryland provides an incentive to seek gainful employment. And by keying the maximum family AFDC grants to the minimum wage a steadily employed head of a household receives, the state maintains some semblance of an equitable balance between families on welfare and those supported by an employed breadwinner.

It is true that in some AFDC families there may be no person who is employable. It is also true that with respect to AFDC families whose determined standard of need is below the regulatory maximum, and who therefore receive grants equal to the determined standard, the employment incentive is absent. But the Equal Protection Clause does not require that a state must choose between attacking every aspect of a problem or not attacking the problem at all. . . . It is enough that the state's action be rationally based and free from invidious discrimination. The regulation before us meets that test.

We do not decide today that the Maryland regulation is wise, that it best fulfills the relevant social and economic objectives that Maryland might ideally espouse, or that a more just and humane system could not be devised. Conflicting claims of morality and intelligence are raised by opponents and proponents of almost every measure, certainly including the one before us. But the intractable economic, social, and even philosophical problems presented by public welfare assistance programs are not the business of this Court. The Constitution may impose certain procedural safeguards upon systems of welfare administration. . . . But the Constitution does not empower this Court to second-guess state officials charged with the difficult responsibility of allocating limited public welfare funds among the myriad of potential recipients. . . .

The judgment is reversed.

On August 8, 1969, President Nixon announced a Family Assistance Plan that would radically alter the present welfare system. In effect, it would abolish the Aid to Families with Dependent Children program (AFDC), an intergovernmental program providing federal funds to state welfare departments, and instead would develop a federal program of income maintenance for families with children. It would increase eligibility and raise income levels for millions of families, but it would also require parents receiving aid to register for employment. Congress had not completed action on the plan by the 1972 presidential elections.

The President's message to the American people is presented here. It is followed by a critique of the plan by George A. Wiley, Executive Director of the National Welfare Rights Organization, a welfare clients' organization.

The Family Assistance Plan

Richard M. Nixon

Whether measured by the anguish of the poor themselves, or by the drastically mounting burden on the taxpayer, the present welfare system has to be judged a colossal failure.

Our states and cities find themselves sinking in a welfare quagmire, as caseloads increase, as costs escalate, and as the welfare system stagnates enterprise and perpetuates dependency. What began on a small scale in the depression thirties has become a monster in the prosperous sixties. The tragedy is not only that it is bringing states and cities to the brink of financial disaster, but also that it is failing to meet the elementary human, social, and financial needs of the poor.

It breaks up homes. It often penalizes work. It robs recipients of dignity. And it grows.

Benefit levels are grossly unequal—for a mother with three children, they range from an average of $263 a month in one state, down to an average of $39 in another state. So great an inequality is wrong; no child is "worth" more in one state than in another. One result of this inequality is to lure thousands more into already overcrowded inner cities, as unprepared for city life as they are for city jobs.

The present system creates an incentive for desertion. In most states, a family is denied welfare payments if a father is present—even though he is unable to support his family. In practice, this is what often hap-

From *Weekly Compilation of Presidential Documents*, August 11, 1969.

pens: a father is unable to find a job at all, or one that will support his children. To make the children eligible for welfare, he leaves home—and the children are denied the authority, the discipline, and the love that come with having a father in the house. This is wrong.

The present system often makes it possible to receive more money on welfare than on a low-paying job. This creates an incentive not to work; it also is unfair to the working poor. It is morally wrong for a family that is working to try to make ends meet to receive less than the family across the street on welfare. This has been bitterly resented by the man who works, and rightly so—the rewards are just the opposite of what they should be. Its effect is to draw people off payrolls and onto welfare rolls—just the opposite of what government should be doing. To put it bluntly and simply—any system which makes it more profitable for a man not to work than to work, and which encourages a man to desert his family rather than stay with his family, is wrong and indefensible.

We cannot simply ignore the failures of welfare, or expect them to go away. In the past eight years, three million more people have been added to the welfare rolls—all in a period of low unemployment. If the present trend continues, another four million will have joined the welfare rolls by 1975. The financial cost will be crushing; the human cost will be suffocating.

I propose that we abolish the present welfare system and adopt in its place a new family assistance system. Initially, this new system would cost more than welfare. But unlike welfare, it is designed to correct the condition it deals with and thus to lessen the long-range burden.

Under this plan, the so-called "adult categories" of aid—aid to the aged, the blind, and disabled—would be continued, and a national minimum standard for benefits would be set, with the federal government contributing to its cost and also sharing the cost of additional state payments above that amount.

But the program now called "Aid to Families with Dependent Children"—the program we normally think of when we think of "welfare"—would be done away with completely. The new family assistance system I propose in its place rests essentially on three principles: equality of treatment, a work requirement, and a work incentive.

Its benefits would go to the working poor, as well as the nonworking; to families with dependent children headed by a father, as well as to those headed by a mother; and a basic federal minimum would be provided, the same in every state.

I propose that the federal government build a foundation under the income of every American family with dependent children that cannot care for itself—wherever in America that family may live.

For a family of four now on welfare, with no outside income, the basic federal payment would be $1,600 a year. States could add to that amount and most would do so. In no case would anyone's present level of benefits be lowered. At the same time, this foundation would be one on which the family itself could build. Outside earnings would be encouraged, not discouraged. The new worker could keep the first $60 a month of outside earnings with no reduction in his benefits, and beyond that his benefits would be reduced by only 50 cents for each dollar earned.

By the same token, a family head already employed at low wages could get a family assistance supplement; those who work would no longer be discriminated against. A family of five in which the father earns $2,000 a year—which is the hard fact of life for many families— would get family assistance payments of $1,260 for a total income of $3,260. A family of seven earning $3,000 a year would have its income raised to $4,360.

Thus, for the first time, the government would recognize that it has no less of an obligation to the working poor than to the nonworking poor; and for the first time, benefits would be scaled in such a way that it would always pay to work.

With such incentives, most recipients who can work will want to work. This is part of the American character.

But what of the others—those who can work but choose not to?

The answer is very simple.

Under this proposal, everyone who accepts benefits must also accept work or training provided suitable jobs are available either locally or at some distance if transportation is provided. The only exceptions would be those unable to work, and mothers of preschool children. Even mothers of preschool children, however, would have the *opportunity* to work—because I am also proposing along with this a major expansion of day-care centers to make it possible for mothers to take jobs by which they can support themselves and their children.

This national floor under incomes for working or dependent families is not a "guaranteed income." Under the guaranteed income proposal, everyone would be assured a minimum income, regardless of how much he was capable of earning, regardless of what his need was, regardless of whether or not he was willing to work.

During the presidential campaign last year I opposed such a plan. I oppose it now, and will continue to oppose it. A guaranteed income would undermine the incentive to work; the family assistance plan increases the incentive to work. A guaranteed income establishes a right without responsibilities; family assistance recognizes a need *and* establishes a responsibility. It provides help to those in need, and in turn requires that those who receive help work to the extent of their capabilities. There is no reason why one person should be taxed so that another can choose to live idly.

In states that now have benefit levels above the federal floor, family assistance would help ease the states' financial burdens. But in twenty states—those in which poverty is most widespread—the new federal floor would be above present average benefit levels, and would mean a leap upward for many thousands of families that cannot care for themselves.

The Nixon Family Assistance Plan: Reform or Repression?

George A. Wiley

"I'm black and I'm beautiful, I'm on welfare and I'm not ashamed—and I'm mad." So said Jennette Washington, one of the New York leaders of the welfare rights movement during the early days of the struggle. This combination of militance, self-awareness, and assertion of dignity has characterized the struggle for welfare rights since its inception. . . .

At the height of the nationwide struggle we have a proposal from President Nixon to "reform" the welfare system. The proposal must be examined in the context of the political forces which produced it. Such an analysis will show the Nixon plan to be a repression against welfare mothers who have been fighting to change their conditions, rather than the reform it is heralded to be.

Historically, welfare was not designed to benefit poor people. It can best be understood as a system designed intentionally to maintain people at as near starvation as conscience or political climate would

From *Black Law Journal*, 1 (Spring 1971), pp. 70–76. George A. Wiley is Executive Director of the National Welfare Rights Organization. Reprinted by permission.

permit, and to maintain them under conditions as humiliating and degrading as possible. The purpose of this design is to insure that no one who is able to work will seek welfare as an alternative to working, no matter how menial or low-paying the job. Indeed the welfare system in the South has been one of the primary institutions that insured the white plantation owners of a ready supply of cheap black labor to work for slave-wage pay and working conditions.

While meager welfare benefits would be offered in the off-season, every able-bodied black including women would be purged from the welfare rolls whenever the cotton chopping or harvest season approached. Welfare laws were always enforced in a selective and discriminatory manner. Moreover the arbitrary rules and regulations of the welfare system facilitated the political subjugation of blacks whose source of subsistence was controlled by white caseworkers. Nor were these techniques the exclusive property of the segregationist South. The welfare system was only slightly better in the North. It operated in a manner that was arbitrary and flagrantly discriminatory. Recipients were subject to the arbitrary will of the caseworker and degraded, humiliated, and harassed in innumerable ways.

Then in mid-1966 came the welfare rights movement spearheaded by a handful of erstwhile civil rights activists who saw in the welfare system a vehicle for organizing a nationwide grassroots political force. They saw the potential for seizing one of the most repressive institutions which subjugates and humiliates millions of black people, and, by organizing against it, fomenting a crisis which would not only pervade the welfare system but which would rock the foundations of all the economic institutions which exploit the labors of blacks and, indeed, many poor whites and other minorities as well.

The techniques of the movement were simple—to learn the rules and regulations of the welfare system so carefully and systematically hidden from the view of recipients and potential recipients. This information was disseminated throughout the ghettos, barrios, and rural areas across the nation. Poor people were encouraged to stand up and fight for the millions and millions of dollars in benefits and entitlements being illegally denied them. At the same time legal challenges were mounted against the eligibility rules and welfare practices which are outside the Constitution, the Social Security Act, or the state and local laws under which welfare is supposed to operate. The objectives of the movement were to build a nationwide grassroots poor people's organization and to mount substantial pressure on the welfare system.

In the ensuing years these techniques proved effective in building a network of more than 700 welfare rights organizations encompassing all fifty states and every major city in the country. These local groups were linked up with the National Welfare Rights Organization. Using militant direct action methods, welfare recipients won campaign after campaign: for school clothing, furniture, special diets, winter clothing, free school lunches, simpler and fairer procedures, speedier treatment, and higher welfare grants in many states. At the same time legal attacks were striking down man-in-house rules and durational residence requirements, establishing the right to privacy and eliminating many of the arbitrary practices and multiple standards where welfare recipients are judged by different criteria of law than the society at large.

The result of this onslaught has been a vast expansion of the numbers of people eligible for welfare. But much more important it opened access to welfare to those who did not know how to apply for welfare, or had applied and were illegally denied.

The result has been dramatic increases in welfare caseloads over the past five years coupled with spectacular increases in welfare costs during the same period of time. The number of people on AFDC has risen from 4.5 million in 1966 to 8.5 million in 1970 with 12.5 million recipients in all categories. Total welfare costs have risen from about 5.5 billion in 1966 to over $12 billion in 1970. . . .

The drastic increases in welfare rolls and welfare costs have caused a hue and cry from the nation's mayors and governors and have precipitated a national debate concerning the ills of the welfare system. Practically every governor in the country is on record for federal takeover of the welfare system. It is in this climate that President Nixon introduced his Family Assistance Plan. A few excerpts from the President's speech of August 8, 1969 will be enlightening. He spoke of the present welfare system in this way—

> Whether measured by the anguish of the poor themselves, or by the drastically mounting burden on the taxpayer, the present welfare system has to be judged a colossal failure.
>
> Our states and cities find themselves sinking in a federal welfare quagmire; as caseloads increase, as costs escalate, and as the welfare system stagnates enterprise and perpetuates dependency. What began on a small scale in the depression thirties has become a monster in the prosperous sixties. And the tragedy is not only that it is bringing states and cities to the brink of financial disaster, but also that it is failing to meet the elementary human, social, and financial needs of the poor. It breaks up homes. It often penalizes work. It robs recipients of dignity. And it grows.

In other places in the speech President Nixon refers to the objective of his Family Assistance proposal: "it aims at getting everyone able to work off the welfare rolls and onto payrolls"—"we cannot legislate our way out of poverty; but this nation can work its way out of poverty." What America needs now is not more welfare but more "workfare."

It should be of little surprise then that the Nixon plan provided little benefit to poor people and in the long run substantial savings to the state and local governments. The basic thrust of the Nixon program is a $1,600 per year federal income floor for a family of four extended only on the condition that the potential recipient accept any offer of employment that is made no matter how menial the job and no matter what working conditions or wages are offered. This forced work program is the heart of the Nixon plan. It is an enshrining in federal law of the basic principles that are the root cause of the horrors of our present welfare system. It is inherent in the approach that the benefit levels must always be inadequate; that the program will be categorical to effectively sort out the "deserving" from the "undeserving" poor; that it will be deficient in real incentives and opportunities for recipients to obtain self-sufficiency; that it will be demeaning to recipients; that it will have a complicated and costly bureaucracy to administer it; and it will deny rights and benefits to millions of people who are in urgent and desperate need.

The Nixon Family Assistance Plan is indeed yet another welfare program for the business community. For it will assure them a supply of cheap labor. An employer need only inform the local welfare office that jobs are available and recipients must work for him at whatever pay is offered or lose their welfare benefits.

. . .

It is [the National Welfare Rights Organization's] belief that the defeat of the Family Assistance Plan, coupled with the stepping up of the grassroots pressure on the welfare system and an active and informed citizens lobby, can force the Congress to start the country on the road toward real welfare reform.

WHAT IS TRUE WELFARE REFORM?

A real welfare reform must meet the following basic tests:

1. Provide an adequate income floor to every person who needs it.
2. Provide the income in a way that is neither degrading to the dignity of recipients nor destructive of family life.
3. Provide a just system that protects the rights of recipients and provides reasonable opportunities for recipients to redress grievances with the system.
4. Provide the income through a simple administrative mechanism.
5. Provide the income in equitable fashion so that it meets the needs of

recipients in the actual conditions in which they live across the country.

6. Provide economic and other incentives for recipients to improve their economic situations.

7. Redistribute income sufficiently to provide poor people a reasonably competitive position in the nation's economy.

The National Welfare Rights Organization has developed a plan which meets these basic tests. The plan has been drafted in legislative form and introduced into the last Congress by Senator Eugene McCarthy. It never received any significant hearing in the Senate in spite of its endorsement by the White House Conference on Food, Nutrition, and Health and a number of major organizations ranging from the United Church of Christ to the United Auto Workers. Another attempt will be made in the next Congress.

ADEQUATE INCOME

Adequate income means providing people with money to meet the basic necessities of life such as food, clothing, housing, health care, transportation, and recreation. The NWRO plan is based upon surveys of actual costs of these items conducted by the Bureau of Labor Statistics of the U.S. Department of Labor and the U.S. Department of Agriculture. It uses the basic needs budget based on the "looser standard budget" of the Bureau of Labor Statistics combined with the "moderate food plan" of the U.S. Department of Agriculture. The moderate food plan was used because Agriculture Department surveys showed that three-quarters of the families living with less money for food did not have a nutritionally adequate diet. From these surveys it is clear that an average urban family of four required $5,500 per year to meet their basic necessities in 1969.

In addition to this income they would have to be provided with free health care, free legal services, and free child care plus special grants for major items of furniture or other emergencies when they arise. Adjustments in the grant of approximately $1,000 per year would be necessary for each additional member of the family. Further, since the $5,500 figure applies to the year 1969, it requires a cost-of-living adjustment to $6,660 per year for the year 1971. The NWRO plan also provides for regional adjustment in the income for different areas of the country where costs of living may vary.

. . .

Not only is the Nixon plan's $1,600 benefit level inadequate, this standard falls below the level of present payments for 90 per cent of the AFDC recipients in forty-three states. It offers states numerous loopholes by which they may cut the pitifully low benefits that AFDC recipients presently receive. The plan is devised in such a way that it clearly regards the poverty line of $3,720 per year as the maximum that ever should be paid in welfare benefits. The poverty line is derived from the U.S. Department of Agriculture's "economy food plan" which the federal government itself recognizes is inadequate to provide a nutritious diet for more than a brief emergency period.

DIGNITY

The second requisite of a welfare reform is to provide the income in such a way that it preserves the dignity of the individual and the integrity of the family. The first prerequisite for dignity is the provision of an adequate income. For poverty itself and the squalid and humiliating living conditions that it requires is inherently demeaning.

The penny-pinching attitude which denies an adequate income usually brings with it a welfare bureaucracy which investigates every aspect of a recipient's personal life. . . . The Nixon Family Assistance Plan was shot through with requirements which would degrade and humiliate recipients. Policing the enforced work requirements, for example, would impose major control by the welfare bureaucracy over recipients' lives, require registration and reregistration for work by recipients, and permit caseworkers to cross-examine them concerning their efforts to find jobs.

In addition, the Family Assistance Plan included payments to third parties as punishment for recipients who do not satisfy the caseworker in their pursuit of work. Absent fathers who may through no fault of their own be unable to support their families would be pursued doggedly by use of federal records not normally available to welfare administrators. Federal benefits they might receive at any time in their lives could be confiscated to replace money paid to their families under Family Assistance. These onerous provisions have been doggedly preserved by the administration through all versions of the bill. A variety of other punitive provisions were advanced by the administration from time to time, although most of them were ultimately repulsed by the welfare rights lobby before the final stages of debate.

In contrast to these demeaning provisions, the NWRO plan simply identifies need as the basic test for whether a person can get assistance and would rely on the person's sworn affidavit analogous to the income tax return as evidence of the need.

JUSTICE

An income maintenance system must recognize and protect the constitutional rights of recipients. Many of the indignities and injustices of our present welfare system result from denial of basic rights of people as citizens. In fact it is a commonplace belief that recipients of public assistance should give up their rights as citizens because they are accepting "public charity." The most basic right of a recipient must be the right to know what his entitlements are and the right to have some voice in determining the policies which affect him. This means that the welfare regulations must be disseminated in simplified form and made available to poor people. This means that organizations of recipients must have access to those regulations and must have a voice in how the policies and regulations are determined. Neither of these principles are recognized in the Nixon plan. As mentioned previously, the Nixon plan includes provisions which erode rights protected, however weakly, in the present Social Security Act. The undermining of the money payment principle, the pursuit of absent parents, the return of the stepfather clause, a version of the man-in-the-house rule, and the forced work provisions are examples of this erosion.

Beyond these protections, recipients must have the right to a fair hearing and, if necessary, court review, before benefits under the plan may be reduced or terminated. This right has been established by several Supreme Court decisions and a weak provision implementing it was included in the Nixon Family Assistance Plan.

. . .

EQUITY

We have already described how the NWRO plan would deal with equitable distribution of resources according to the needs in various parts of the country, the needs of various family sizes, and the changes in needs resulting from changes in the cost of living.

The basic framework of the Nixon plan perpetuates the categorical approach which is at the heart of the inequities of the present system. It basically establishes four categories: the aged, disabled, and blind make up one category. A single recipient in this category could receive as much as $1,560 a year compared with the $1,600 for family of *four* under the family category. The second category for families at least has the virtue of bringing working and nonworking recipients as well as female- and male-headed families under a single part of the plan, but it provides the benefits at such a low level that most of the present inequity in benefit levels from state to state would continue.

The third program would be a state-run supplementation program which would maintain present AFDC recipients at their present benefit levels (except for cuts which are permitted under the loopholes described earlier); in addition in some versions of the bill an unemployment parent program was mandated to require states to supplement families with two parents but with an unemployed father at least at their present AFDC level. And finally, the fourth category would include single individuals and couples without children who would be totally excluded from any benefits under any of the federal programs. Thus the Nixon plan would project an extension of the complicated hodgepodge of programs with varying payments and requirements from one category to another and with varying payments and eligibility requirements from one state to another. The NWRO proposal would erect a single category which would cover all persons in need in all parts of the country at an adequate income level for their family size and region of the country. It would not arbitrarily and categorically distinguish between young and old, disabled or nondisabled, working or nonworking, two-parent or single-parent families.

INCENTIVES

The question of incentives is a controversial part of income maintenance. On the one hand the inclusion of provisions to allow recipients to keep a portion of earned income adds a very large apparent cost to the plan. If one is concerned about the total cost of a program, then the inclusion of a large "work incentive," that is permitting the welfare recipient to keep a large portion of earned income without losing his benefits, adds considerably to the cost of the program. The NWRO plan would cost approximately $20 billion to simply supplement the present income of poor people from work or other sources up to the adequate income standard for his family size. It would cost an additional $45 billion to allow recipients to keep 50 per cent of earned income. In the NWRO plan we propose a lower "work incentive" in order to allow adequate basic payment levels without raising the cost unduly.

The NWRO plan provides an earnings exemption of 33⅓ per cent. This adds about $30 billion to the cost. It provides a smooth transition between total dependency on the income plan to total self-sufficiency. That is to say a recipient does not feel that if he goes out and earns an additional $10, $10 will be deducted from his check. Under our plan for every $100 earned he would lose $67 from his payment or, conversely, he would be able to keep $33 of each $100 earned. This means that a family would continue to benefit from a plan until its total income reaches $8,246 a year. Because of the way the tax system would be adjusted, any family of four earning less than $10,000 would benefit from the NWRO program.

Under the Nixon plan work incentives would be very complicated. Ostensibly, a 50 per cent earnings exemption was proposed. However, when one read the fine print one found that the earning exemption varied widely in the various versions and for people in the various categories. For some categories of some people in some parts of the country the exemption was actually less than 10 per cent; for most people it ranged between 20 and 30 per cent. A uniform 33⅓ per cent income exemption is clearly more equitable and more desirable.

REDISTRIBUTION OF INCOME

If an income maintenance plan fails to redistribute wealth in the country in the direction of poor people, it cannot fulfill the basic objective of eliminating poverty. For poverty is a relative thing, related in part to the vast discrepancy between those people who have and those who have not. In the United States the wealthiest 20 per cent of the population receive 40 per cent of all income received in a given year and the poorest 20 per cent of the population receive less than 6 per cent of the total income. This is a condition that has existed for the last hundred years. It was very little affected by the introduction of the income tax system in 1913. And, needless to say, it would be virtually unaffected by the Nixon Family Assistance Plan. Since under the NWRO plan only persons earning above $10,000 would bear the cost of the plan and everyone earning $10,000 or less would benefit, the result is that the one-third of the population with incomes above $10,000 would have their wealth trimmed somewhat to increase the share for persons below $10,000, with the heaviest benefit going to those people below $5,500. We estimate that the share going to the bottom 20 per cent should more than double while the share going to the top 20 per cent would be trimmed perhaps by as much as 50 per cent.

What we have, therefore, in the Family Assistance Plan is a plan which fails to redistribute wealth, which perpetuates the inequities of our present welfare system, and which adds onerous forced work provisions designed to subjugate poor people and harass them.

It is discouraging to us that so many white liberals and so many black leaders were duped by the sham of the Nixon plan. Toward the end of 1970, however, the welfare rights lobby turned the tide of battle against the Family Assistance Plan. The task for 1971 is to consolidate our forces and drive for a guaranteed adequate income for all Americans.

4 SEXISM

American political, social, and economic life excludes 51 per cent of the population from meaningful participation. Women were not referred to in the Declaration of Independence, which referred only to the "self-evident" truth that "all *men* are created equal." Women did not gain the right to vote when the Constitution was adopted, nor did they participate in its drafting or ratification. Due process of law and equal protection of the laws, applied to the states through the Fourteenth Amendment, referred to men; women did not gain the right to vote until passage of the Nineteenth Amendment in 1920.

Even though the suffrage movement culminated in the adoption of the Nineteenth Amendment giving women the right to vote, the inferior status of women in America remained unchanged. "Protective" legislation based on sex prevented some exploitation of women in industry, but other legislation made it difficult for women to hold certain jobs or conduct business, provided for lower pay scales, and kept married women from conducting their own business affairs. The educational system discouraged women from entering the professions, while employers were permitted to exploit educated women in low-paying positions. Today fewer than 10 per cent of the scientists, 7 per cent of the doctors, 4 per cent of the lawyers, and 20 per cent of the college teachers, are women. Few women are in the management levels of civil service or the corporate world, although many perform managerial tasks with the rank (and low salary) of "Assistant to Mr. Big."

And this does not exhaust the inequities. Women are "excused" from jury duty, the military, and even from intercollegiate athletics. Women are discharged from work for being pregnant (even if married), and they are denied maternity leaves, child care facilities, and time off from work to care for sick children. Work schedules in male-dominated organizations are rarely arranged so that women can supervise their households and also work. (Nor do males usually share in the supervision of children after the children return from school for the day.) Women are denied control over their own bodies: abortion laws, contraception and birth control policies and programs, and sterilization programs are all legislated and funded (if at all) by male-dominated legislatures and administrative bodies.

The participation of women in politics is minimal. Between 1959 and 1969 the number of women in Congress decreased from 17 to 11; in state elective offices the number declined from 41 to 30; in state legislatures it went down from 347 to 305. And in 1969 there were only two women federal judges. There has never been a female justice on the

Supreme Court, a female ambassador to the United Nations, or a female vice president. In 1972 there were no women in the cabinet or in key positions on the White House staff.

In recent years there have been minimal changes. In 1963 Congress passed the *Equal Pay Act* (an amendment to the *Fair Labor Standards Act*), and forty states have also passed measures providing equal pay for equal work. None of this legislation is enforced very effectively, but courts have begun to award compensatory back pay when cases of sex-based discrimination in pay scales are proven. Title VII of the *Civil Rights Act of 1964* prohibits discrimination in employment based on sex (among other things). But the Equal Employment Opportunity Commission, which is charged with the enforcement of the title, has until recently had no power other than to conciliate between the employer and prospective employees. In 1972 it finally received the power to sue in Federal District Court when conciliation fails.

A series of executive orders issued by Presidents Johnson and Nixon bar discrimination in employment involving the federal government or federal contractors. The Office of Civil Rights of the Department of Health, Education, and Welfare has been delegated enforcement of these orders as they apply to colleges and universities. Negotiations with Columbia University are expected by HEW officials to serve as a prototype for the "affirmative action" that will be required in many of the nation's universities. The Department of Labor may eventually take action against unions and corporations that discriminate against women.

There are over one thousand state statutes which involve sex-based distinctions. At present civil rights organizations and women's liberation groups are attempting individual attacks, state by state, on the statutes. A proposed Women's Rights Amendment, if adopted, would end the need for such efforts by eliminating all sex-based distinctions in American public law. Until such an amendment is passed, however, individual lobbying and litigation will be necessary. The American Civil Liberties Union, realizing this fact, adopted "Women's Rights" as its top priority for 1972.

An interesting notion for men to ponder is *male* liberation. If women were drafted, fewer men would have to serve in the military. In divorce proceedings, men would not be expected to pay alimony nor women to take custody of the children without more careful consideration of individual circumstances. Husbands would no longer be liable for the debts of their wives. Ending differential pay rates and phony job classifications would mean that families would receive more income when the wife worked. Many jobs now held mostly by women would be open to men: They could become nurses, elementary school teachers, and airline stewards (there would not be only stewardesses).

Finally, an end to sexism means an end to the hypocrisy of social relations in American society. Not only will women be free to reject confining roles, but men will be free as well to reject the *machismo* image. The end of role-playing is long overdue, and may be the greatest benefit women's liberation brings to the other 49 per cent of the population.

The following article by Betty Friedan is intended as a brief introduction to the political aspects of the women's liberation movement.

Our Revolution Is Unique

Betty Friedan

... We new feminists have begun to define ourselves—existentially— through action. We have learned that while we had much to learn from the black civil rights movement and their revolution against economic and racial oppression, our own revolution is unique: it must define its own ideology.

We can cut no corners; we are, in effect, where the black revolution was perhaps fifty years ago; but the speed with which our revolution is moving now is our unearned historical benefit from what has happened in that revolution. Yet there can be no illusion on our part that a separatist ideology copied from black power will work for us. Our tactics and strategy and, above all, our ideology must be firmly based in the his-

From President's Report to The National Conference of NOW, delivered in Atlanta, Georgia, December 6, 1968. Reprinted from *Voices of the New Feminism,* edited by Mary Lou Thompson, by permission of Curtis Brown, Ltd. All rights reserved. Betty Friedan is the founder and first president of the National Organization for Women.

torical, biological, economic, and psychological reality of our two-sexed world, which is not the same as the black reality and different also from the reality of the first feminist wave.

Thanks to the early feminists, we who have mounted this second stage of the feminist revolution have grown up with the right to vote, little as we may have used it for our own purposes. We have grown up with the right to higher education and to employment, and with some, not all, of the legal rights of equality. Insofar as we have moved on the periphery of the mainstream of society, with the skills and the knowledge to command its paychecks, even if insufficient, and to make decisions, even if not consulted beyond housework, we begin to have a self-respecting image of ourselves, as women, not just in sexual relation to men, but as full human beings in society. We are able, at least some of us, to see men, in general or in particular, without blind rancor or hostility, and to face oppression as it reveals itself in our concrete experience with politicians, bosses, priests, or husbands. We do not need to suppress our just grievances. We now have enough courage to express them. And yet we are able to conceive the possibility of full affirmation for man. Man is not the enemy, but the fellow victim of the present half-equality. As we speak, act, demonstrate, testify, and appear on television on matters such as sex discrimination in employment, public accommodations, education, divorce-marriage reform, or abortion repeal, we hear from men who feel they can be freed to greater self-fulfillment to the degree that women are released from the binds that now constrain them.

. . .

Another point we are conscious of in the new feminism is that we are a revolution for all, not for an exceptional few. This, above all, distinguishes us from those token spokeswomen of the period since women won the vote, the Aunt Toms who managed to get a place for themselves in society, and who were, I think, inevitably seduced into an accommodating stance, helping to keep the others quiet. We are beginning to know that no woman can achieve a real breakthrough alone, as long as sex discrimination exists in employment, under the law, in education, in mores, and in denigration of the image of women.

Even those of us who have managed to achieve a precarious success in a given field still walk as freaks in "man's world" since every profession—politics, the church, teaching—is still structured as man's world. Walking as a freak makes one continually self-conscious, apologetic, if not defiant, about being a woman. One is made to feel there are three sexes—men, other women, and myself. The successful woman may think, "I am the exception, the 'brilliant' one with the rare ability to be an anthropologist, author, actress, broker, account executive, or television commentator; but you drones out there, you watch the television set. And what better use can you make of your life than doing the dishes for your loved ones?"

We cannot say that all American women want equality, because we know that women, like all oppressed people, have accepted the traditional denigration by society. Some women have been too much hurt by denigration from others, by self-denigration, by lack of the experiences, education, and training needed to move in society as equal human beings, to have the confidence that they can so move in a competitive society. They say they don't want equality—they have to be happy, adjust to things as they are. Such women find us threatening.

. . .

Perhaps the least understood fact of American political life is the enormous buried violence of women in this country today. Like all oppressed people, women have been taking their violence out on their own bodies, in all the maladies with which they plague the doctors' offices and the psychoanalysts. They have been taking out their violence inadvertently and in subtle and in insidious ways on their children and on their husbands. And sometimes, they are not so subtle, for the battered child syndrome that we are hearing more and more about in our hospitals is almost always to be found in the instance of unwanted children, and women are doing the battering, as much or more than men.

Man, we have said, is not the enemy. Men will only be truly liberated, to love women and to be fully themselves, when women are liberated to be full people. Until that happens, men are going to bear the burden and the guilt of the destiny they have forced upon women, the suppressed resentment of that passive stage—the sterility of love, when love is not between two fully active, fully participant, fully joyous people, but has in it the element of exploitation. And men will also not be fully free to be all they can be as long as they must live up to an image of masculinity that denies to a man all the tenderness and sensitivity that might be considered feminine. Men have in them enormous capacities that they have to repress and fear in themselves, in living up to this obsolete and brutal man-eating, lion-killing, Ernest Hemingway image of masculinity— the image of all-powerful masculine superiority. All the burdens and responsibilities that men are supposed to shoulder alone, make them, I think, resent women's pedestal, while the burden to women is enforced passivity.

So the real sexual revolution is not the cheap headlines in the papers —at what age boys and girls go to bed with each other and whether they do it with or without the benefit of marriage. That's the least of it. The real sexual revolution is the emergence of women from passivity, from thingness, to full self-determination, to full dignity. And insofar as they can do this, men are also emerging from the stage of identification with brutality and masters to full and sensitive complete humanity.

A revolutionary theory that's adequate to the current demand of the sexual revolution must also address itself to the concrete realities of our society. We can only transcend the reality of the institutions that oppress us by confronting them in our actions now; confronting reality, we change it; we begin to create alternatives, not in abstract discussion, but here and now.

. . .

If we are going to address ourselves to the need for changing the social institutions that will permit women to be free and equal individuals, participating actively in their society and changing that society —with men—then we must talk in terms of what is possible, and not accept what is as what must be. . . .

. . .

We need not accept marriage as it's currently structured with the implicit idea of man, the breadwinner, and woman, the housewife. There are many different ways we could posit marriage. But there seems to be a reasonable guess that men and women are going to want relationships of long-term intimacy tied in with sexual relationship, although we can certainly posit a large variety of sex relationships than now seem conventional. And it's not possible, much less conducive to health, happiness, or self-fulfillment, for women or men to completely suppress their sexual needs.

We can change institutions, but it is a fantasy deviation from a really revolutionary approach to say that we want a world in which there will be no sex, no marriage, that in order for women to be free they must have a manless revolution. We have to deal with the world of reality if we are going to have a real revolution.

I don't happen to think that women and men are so completely different that it is impossible for us to see each other as human beings. I think that it is as possible for men to put themselves finally in woman's place by an act of empathy or by guilt or by awareness of human rights as it has been possible for some whites to do for blacks. But it's perhaps not much more possible than that, though there are more bonds between men and women, and really men's stake in this revolution is greater, because a woman can make a man's life hell if it isn't solved. But I think it would be as much of a mistake to expect men to hand this to women as to consider all men as the enemy, all men as oppressors. This revolution can have the support of men, but women must take the lead in fighting it as any other oppressed group has had to.

. . .

On the question of self-determination, we became painfully aware, in our attempts to get a bill of rights for women into the platforms of both political parties at the last presidential election and as a major issue in the election for all candidates for national office, that we need *political power.* Our only success then was getting the word "sex" added to a rather vague antidiscrimination sentence in the Republican platform.

We must overcome our diversity of varied political beliefs. Our common commitment is to equality for women. And we are not single-issue people; we want a voice for all women, to raise our voices in decision-making on all matters from war and peace to the kinds of cities we're going to inhabit. Many large issues concern all of us; on these things we may differ. We will surmount this. Political power is necessary to change the situation of the oppressed 51 per cent, to realize the power potential in the fact that women *are* 51 per cent.

We will do it by getting into city hall ourselves, or by getting into Congress ourselves, regardless of whether our political party is Republican or Democratic or Peace and Freedom. We're only going to do it by getting there ourselves; that's the nitty-gritty of self-determination for us—not to rely on Richard Nixon or a Senate with only one female or a House with only a few women to do it for us.

In this we can be united. We had notable successes, in spite of a general political failure on our part in respect to the platforms in the presidential election. In California through the initiative of one member of NOW, the NOW Bill of Rights for Women was incorporated into the state platform of the California Democratic Party. In other cities (Pittsburgh, Syracuse, New York) and states where we had active chapters and where those chapters took advantage of hearings that were held on platforms to raise these issues, we began to get *an awareness* of woman's existence from politicians to whom previously women were simply invisible people. Though it's not going to be easy, by 1972 I think we must be determined that we will have our own Julian Bonds, that we will find some way to confront and break through the travesty of women's visibility in American political conventions only as mini-skirted greeters or at ladies' luncheons.

We must begin to use the power of our actions: to make women finally *visible* as people in America, as conscious political and social power; to change our society *now,* so all women can move freely, as people, in it.

The two political programs reproduced below describe some of the political goals of the women's liberation movement. Local women's groups, aided by various national organizations, develop their own local demands and political strategies.

Bill of Rights

National Organization for Women

I. Equal Rights Constitutional Amendment
II. Enforce Law Banning Sex Discrimination in Employment
III. Maternity Leave Rights in Employment and in Social Security Benefits
IV. Tax Deduction for Home and Child Care Expenses for Working Parents
V. Child Day Care Centers
VI. Elimination of Discrimination in Education
VII. Anti-Poverty Measures Which Protect Human Dignity
VIII. The Right of Women to Control Their Reproductive Lives
IX. Equal Access to Public Accommodations and Housing
X. Partnership Marriages of Equalized Rights and Shared Responsibilities

We Demand:
I. That the Equal Rights Amendment to the Constitution, passed by the Congress, be immediately ratified by the several states to provide that "Equality of rights under the law shall not be denied or abridged by the United States or by any State on account of sex."
II. That equal employment opportunity be guaranteed to all women, as well as men, by insisting that the Equal Employment Opportunity Commission enforces the prohibitions against sex discrimination in employment under Title VII of the Civil Rights Act of 1964 with the same vigor as it enforces the prohibitions against racial discrimination.
III. That women be protected by law to ensure their rights to return to their jobs within a reasonable time after childbirth without loss of seniority or other accrued benefits, and be paid maternity leave as a form of social security and/or employee benefit.
IV. Immediate revision of tax laws to permit the deduction of home and child care expenses for working parents.

V. That child care facilities be established by law on the same basis as parks, libraries, and public schools, adequate to the needs of children from the pre-school years through adolescence, as a community resource to be used by all citizens from all income levels.

VI. That the right of women to be educated to their full potential equally with men be secured by Federal and State legislation, eliminating all discrimination and segregation by sex, written and unwritten, at all levels of education, including colleges, graduate and professional schools, loans and fellowships, and Federal and State training programs such as the Job Corps.

VII. The right of women in poverty to secure job training, housing, and family allowances on equal terms with men, but without prejudice to a parent's right to remain at home to care for his or her children; revision of welfare legislation and poverty programs which deny women dignity, privacy, and self-respect.

VIII. The right of women to control their own reproductive lives by removing from penal codes laws limiting access to contraceptive information and devices and laws governing abortion.

IX. Amendment of Title II of the Civil Rights Act and state laws to include prohibition of sex discrimination in places of public accommodation, housing.

X. Revision of marriage, divorce and family laws to equalize the rights of men and women to own property, establish domicile, maintain individual identity and economic independence, etc., and promote marriage as an equal partnership of shared responsibility in all its aspects.

Women Unite for Revolution

Congress to Unite Women

The Congress to Unite Women is a historic event in the unfinished revolution for women's liberation. Over 500 women from the eastern United States met in New York November 21–23 to set up a Congress to Unite Women. A Continuing Committee was established to carry out

Reprinted from Leslie B. Tanner, ed., *Voices from Women's Liberation,* New York: The New American Library, 1971. Appeared originally in *Woman's Monthly,* November 28, 1969.

the decisions of the Congress and to set in motion procedures for a permanent nationwide coalition for women's liberation.

The Congress to Unite Women is committed to the liberation of all women now. We know that only with power can we end the oppression of women. Together, in a united Congress we will fight for what is good for women.

1. With regard to early childhood education and care: We demand nationwide free twenty-four-hour-a-day child-care centers for all children from infancy to early adolescence, regardless of their parents' income or marital status, with child-care practices decided by those using the centers. To encourage the breakdown of sex-role stereotypes, these centers must be staffed equally by women and men. Their wages should be equal to those of public school teachers.

Until these free child-care centers are established, we demand immediate national and state legislation for deduction of child-care expenses from income before taxes.

2. In the field of education, we are against the tracking system. We believe high school and college guidance counseling must not restrict individuals to sex-determined roles. Home economics, shop, and other vocational courses must be made available to all without regard to sex. History texts and anthologies of literature must be changed to represent fairly and correctly the achievements of women. Workshops on women's problems should be conducted for parents, teachers, and teachers-in-training, and be included in adult and continuing education courses.

Women, regardless of marital status or pregnancy, must be guaranteed the right to attend school.

We demand a women's studies section in all public libraries and school and university libraries.

We encourage the academic community to restructure language to reflect a society in which women have equal status with men.

Educational institutions must no longer be exempt from Title VII of the 1964 Civil Rights Act.

We demand the elimination of nepotism rules from colleges and universities.

We demand that all educational institutions set up day-care centers for all students, faculties, and staff.

Woman's study programs should be established in all colleges and universities.

3. On the subject of employment, we demand that working hours be made flexible for both men and women.

We demand legal steps to open trade schools and unions to women.

We support ACLU Women's Rights Project, and intend to create dossiers analyzing individual companies and the per cent of women hired in each job category.

Part-time employment must be made available for women who want it.

All women are oppressed as women and can unite on that basis; however, we acknowledge that there are differences among women—male-created—of economic and social privilege, race, education, etc., and that these differences are real, not imaginary. Such divisions must be eliminated. They can only be eliminated by hard work and concrete action, not by rhetoric.

POLITICAL POWER

The Congress to Unite Women announces the formation of a women's political power block to fight for women's liberation. We now expand the definition of political to include women's "personal" lives, meaning both the structure of government in the present society, and new alternatives on which women unite. While we demand representation on all such bodies in proportion to our numbers (presently fifty-one per cent), we see this only as a means to an even larger end—the total liberation of women by every avenue available.

1. We will work against people in politically powerful positions who have demonstrated that they oppose our interest.

2. We are determined to get priority in political attention for our issues, particularly child care, abortion, civil rights, and the Equal Rights Amendment.

SEX ROLES

We must proceed on the assumption that there are *no* biological bases for any sex-role differentiation beyond the basic reproductive functions. If we are truly free we will soon find out what differences there are, if any.

Children should be given *human* models to emulate, not just male and female models.

We must each have the courage to fight to live our own beliefs in undifferentiated sex roles.

WOMEN AND THE LAW

We resolve to direct attention to two issues now:

1. The Civil Rights Act of 1964 includes sex in only Title VII, which

covers employment. There is no provision for penalty against discrimination or enforcement of the act. There is no money available for suits, which must be instituted at the expense of the plaintiff.

2. An Equal Rights Amendment is essential. While the Fourteenth Amendment guarantees equal protection under the law to all persons who are citizens, the Supreme Court has refused to rule on the issue of whether women are persons.

ABORTION

The Congress to Unite Women recognizes women's basic human right to decide whether to have children and opposes in the courts, in the legislature, and in direct action all attitudes, practices, and laws that would compel any woman to bear a child against her will. We not only demand the *total* repeal *now* of all laws restricting access to contraception, sterilization, and abortion, and in the free public provision of such birth control services in all hospitals and clinics; but, concomitantly, we insist that appropriate safeguards be developed so that women are not coerced or in any way pressured into birth control, sterilization, or abortion.

We protest the derogatory image of women presented by the media. This Congress deplores the misrepresentation of the movement for women's liberation to the women of America.

The Women's Rights Amendment has been introduced in every session of Congress since 1923, yet only in recent years has it been taken seriously. It finally reached floor action in Congress and on March 22, 1972, was passed by the necessary two-thirds of the members in each house. It must now be ratified by three-fourths of the state legislatures.

The selections that follow the text of the amendment discuss some of the arguments in favor of and against its adoption.

Equal Rights Amendment

Equality of rights under the law shall not be denied or abridged by the United States or by any state on account of sex. Congress and the several states shall have the power, within their respective jurisdictions, to enforce this article by appropriate legislation.

Equal Rights Amendment: A Historic Step Backward

Emanuel Celler

Mr. Speaker, I yield myself such time as I may require. I rise in opposition to House Joint Resolution 264.

Mr. Speaker, remember that the joint resolution would create equal rights for men as well as equal rights for women. If a right is accorded to a woman and not to a male, that male has a right to object to that woman's right as not accorded to him.

Where would that apply? It would apply to the state laws of alimony. Strangely, it may relate to state laws concerning rape, to military service, support of the family, domicile, age of consent, the bastardy laws, and a whole slew of other laws that time does not permit me to mention.

We have assiduously in the Congress avoided giving jurisdiction to the federal government in domestic relations, marital, and divorce mat-

Senate Joint Resolution 8, 92nd Congress, 1st Session.
From *Congressional Record*, August 10, 1970, H28012-14. Emanuel Celler is a Democratic Representative from New York.

ters. But we would be plunged into that cockpit by the adoption of this amendment, because one of the provisions of the amendment states that the federal government has the right to enforce the provisions of the amendment. The intrusion of the hand of the federal legislature and the federal courts into the very delicate personal relationships of husband and wife and their relationship to their children, including custody and bastardy laws, as I said before, age of consent, and so forth, would bring grief untold.

Remember also that there is no time limit specified for ratification of the amendment. Examine House Joint Resolution 264 and you will see how loosely it has been drawn, how incompletely it has been conceived. This amendment could roam around state legislatures for fifty years. Customarily we provide that ratification must occur within seven years of its submission to the states. But there is no provision of that sort in this resolution. There is unlimited time for the states to ratify it. Ultimately, the Congress will be confronted with the responsibility of determining the validity of state legislature approval.

Do you want to approve an amendment of that sort with such a loose end? Think carefully about that, ladies and gentlemen.

It has been said by the distinguished Speaker—and I have the highest regard for his opinion, but even a cat can look at a king—he says it is a historic step forward. I say it is a historic step backward. Labor spent years and years to get protective legislation for factoryworkers and farmworkers.

At one fell swoop this amendment would wipe out all those protective laws that we, after arduous toil, sought to put on the statute books. And the feminists cavalierly, as I said before, would say, "We do not want protection, we want liberation." I say "Tell that to the Marines." Tell that to the female farmworkers. Tell that to the female factoryworkers. Then get your reply. They want these protections: protection against arduous labor; protection against manual and heavy weightlifting requirements; protection against night work; protection in reference to certain rest periods. These all would go by the board, because they are not accorded to men. Think about that before you vote for this amendment.

As I said, we would just dump the Congress into the cockpit of domestic and marital relations concerning alimony, divorce, domicile, and community property as well as child custody, support, and maintenance. We have addressed ourselves over many years against specific wrong leveled against women. We have arrested many kinds of discriminations against women. That has been done with the help of men. I have been in the forefront of that kind of battle. I struggled long and arduously for passage of title VII of the Civil Rights Act of 1967, giving equality to women in employment. We passed the equal pay law for equal work for women. We passed hundreds of statutes. Hundreds have been passed in the states and in the federal government.

That is the way to proceed in these matters and not by using this blunderbuss proposal that will wipe out all the good as well as the bad. I do not want to wipe out the good. This unfortunately would wipe out the good.

There are over 20 million married women who are nonworking full-time homemakers. What about those homemakers? I am not speaking of the professional women who are in the forefront of this demand for this amendment. What about the homemakers? We do not hear from them, but they are vitally interested. Close to 60 per cent of the women in the labor force are married and must depend upon their husbands for the majority of the family income. Thus, there are approximately 44 million who depend upon their husbands to provide the primary support for the family, and eminent authorities maintain that the equal rights amendment would abolish the common rule whereby a husband has the primary right to support his family.

Thus, I hope that the amendment will be voted down.

Mr. Speaker, I do not oppose this proposed amendment lightly; I have devoted many years of my life pursuing the goal of equality of opportunity for all people. Nor do I oppose the so-called equal rights amendment with the patronizing smugness of the male. Discriminations against women do exist as has been time and time again conclusively shown. The inequality in pay scales, the inequality to access to higher education, to high posts in business and government, to cite but a few, cannot be justified or defended and the understandable passion to break these barriers to equality cannot be dismissed.

If the Equal Rights Amendment supplied the remedy I would be among the first to rise in its support. It does not. It is, I am sorry to state, a deft, vague ear- and eye-catching slogan, deceiving in its simplicity and dangerous because of its very simplicity. It is an abstraction, the words of which are not susceptible to definition or to clarity of meaning. Even the proponents of the legislation disagree on intent. There are those supporting the amendment who believe that that which differentiates necessarily discriminates, that only identity of treatment can destroy discrimination. Other proponents declare that it will in no wise affect operation of law based on functional differences.

It interests me greatly that the Citizens' Advisory Council on the Status of Women, in a statement issued in March of 1970 in defense of the Equal Rights Amendment, talks about the "probable meaning and effect" of that amendment. We are asked to throw a rock into a churning sea with only guesswork as to what the waves will bring to the shores. It states unequivocally:

> The amendment would restrict only governmental action and would not apply to purely private action.

Yet we know that the courts more and more have extended right of suits to private action. Quo vadis? Possibly into the private quarrels, private wishes, private adjustment of two joined in matrimony?

I read with amazement the following quotation taken directly from the aforesaid Citizens' Advisory Council on the Status of Women:

> 3. *Removal of Age Distinctions Based on Sex:* Some laws which apply to both sexes make an age distinction by sex and thereby discriminate as to persons between the ages specified for males and females. Under the foregoing analysis, the ages specified in such laws would be equalized by the amendment by extending the benefits, privileges, or opportunities under the law to both sexes. This would mean that as to some such laws, the *lower* age would apply to both sexes. For example: a lower minimum age for marriage for women would apply to both sexes; a lower age for boys under child labor laws would apply to girls as well. In other words, the *privileges* of marrying or working would be *extended* and the sex discrimination removed.
>
> As to other laws, the *higher* age would apply to both sexes. For example: a higher cutoff age for the right to paternal support for boys would apply to girls as well; a higher age for girls for juvenile court jurisdiction would apply also to boys. In these cases, the *benefits* of paternal support or juvenile court jurisdiction would be *extended* to both sexes,
>
> Thus, the test in determining whether these laws are to be equalized by applying the lower age or by applying the higher age to both sexes is as follows:
>
> "If the age limitation restricts individual liberty and freedom the lower age applies; if the age limitation confers a right, benefit, or privilege to the individuals concerned and does not limit individual freedom, the higher age applies."

I defy any legislator, any court, any man, any woman, to tell me not only the meaning of the paragraphs but how such assumptions were arrived at. How easily are the problems of the ages put to rest. Wars have been fought on differing interpretations of words and phrases like "individual freedom," "privileges," "rights," and "benefits."

There are proponents who admit that the Fifth and Fourteenth Amendments to the Constitution are adequate to achieve the objective sought. Adding an additional constitutional amendment, albeit surplus, could not hurt. Well, I wonder.

Let us turn, for a moment, to consider the area of domestic relations.

There are over 28 million married women who are nonworking full-time homemakers. Close to 60 per cent of the women in the labor force are married and must depend upon their husbands for a majority of the family income. Thus, there are approximately 44 million women who depend upon their husbands to provide the primary support for the family. Eminent authorities maintain that the Equal Rights Amendment could abolish the common rule whereby a husband has the primary duty of support toward his family. In many jurisdictions, as I will show subsequently, failure to give such support is a ground for separation and divorce. Hence, we must keep clearly in mind that the concept of a primary duty does not lend itself easily to a rule of identity of treatment. Here I am reminded of what Anatole France once stated:

> The law in its majestic equality forbids the rich as well as the poor to sleep under bridges, to bet in the streets, and to steal bread.

Putting it more colloquially, "Each man for himself. Lord help us all, cried the elephant as he danced among the chickens."

I am speaking for the 44 million homemakers. I am speaking for the widows; I am speaking for the children who, if this amendment is enacted, could be removed as beneficiaries of the protective legislation accorded them by state legislatures.

Most women's lives, unlike that of men, can be divided into three phases: first, the preparation toward gainful employment; second, the functioning in the role of wife and mother as homemaker; and third, the return in many instances to some kind of gainful employment after the children have left the household. It is in the second and third phases of a woman's life when the protective measures of which I speak are paramount.

The Equal Rights Amendment may require changes in the traditional roles of the husband as breadwinner and the wife as householder, but the manner in which it will do this leaves room for speculation. Any of several results may occur. First, failure to support may disappear as a ground for divorce. If the duty to support remains viable in domestic relations law, it may at least spread to both spouses equally, and as a result the courts will have to consider in each case the relative ability of each spouse to contribute his or her income to the support of the family. Thus, the duty to support may evolve into the duty to contribute, and failure of either spouse to contribute to a reasonable extent of his or her ability will either directly provide grounds for divorce to the other spouse, or result in a "constructive desertion," which would accomplish the same effect indirectly.

The other area of divorce grounds which may feel the most effect of the Equal Rights Amendment is that which emerges from the husband's now generally acknowledged role as head of the household. In California, his role is expressed by statute; in Alaska, Colorado, and the District of Columbia, it is reflected by court decisions. Because the husband is head of the household, he has the right to choose and change the marital domicile, and refusal of the wife, without reasonable grounds, to accompany the husband makes her guilty of desertion. The courts may take either of two distinct tacks in dealing with this problem. First, they may overturn the cases and statutes recognizing the husband as head of the household, and thereby allocate the role in each marriage before them, or second, they may do away entirely with the concept of head of the household. In either case, the courts may become involved in new considerations of unprecedented complexity. In the one instance, the courts will have to decide, on the basis of such considerations as comparative income and family responsibility, which spouse actually deserves the title of head of the household. In the other instance, the courts will have to assess the same considerations to determine who is deserting whom when one spouse desires to move the family domicile in pursuit of a different or better job, or a more healthful climate, and the other spouse refuses to move because of his or her own job, or own health.

The intrusion of the hand of government into the delicate personal relationship of husband and wife and their relationship to their children, including custody and bastardy laws, age of consent, and so forth, would bring grief untold. We are asked to put emotion and sentiment on a checkerboard, to be moved about by federal and state governmental authorities.

Do we know, I ask, what we are doing in the area of divorce, separation, alimony, support, custody of minor children? So far as I can ascertain no definitive legal analysis has ever been undertaken which purports to examine in detail any of the ramifications of these problems. Do we use the hatchet when the scalpel will suffice?

I maintain that when the amendment was introduced some forty-seven years ago, it raised the same questions. No answers have been supplied. Yet we have seen how the specific remedy applied to the specific wrong has been made to work. We have the enactment of the equal pay law in 1963, Title VII of the Civil Rights Act of 1964, the issuance of a series of executive orders that prohibit discrimination on the basis of sex by federal contractors, in federal employment on federally assisted construction projects. Equal pay is now required by law in thirty-five states; twenty-one states and the District of Columbia have fair employment practices laws, which prohibit discrimination in employment on the basis of sex. There are now no restrictions on voting, holding of public office, jury service. There are no restrictions now with respect to property rights which apply to married women that do not also apply to married men, but discriminations do exist, as I said earlier. And to them we can and must apply the concrete remedy, a remedy clearly understood by all which would not throw out the baby with the bath.

There are bills before us; namely, H.R. 18278, introduced by the gentleman from Illinois (Mr. Mikva); H.R. 18317, introduced by the gentlewoman from Michigan (Mrs. Griffiths), and H.R. 18427, introduced by the gentleman from New York (Mr. Ryan), which by statutory law does carry out the recommendations of the Presidential Task Force on Women's Rights and Responsibilities. Unlike the Equal Rights Amendment the proposal would not affect the status of women in the areas of domestic relations, and possibly military training. It would supply women with the legal leverage they rightfully seek. In attacking sex discrimination in the areas with which they are most concerned, such as equal job opportunity, equal pay, and equal rights for education, it specifically attacks those areas of greatest discrimination while not involving itself in the delicate, intricate problems of adjudging a married woman's status as a wife and mother.

Furthermore, the bill would require the Secretary of Health, Education, and Welfare to make recommendations which would attempt to equalize the treatment of the sexes in such areas as taxation, social security, and the Family Assistance Act. Upon passage of such a bill six of the ten proposals would be directly enacted into law without the uncertainty, vagueness, invitation to litigation and chaos that would attend the passage of the Equal Rights Amendment. These are:

1. Title VII of the Civil Rights Act of 1964 would be amended to:
   a. empower the Equal Employment Opportunity Commission to enforce bans against discrimination based on sex.
   b. extend the act's coverage to state and local governments and teachers.
2. Titles IV and IX of the Civil Rights Act will be amended to authorize the Attorney General to assist women in seeking equal access to public education facilities.
3. Title II of the Civil Rights Act would be amended to prohibit discrimination because of sex in public accommodations.
4. The Civil Rights Act of 1957 would be amended to extend the jurisdiction of the Civil Rights Commission to include denial of civil rights because of sex.
5. The Fair Labor Standards Act would be amended to extend coverage of its equal pay provisions to executive, administrative, and professional employees.

6. Legislation would be enacted which would authorize federal grants on a matching basis for financing state commissions on the status of women.

I believe that Paul Freund, speaking for many eminent constitutional authorities, has put it most succinctly:

> If anything about this proposed amendment is clear, it is that it would transform every provision of law concerning women into a constitutional issue to be ultimately resolved by the Supreme Court of the United States. Every statutory and common-law provision dealing with the manifold relation of women in society would be forced to run the gantlet of attack on constitutional grounds. The range of such potential litigation is too great to be readily foreseen, but it would certainly embrace such diverse legal provisions as those relating to a widow's allowance, the obligation of family support and grounds for divorce, the age of majority and the right of annulment of marriages, and the maximum hours of labor for women in protected industries.

I urge that this amendment be voted down. I urge that we resist the magic of catch phrases which could induce havoc rather than command rights. I urge that we seek equality for all with the precision all good law demands. I urge we do not open this Pandora's box.

Set Future Generations Free

Shirley Chisholm

Mr. Speaker, House Joint Resolution 264, before us today, which provides for equality under the law for both men and women, represents one of the most clear-cut opportunities we are likely to have to declare our faith in the principles that shaped our Constitution. It provides a

From *Congressional Record*, August 10, 1970, H28028-29. Shirley Chisholm is a Democratic Representative from New York.

legal basis for attack on the most subtle, most pervasive, and most institutionalized form of prejudice that exists. Discrimination against women, solely on the basis of their sex, is so widespread that it seems to many persons normal, natural, and right. Legal expression of prejudice on the grounds of religious or political belief has become a minor problem in our society. Prejudice on the basis of race is, at least, under systematic attack. There is reason for optimism that it will start to die with the present older generation. It is time we act to assure full equality of opportunity to those citizens who, although in a majority, suffer the restrictions that are more commonly imposed on minorities, to women.

The argument that this amendment will not solve the problem of sex discrimination is not relevant. If the argument were used against a civil rights bill—as it has been used in the past—the prejudice that lies behind it would be embarrassing. Of course laws will not eliminate prejudice from the hearts of human beings. But that is no reason to allow prejudice to continue to be enshrined in our laws—to perpetuate injustice through inaction.

The amendment is necessary to clarify countless ambiguities and inconsistencies in our legal system. For instance, the Constitution guaranteees due process of law, in the Fifth and Fourteenth Amendments. But the applicability of due process to sex distinctions is not clear: Women are excluded from some state colleges and universities. In some states, restrictions are placed on a married woman who engages in an independent business. Women may not be chosen for some juries. Women even receive heavier penalties than men who commit the same crime.

What would the legal effects of the Equal Rights Amendment really be? The Equal Rights Amendment would govern only the relationship between the state and its citizens—not relationships between private citizens.

The amendment would be largely self-executing, that is, any federal or state laws in conflict would be ineffective one year after date of ratification without further action by the Congress or state legislatures.

Opponents of the amendment claim its ratification would throw the law into a state of confusion and would result in much litigation to establish its meaning. This objection overlooks the influence of legislative history in determining intent and the recent activities of many groups preparing for legislative changes in this direction.

State labor laws applying only to women, such as those limiting hours of work and weights to be lifted, would become inoperative unless the legislature amended them to apply to men. As of early 1970 most states would have some laws that would be affected. However, changes are being made so rapidly as a result of Title VII of the Civil Rights Act of 1964, it is likely that by the time the Equal Rights Amendment would become effective, no conflicting state laws would remain.

In any event, there has for years been great controversy as to the usefulness to women of these state labor laws. There has never been any doubt that they worked a hardship on women who need or want to work overtime and on women who need or want better-paying jobs, and there has been no persuasive evidence as to how many women benefit from the archaic policy of the laws. After the Delaware hours law was repealed in 1966, there were no complaints from women to any of the state agencies that might have been approached.

Jury service laws not making women equally liable for jury service would have to be revised.

The selective service law would have to include women, but women would not be required to serve in the armed forces where they are not fitted any more than men are required to serve. Military service, while a great responsibility, is not without benefits, particularly for young men with limited education or training. Since October 1966, 246,000 young men who did not meet the normal mental or physical requirements have been given opportunities for training and correcting physical problems. This opportunity is not open to their sisters. Only girls who have completed high school and meet high standards on the educational test can volunteer. Ratification of the amendment would not permit application of higher standards to women.

Survivorship benefits would be available to husbands of female workers on the same basis as to wives of male workers. The Social Security Act and the civil service and military service retirement acts are in conflict.

Public schools and universities could not be limited to one sex and could not apply different admission standards to men and women. Laws requiring longer prison sentences for women than men would be invalid, and equal opportunities for rehabilitation and vocational training would have to be provided in public correctional institutions.

Different ages of majority based on sex would have to be harmonized.

Federal, state, and other governmental bodies would be obligated to follow nondiscriminatory practices in all aspects of employment, including public school teachers and state university and college faculties.

What would be the economic effects of the Equal Rights Amendment? Direct economic effects would be minor. If any labor laws applying only to women still remained, their amendment or repeal would provide opportunity for women in better-paying jobs in manufacturing. More opportunities in public vocational and graduate schools for women would also tend to open up opportunities in better jobs for women.

Indirect effects could be much greater. The focusing of public attention on the gross legal, economic, and social discrimination against women by hearings and debates in the federal and state legislatures would result in changes in attitude of parents, educators, and employers that would bring about substantial economic changes in the long run.

Sex prejudice cuts both ways. Men are oppressed by the requirements of the Selective Service Act, by enforced legal guardianship of minors, and by alimony laws. Each sex, I believe, should be liable when necessary to serve and defend this country.

Each has a responsibility for the support of children.

There are objections raised to wiping out laws protecting women workers. No one would condone exploitation. But what does sex have to do with it? Working conditions and hours that are harmful to women are harmful to men; wages that are unfair for women are unfair for men. Laws setting employment limitations on the basis of sex are irrational, and the proof of this is their inconsistency from state to state. The physical characteristics of men and women are not fixed, but cover two wide spans that have a great deal of overlap. It is obvious, I think, that a robust woman could be more fit for physical labor than a weak man. The choice of occupation would be determined by individual capabilities, and the rewards for equal work should be equal.

This is what it comes down to: artificial distinctions between persons must be wiped out of the law. Legal discrimination between the sexes is, in almost every instance, founded on outmoded views of society and the prescientific beliefs about psychology and physiology. It is time to sweep away these relics of the past and set future generations free of them.

Federal agencies and institutions responsible for the enforcement of equal opportunity laws need the authority of a constitutional amendment. The 1964 Civil Rights Act and the 1963 Equal Pay Act are not enough; they are limited in their coverage—for instance, one excludes teachers, and the other leaves out administrative and professional women. The Equal Employment Opportunity Commission has not proven to be an adequate device, with its powers limited to investigation, conciliation, and recommendation to the Justice Department. In its cases involving sexual discrimination, it has failed in more than one-half. The Justice Department has been even less effective. It has intervened in only one case involving discrimination on the basis of sex, and this was on a procedural point. In a second case, in which both sexual and racial discrimination were alleged, the racial bias charge was given far greater weight.

Evidence of discrimination on the basis of sex should hardly have to be cited here. It is in the Labor Department's employment and salary figures for anyone who is still in doubt. Its elimination will involve so many changes in our state and federal laws that, without the authority and impetus of this proposed amendment, it will perhaps take another 194 years. We cannot be parties to continuing a delay. The time is clearly now to put this House on record for the fullest expression of that equality of opportunity which our founding fathers professed.

They professed it, but they did not assure it to their daughters, as they tried to do for their sons.

The Constitution they wrote was designed to protect the rights of white, male citizens. As there were no black founding fathers, there were no founding mothers—a great pity, on both counts. It is not too late to complete the work they left undone. Today, here, we should start to do so.

In closing I would like to make one point. Social and psychological effects will be initially more important than legal or economic results. As Leo Kanowitz has pointed out:

> Rules of law that treat of the sexes per se inevitably produce far-reaching effects upon social, psychological, and economic aspects of male-female relations beyond the limited confines of legislative chambers and courtrooms. As long as organized legal systems, at once the most respected and most feared of social institutions, continue to differentiate sharply, in treatment or in words, between men and women on the basis of irrelevant and arti- ficially created distinctions, the likelihood of men and women coming to regard one another primarily as fellow human beings and only secondarily as representatives of another sex will continue to be remote. When men and women are prevented from recognizing one another's essential humanity by sexual prejudices, nourished by legal as well as social institutions, society as a whole remains less than it could otherwise become.

Working Women and the Equal Rights Amendment

Joan Jordan

In the spring of 1970, scenes from the early period of industrialization sprang to life again in Antioch and Stockton, California. Forced by Fireboard Corporation under threat of job loss to break the state protective laws for women, women worked sixteen hours straight, lifted 150 pounds a minute, gave up rest periods and lunch hours, and to add insult to injury, all this was done in the name of "equality."

Women workers are in danger of exposure to hazard and extreme economic exploitation if California employers and corporations have their way. They are trying to destroy the state's protective laws for women, claiming that they are in conflict with the federal law, Title VII of the Civil Rights Act of 1964, which calls for equality between the sexes on the job. The corporations' idea of equality is greater exploitation through suspension of the protective laws for women. The women workers' idea of equality is (or should be) to extend the state protective laws to men. . . .

SWEATING THE WOMEN

The absence of equality in employment opportunity for women is grounded in the profit motive of production. Using 1950 census reports, and figures from the Federal Reserve Board and also from the Securities and Exchange Commission, Grace Hutchins calculates that manufacturing companies realized a profit of $5.4 billion in 1950 by paying women less per year than the wages paid to men for similar work. The extra profits from employing women at lower rates than men formed 23 per cent of all manufacturing company profits.

The removal of protective legislation will not insure equality; only changing the profit motive of production will do that. But their removal will increase profits through greater exploitation and inequality than currently exist. Attempts to break the laws began about three years ago. The tocsin sounded in November 1967 when the women's eight-

From transaction (November/December 1970), pp. 16–21. Copyright © November 1970 Society Magazine by Transaction, Inc., New Brunswick, New Jersey. Joan Jordan is a working woman and a student.

hour law was amended for the first time in half a century to allow women to work up to ten hours a day or fifty-eight hours per week. California, with more working women than any other state, then had the best protective laws for workers. But it was clear they were in for a siege of attacks. The reaction of some union leaders such as Ray Pappert of the Lithographers was to say, "So we will just have to write more 'laws' into our contracts." However, the vast majority of women workers, 85 per cent nationally, 80 per cent in California, aren't organized in unions and so won't be covered by "laws" written into negotiated contracts. In addition, the rising recesssion, causing increasing unemployment in a contracting labor market, weakens the position of the workers and pushes the unions into headlong conflict with the employers. Under these conditions the employers have chosen to attack what they believe to be the weakest link in the working class—the women.

They are doing it in three ways. The first entails direct concrete attempts to destroy established working conditions on the job. The second way is to aim legal and political assaults on the laws covering women's working conditions. The third way is to divide the women themselves, to maneuver some women into the position of fighting the companies' battles for them, thus providing a screen behind which the corporations can preserve their image of selflessness. To do this they have set in motion a public relations campaign for "equality," the chief advocates of which turn out to be that section of the working women most closely associated with management, the business and professional women. They have been successful in creating confusion among working women and the women's liberation movement, so much so that many women, especially in the National Organization for Women (NOW), believe that protective laws are a threat to women's equality. Some women cannot seem to grasp the idea that equality doesn't mean greater exploitation but could mean extension of the protective laws to men.

NOW's position seems to be particularly ambiguous. Nationally, it calls for passage of the Equal Rights Amendment to the Constitution but refuses to amend it in a way that would extend the state protective laws to men. If passed without such a proviso the Equal Rights Amendment could be interpreted in the courts to break state protective laws for women. If, however, it were amended to extend the state protective laws to men, it would be clear that "equality" did not and could not mean greater exploitation. . . .

EQUAL PROTECTION

The campaign in NOW is particularly insidious as it pushes the California state Fair Employment Practices sex amendment and the federal Equal

Rights Amendment without explaining their possible effects on working women and especially on unorganized, nonunion working women. However, there is also a wing of working-class women within the women's liberation movement which is trying to air these questions publicly and to clearly pose the dangers involved. These women call for extending the state protective laws to men and ask that no support be given to the federal Equal Rights Amendment unless it is amended to extend the state protective laws to men.

At this point, the relationship between economics and politics, the question of power, begins to be expressed more clearly. Women, especially working-class women, simply don't hold power. In California there are no women in the Senate, and the ratio of men to women in the Assembly is 39 to 1. The laws affecting women, such as those dealing with abortion, divorce, alimony, protective laws and so on, are all made and unmade by men. In addition, most of the politicians are also employers, sympathizing and identifying with the corporations.

Out of this legislature constituted primarily of white Anglo-Saxon (capitalist) males, the Assembly Committee on Labor Relations called a public hearing on California's Protective Labor Laws for Women on Thursday, 26 February 1970, at the state capitol. The call was based on the assumption that some or all of the protective legislation will be struck down by the courts. It included four alternatives that testimony might be addressed to: (1) eliminating all protective legislation immediately, (2) operating under or (3) suspending present laws until the court decisions are in or (4) extending the laws to cover everybody.

The agenda of the hearings spelled it out:

> The federal Civil Rights Act of 1964, Title VII, and several recent court cases such as *Rosenfeld* v. *Southern Pacific and the State of California* have cast doubt upon the validity of California's historic protective labor laws for women. It is probable that some and possible that all of these laws—the minimum wage, the hours limitations, and over twenty standard conditions of labor—will be held invalid in the near future. The purpose of the committee's hearing today is to receive testimony relating to the general question: what action should the Legislature take if some or all of California's protective labor laws for women are held invalid? Witnesses may speak specifically to one or a few laws, or generally; they may propose legislation or simply suggest an approach. . . .
>
> Aside from the legal issue, many people feel that some of the state's protective laws are outmoded, discriminatory, inadequate, or otherwise imperfect and should therefore be changed. The committee will also receive testimony relating to these concerns . . .

Representatives of six employers' associations including the California Conference of Employer Associations, Restaurant, Laundry, Linen Supply, Dry Cleaners and Processors and Can Companies Associations testified at the hearing and were in general agreement in calling for suspension of all state protective laws in litigation. These included the eight-hour day, forty-hour week, rest periods, lunch hours and lifting requirements especially. The restaurant workers are on a forty-eight-hour week now. The employers also called for a uniform national minimum wage law under the National Fair Labor Standards Act. This sounds magnanimous after their calls for suspension of all the other laws, at least until one discovers that the national minimum wage is five cents lower than the California minimum wage and could subject Californians to the depressing effects of bad job conditions and low wages as in such reactionary areas of the country as Mississippi. Decisions on wages, moreover, would henceforth be controlled by Congress, which under the seniority system is dominated by old white male Southerners.

In the past, all these employer association representatives supported enforcement of the protective laws. Why this shift to a call for suspension now? Is it only because of the so-called conflict between state and federal laws? I suspect that the shift has more to do with the changed conditions of the labor market. In an expanding labor market with a need to attract workers, it was necessary to maintain good working conditions. Each employer wanted to make sure his competitor had to bear the same costs of production by providing the same working conditions. Now there is a recession, a contracting labor market. With many people looking for jobs and willing to do anything to get them, the employers see the opportunity of cutting costs and increasing profits through exploitation by breaking the standards of decent working conditions that have been so dearly fought for and won over the years.

The employers' attacks on the state protective laws for women were carried out on a national as well as state level. At the three-day fiftieth anniversary conference of the Women's Bureau of the Department of Labor on 11–13 June 1970 support for the Equal Rights Amendment was pushed and passed. However, the working women there caucused, and a majority emerged which was opposed to supporting the amendment. A number of these working women, along with other allies, issued a minority report that protested the way in which the conference was used to ram through support for the Equal Rights Amendment without adequate discussion that would enable the working women to develop their position. (The authors of the report knew this was so because they polled people from every workshop as to what had happened.) The minority report also called for including language in the amendment clearly stating that "existing labor standards would not be destroyed." It further objected to the composition of a conference whose purpose was to establish priorities, goals, and standards for working women but whose invited guests were predominantly business, professional, and college-educated women who would hardly be affected by the destruction of the protective laws.

Those women, and particularly those in NOW, consistently stated that they were in favor of extending the protective laws to the entire work force. Yet each time they were asked to include language to that effect in the amendment, they refused, claiming that it could only be interpreted that way anyhow and wouldn't pass at all if any additions were made. The attorney general has clearly stated that his interpretation is the opposite—immediate suspension of the protective laws upon passage of the Equal Rights Amendment. The working women's amendment leaves no doubt as to interpretation—the intent of the constitutional amendment would not be to expose women to increased exploitation and hazard; equality could only mean that no workers could be exposed to exploitation and hazard. If it is true, as NOW claims, that the amendment wouldn't pass with this clarification added, then one has to conclude that the legislators are prepared to accept the coming of a new dark age of industrial exploitation.

. . .

THE EMPLOYERS MOVE

Since 1964 six states have repealed hours laws for women, and another six have substantially amended such laws. Laws regulating the weights that women can be required to lift have been weakened. State courts in California and Oregon ruled that their weight regulations violated the Civil Rights Act. Georgia recently removed any specific limitation from its weight law and also applied the law to men as well as women; the new law simply relieves both sexes from lifting weights that could cause "strains or undue fatigue." The problem with this law is that in a contracting labor market with many people looking for jobs it will be easy for employers to coerce workers into lifting excessive weights for fear of losing their jobs.

Ohio has recently announced it wouldn't prosecute alleged violations of its many women's protective laws because they may be in conflict with the Civil Rights Act. North Dakota has announced the same. In six other states, attorneys general have ruled that these special laws have been superseded by either the Civil Rights Act or new state fair employment laws.

A federal court in Illinois recently upheld the positions of Illinois Bell Telephone Company, the Chicago subsidiary of American Telephone & Telegraph Company, and Caterpillar Tractor Company of Peoria in a pair of suits filed last March. The companies charged that the sixty-one-year-old Illinois Maximum Hours Act—restricting women to eight-hour days—conflicted with the Federal Civil Rights Act. In its suit Illinois Bell, the largest employer of women in the state with 22,000 women workers, said the Illinois law was proving to be a costly one for employers in many cases where it would be more economical to pay women for overtime rather than hire additional workers. A company spokesman also said the suits in no way reflected the pressure from women's rights groups. These statements are a key to the whole struggle nationally.

Mrs. Eloise M. Basto, a Lansing, Michigan, special representative for the Communications Workers of America, suggests that a glimpse of what will happen once the economy picks up was provided in 1968, when Michigan's attorney general initially ruled against the state's hours law. (His ruling was later reversed by the courts, although a similar action by him last year has yet to be challenged.) "At that time, women in some auto and meat-packing plants were forced to work seventy to eighty hours a week," says Mrs. Basto. "Many women simply had to leave their jobs."

No support should be given by the women's liberation movement for passage of the Equal Rights Amendment as it now stands. It should be backed only if it is amended to state clearly that existing labor standards shall not be destroyed. NOW members must be made aware of the implications of their narrow self-interests. National offensives to amend the Equal Rights Amendment and state battles to extend the protective laws to all workers must be organized with alliances and coalitions between women's liberation and working women and men. When and if the Equal Rights Amendment comes to a vote next year, it must be amended or again voted down. At the same time, women must also fight on the state level against the suspension and invalidation of the protective laws. In the process of such action and struggle, a strong woman's movement can be built. The dynamic of it will swing a growing sector of the working class, the working women, into the total movement for social change. This in turn will begin to influence the white male skilled trade unionists, who are also being affected by the squeeze of inflation, to join the rising tide of people who want production based on use and human need rather than profit.

How does an institution end discrimination against women? Does it simply decide to end discriminatory practices and pledge to consider all people on their merits? Or must it take some form of "affirmative action" and create some set of deliberate procedures to ensure against discrimination? If the latter, what specifically should these procedures aim to accomplish, and what should they involve?

Universities are attempting to resolve these questions. Individual departments have traditionally made academic appointments subject to little interference by the central administration or the board of trustees. The concept of "academic freedom" suggests, at the least, that political factors should not enter into appointments, but only scholarly competence and (one would hope) a respectable performance in the classroom. Government prodding of universities creates two issues: First, is there to be a quota or preference given to women in hiring, and if so, how can that be squared with scholarly standards and academic freedom? Second, does government intrusion on university functions for benign purposes (as in this case) portend the possibility of future intervention by the government for malign purposes, such as ideological purges?

In the following selection, a male faculty member presents the problem forcefully. His conclusions need not be accepted but should be appreciated as a candid expression of concern that reflects the views of many members of university faculties.

HEW and the Universities

Paul Seabury

Old Howard Smith, Virginia swamp fox of the House Rules Committee, was a clever tactical fighter. When Dixiecrats in 1964 unsuccessfully tried to obstruct passage of the Civil Rights bill, Smith in a fit of inspired raillery devised a perverse stratagem. He proposed an amendment to the bill, to include women as an object of federal protection in employment, by adding sex to the other criteria of race, color, national origin, and religion as illegitimate grounds for discrimination in hiring. This tactical maneuver had far-reaching effects; calculated to rouse at least some Northern masculine ire against the whole bill, it backfired by

From *Commentary*, 53 (February 1972), pp. 38–44. Copyright © 1972 by the American Jewish Committee. Reprinted by permission of the author and *Commentary*. Paul Seabury is Professor of Political Science, University of California, Berkeley.

eliciting a chivalrous rather than (as we now call it) sexist response: the amendment actually passed!

Smith, however, had greater things in mind for women's rights. As a fall-back strategy, they would distract federal bureaucrats from the principal object of the bill, namely, to rectify employment inequities for Negroes. In this, at least in higher education, Smith's stratagem is paying off according to expectations. The middle-range bureaucrats staffing the HEW Civil Rights office, under its Director, J. Stanley Pottinger, now scent sexism more easily than racism in the crusade to purify university hiring practices. Minority-group spokesmen grumble when this powerful feminine competitor appears, to horn in. In the dynamics of competition between race and sex for scarce places on university faculties, a new hidden crisis of higher education is brewing. As universities climb out of the rubble of campus disorders of the 1960s, beset by harsh budgetary reverses, they now are required to redress national social injustices within their walls at their own expense. Compliance with demands from the federal government to do this would compel a stark remodeling of their criteria of recruitment, their ethos of professionalism, and their standards of excellence. Refusal to comply satisfactorily would risk their destruction.

. . .

Let us begin the story, then, with a brief history of the Civil Rights Act of 1964. This act, in the view of its principal sponsors, purposed (among other things) to engage the force of the federal government in battle to diminish or to rectify discriminatory hiring practices in firms and institutions having or seeking contracts with the federal government. Title VII of the act expressly forbids discrimination by employers on grounds of race, color, religion, and national origin, either in the form of preferential hiring or advancement, or in the form of differential compensation. Contracting institutions deemed negligent in complying with these provisions could be deemed ineligible for such contracts, or their contracts could be suspended, terminated, or not renewed.

. . .

The first steps in implementing the new act were based on executive orders of the president. . . . President Johnson's Executive Order No. 11375 (1967) stated that

> The contractor will not discriminate against any employee or applicant because of race, color, religion, sex, or national origin. The contractor *will take affirmative action* [italics added] to ensure that employees are treated during employment, without regard to their race, color, religion, sex, or national origin.

Under such plausible auspices, "affirmative action" was born, and with a huge federal endowment to guarantee its success in life. Since

1967, however, this child prodigy—like Charles Addams's famous nursery boy with the test tubes—has been experimenting with novel brews, so as to change both his appearance and his behavior. And it is curious to see how the singleminded pursuers of an ideal of equity can overrun and trample the ideal itself, while injuring innocent bystanders as well. . . .

Affirmative action was altered by a Labor Department order (based not on the Civil Rights Act but on revised presidential directives) only months after the Johnson order was announced. This order reshaped it into a weapon for discriminatory hiring practices. If the reader will bear with a further recitation of federal prose, let me introduce Order No. 4, Department of Labor:

> An affirmative-action program is a set of specific and result-oriented procedures to which a contractor commits himself to apply every good faith effort. The objective of these procedures plus such efforts is equal employment opportunity. Procedures without effort to make them work are meaningless; and effort, undirected by specific and meaningful procedures, is inadequate. An acceptable affirmative-action program must include an analysis of areas within which the contractor is deficient in the utilization of minority groups and women, and further, *goals and timetables to which the contractor's good faith efforts must be directed to correct the deficiencies and thus, to increase materially the utilization of minorities and women, at all levels and in all segments of his work force where deficiences exist.*

This directive is now applicable through HEW enforcement procedures to universities by delegation of authority from the Labor Department. By late 1971, something of a brushfire, fanned by hard-working HEW compliance officers, had spread through American higher education, the cause of it being the demand that universities, as a condition of obtaining or retaining their federal contracts, establish hiring goals based upon race and sex. . . .

Universities, for a variety of singular reasons, are extremely vulnerable to this novel attack. As President McGill of Columbia remarked recently, "We are no longer in all respects an independent private university." As early as 1967, the federal government was annually disbursing contract funds to universities at the rate of three-and-a-half billion dollars a year; recently the Carnegie Commission suggested that federal contract funding be increased by 1978 to thirteen billion dollars, if universities are to meet their educational objectives. Individual institutions, notably great and distinguished ones, already are extraordinarily dependent on continuing receipt of federal support. The University of California, for instance, currently (1970–71) depends upon federal contract funds for approximately $72 million. The University of Michigan, periodically harassed by HEW threats of contract suspension, cancellation, or nonrenewal, would stand to lose as much as $60 million per annum. The threat of permanent disqualification, if consummated, could wholly wreck a university's prospects for the future.

In November 1971, HEW's Office for Civil Rights announced its intent to institute proceedings for Columbia's permanent debarment—*even though no charges or findings of discrimination had been made:* Columbia had simply not come up with an acceptable affirmative-action program to redress inequities which had not even been found to exist. When minor officials act like Alice in Wonderland's Red Queen, using threats of decapitation for frivolous purposes; when they act as investigator, prosecutor, and judge rolled into one, there may be no cause for surprise. But one can certainly wonder how even they would dare pronounce sentence—and a sentence of death at that—even before completion of the investigatory phase. Such, however, appears to be the deadly logic of HEW procedures. As J. Stanley Pottinger, chief of HEW's office, said at a West Coast press conference recently, "We have a whale of a lot of power and we're prepared to use it if necessary." In known circumstances of its recent use, the threat resembles the deployment of MIRV missiles to apprehend a suspected embezzler. . . .

As the federal government of the United States moves uncertainly to establish equitable racial patterns in universities and colleges, it does so with few guidelines from historical experience. The management, manipulation, and evaluation of quotas, targets, and goals for preferential hiring are certainly matters as complex as are the unusual politics which such announced policies inspire. How equitably to assuage the many group claimants for preference, context-by-context, occasion-by-occasion, and year-by-year, as these press and jostle among themselves for prior attention in preference, must by now occasion some puzzlement even among HEW bureaucrats. On a recent Inspector General's tour of California, J. Stanley Pottinger found himself giving comfort to militant women at Boalt Hall Law School of the University of California; yet at Hayward State College, he was attacked by Chicanos for giving preference to blacks! Leaders of militant groups, needless to say, are less interested in the acute dilemmas posed to administrators by this adventure than in what they actually want for themselves. . . .

. . .

To remain eligible for federal contracts under the new procedures, universities must devise package proposals, containing stated targets for preferential hiring on grounds of race and sex. HEW may reject these goals, giving the university thirty-day notice for swift rectification, even though no charges of discrimination have been brought. Innocence must either be quickly proved, or acceptable means of rectification devised. But how does one *prove* innocence?

"Hiring practices" (i.e., faculty recruitment procedures) are decentralized; they devolve chiefly upon departments. At Columbia, for instance, seventy-seven units generate proposals for recruitment. Faculties resent (most of the time quite properly) attempts of administrators to tell them whom to hire, and whom not. Departments rarely keep records of the communications and transactions which precede the making of an employment offer, except as these records pertain to the individual finally selected. Still, the procedure is time-consuming and expensive. The Department of Economics of the San Diego campus of the University of California estimates that it costs twenty to forty man hours, plus three to five hundred dollars, to screen *one* candidate sufficiently to make an offer. Typically, dozens of candidates are reviewed in earlier stages.

Compliance data thus tend to be scanty and incomplete. "Columbia's problem," President McGill recently observed, "is that it is difficult to prove what we do because it is exceedingly difficult to develop the data base on which to show, in the depth and detail demanded [by HEW], what the University's personnel activities in fact are." Yet HEW demands such data from universities on thirty-day deadlines, with contract suspension threatened. Moreover, on its finding of discrimination (usually based on statistical, not qualitative, evidence), it may demand plans for rectification which oblige the university to commit itself to abstract preferential goals without regard to the issue of individual merit.

The best universities, which also happen to be those upon which HEW has chiefly worked its knout, habitually and commonsensically recruit from other best institutions. The top universities hire the top 5 per cent of graduate students in the top ten universities. This is the "skill pool" they rely upon. Some may now deem such practices archaic but they have definitely served to maintain quality. Just as definitely they have not served to obtain "equality of results" in terms of the proportional representation of sociological categories. Such equality assumes that faculties somehow must "represent" designated categories of people on grounds other than those of professional qualification. As Labor Department Order No. 4 states, special attention "should be given to academic, experience and skill requirements, to ensure that the requirements in themselves do not constitute inadvertent discrimination." Indeed, according to four professors at Cornell writing in the *Times* (Letters to the Editor, January 6), deans and department chairmen have been informed by that university's president that HEW policy means the " 'hiring of additional minority persons and females' even if 'in many instances, it may be necessary to hire unqualified or marginally qualified people.' "

If departments abandon the practice of looking to the best pools from which they can hope to draw, then quality must in fact be jeopardized. To comply with HEW orders, every department must come up not with the *best* candidate, but with the best-qualified *woman* or *nonwhite* candidate. For when a male or a white candidate is actually selected or recommended, it is now incumbent on both department and university to *prove* that no qualified woman or nonwhite was found available. Some universities already have gone so far in emulating the federal bureaucracy as to have installed their own bureaucratic monitors, in the form of affirmative-action coordinators, to screen recommendations for faculty appointments before final action is taken.

A striking contradiction exists between HEW's insistence that faculties prove they do not discriminate and its demand for goals and timetables which require discrimination to occur. For there is no reason to suppose that equitable processes in individual cases will automatically produce results which are set in the timetables and statistical goals universities are now required to develop. If all that HEW wishes is evidence that universities are bending over backward to be fair, why should it require them to have statistical goals at all? Do they know something no one else knows, about where fairness inevitably leads?

Yet another facet of HEW's procedures goes to the very heart of faculty due process: its demand of the right of access to faculty files, when searching for evidence of discrimination. Such files have always been the most sacrosanct documents of academia, and for good reason: it has been assumed that candor in the evaluation of candidates and personnel is best guaranteed by confidentiality of comment; and that evasiveness, caution, smokescreening, and grandstanding—which would be the principal consequences of open files—would debase standards of judgment. In the past, universities have denied federal authorities— the FBI for instance—access to these files. Now HEW demands access. And it is the recent reluctance of the Berkeley campus of the University of California to render unto this agent of Caesar what was denied to previous agents, which occasioned the HEW ultimatum of possible contract suspension: $72 million. One might imagine the faculty would be in an uproar, what with Nixon's men ransacking the inner temple. But no. In this as in other aspects of this curious story, the faculty is silent. . . .

"In respect of civil rights, common to all citizens, the Constitution of the United States does not, I think, permit any public authority to know the race of those entitled to be protected in the enjoyment of such rights. . . . Our Constitution is color-blind, and neither knows nor tolerates classes among citizens." This is Justice Harlan, dissenting in

Plessy v. *Ferguson* in 1896, when the Supreme Court endorsed the "separate but equal" doctrine.

Some of us in the league of lost liberals are still wont to say that the Constitution is color-blind. Yet now under the watchful eye of federal functionaries, academic administrators are compelled to be as acutely sensitive as Kodachrome to the outward physical appearance of their faculty members and of proposed candidates for employment. Forms supplying such information are now fed into data-processing machines; printouts supply ethnic profiles of departments, colleges, and schools, from which compliance reports may be sent to HEW, and university affirmative-action goals are approved or rejected.[1]

All of this is done in some uneasiness of mind to put it mildly. In many states, Harlan-like blue laws of a recent innocent epoch still expressly prohibit employers from collecting and maintaining data on prospective employees with respect to race, religion, and national origin. The crafty practices contrived to elude the intention of such laws, while at the same time complying with HEW, vary from campus to campus. At the University of Michigan, the procedure entails what is known as "self-designation"—the employee indicates on a form the race or ethnic group of which he considers himself a part.[2] These forms are collected and grouped according to job-classifications, departments, etc., and then they are burned, so as to disappear without a trace. Other universities, less anxious to cover their traces, simply file the forms separately from regular personnel files, without the names of the individuals concerned. In New York, the CUNY system resorts to a quite different practice invented and perfected by South African Boers: "visual identification." Affirmative-action coordinators are told to proceed as follows: "The affirmative-action inventory is to be done by a *visual* survey [italics in original]. There *should not be a notation of any kind* as to ethnic background in either personnel records or permanent files. This is against the law. . . . Identification of Italian Americans will be done visually and by name. . . . Please remember, however, that each individual is to be listed in only one ethnic group."

The number of categories established on behalf of affirmative action, though at present finite, already betrays accordion-like expansibility. The affirmative-action program at San Francisco State College, typical of most, is now confined to six racial groups: Negroes; Orientals; other

---

[1] Since HEW has divulged no reliable standards of its own, the well-intentioned administrator is like a worshiper of Baal, propitiating a god who may punish or reward, but who is silent.

[2] Self-designation is not always reliable. At Michigan, the amused or disgusted members of one of the university's maintenance crews all self-designated themselves as American Indians (bureaucratese: Native American); their supervisor was quietly asked to redesignate them accurately.

Non-White; persons of Mexican, Central or South American ancestry ("except those who have physical characteristics of Negro, Oriental, or other Non-White races"); Native American (American Indian); and All Others, ". . . including those commonly designated as Caucasian or White." All but the last category are eligible for discriminatory preference.[3]

As the above CUNY memorandum signals, however, this last category of "those commonly designated as Caucasian or White" is a Pandora's box inside a Pandora's box. Now that the Italians have escaped from it in New York, the lid is open for others—all the many different groups now fashionably known as "ethnics"—to do likewise. A far-seeing administrator, even as under HEW's gun he hastily devises future-oriented hiring quotas ("goals") to muffle the noise of one or two squeaky wheels, might wonder how he will be able to gratify subsequent claimants on the dwindling capital of reserved quotas still at his disposal.

Yet the administrator in practice has no choice but to act on the "sufficient unto the day is the evil thereof" principle. HEW ultimata, when they come, are imperious and immediate. Thirty-day rectifications are in order. At Johns Hopkins, MIT, Columbia, Michigan, and the University of California, an acute agony arises from no such philosophical long-range speculations, but from how to put together attractive compliance reports fast enough to avoid the threatened withholding of vast funds, the closing-down of whole facilities, the dismissal of thousands of staff workers, and the irreparable damage done to important ongoing research, especially to laboratory experiments. Crocodile tears do flow, from the gimlet eyes of HEW investigators, who observe these sufferings from distant federal offices. Even J. Stanley Pottinger recently noted, in appropriate Pentagonese, that the act of contract suspension at Berkeley, for instance, might constitute "overkill." Yet no sooner had he voiced this note of sadness than his regional compliance director recommended to Washington precisely such action. . . .

While deans, chancellors, and personnel officials struggle with these momentous matters, faculties and graduate students with few exceptions are silent. HEW is acting in the name of social justice. Who in the prevailing campus atmosphere would openly challenge anything done in that name? Tenured faculty perhaps consult their private interests and conclude that whatever damage the storm may do to less protected colleagues or to their job-seeking students, prudence suggests a posture of silence. Others perhaps, refusing to admit that contending interests

[3] One object of current discriminatory hiring practices at San Francisco State is to make the institution's non-academic personnel ethnically mirror the population of the Bay Area.

are involved, believe that affirmative action is cost-free, and that all will benefit from it in the Keynesian long run. But someone *will* pay: namely very large numbers of white males who are among those distinguishable as "best qualified" and who will be shunted aside in the frantic quest for "disadvantaged qualifiables."

The inequities implied in affirmative action, and the concealed but real costs to individuals, would probably have had less damaging effects upon such highly skilled graduate students had they been imposed in the early 1960s. Then, the sky was the limit on the growth and the affluence of higher education. If a pie gets bigger, so may its slices enlarge; nobody *seems* to lose. Such is today not the case. The pie now shrinks. One West Coast state college, for example, last year alone lost nearly seventy budgeted faculty positions due to financial stringency. Yet this same college has just announced the boldest affirmative-action program in California higher education. "Decided educational advantages can accrue to the college," it said, "by having its faculty as well as its student body be more representative of the minority population of the area. *It is therefore expected that a substantial majority of all new faculty appointments during the immediate academic years will be from minorities, including women, until the under-utilization no longer exists.*" (Italics added.) Departments which refuse to play the game will have their budgets reviewed by university officials.

It is hard to say how widely such pernicious practices have been institutionalized in other colleges and universities. But were they to be generalized across the nation, one thing is certain: either large numbers of highly qualified scholars will pay with their careers simply because they are male and white, *or*, affirmative action will have failed in its benevolent purposes.

To what extent does the Fourteenth Amendment protect women against sex-based discrimination? The record of the Supreme Court is not encouraging. In 1908, in Muller v. Oregon, state "protective legislation" was upheld. At that time such legislation was strongly supported by Progressives and women. In 1948, in Goesaert v. Cleary, and later in similar cases, the Court refused to apply the Fourteenth Amendment to strike down legislation that excluded women from certain occupations. In 1961, in Hoyt v. Florida, a statute that excused women from jury duty was upheld.

Even the first "victory" in the Supreme Court for the women's liberation movement is illusory. In Reed v. Reed, decided in 1971, the Supreme Court used the Fourteenth Amendment to strike down state legislation. But the Court decided the case by using a "reasonableness" standard. In other words, instead of deciding that all **sex-based legislation is unconstitutional (or at least always suspect, a position taken by the ACLU)**, the Court determined that this particular piece of legislation was not a reasonable exercise of legislative power. Thus, each separate piece of state legislation would have to be considered separately, given the application of the Fourteenth Amendment in Reed.

Reed v. Reed

Mr. Chief Justice Burger delivered the opinion of the Court.

Richard Lynn Reed, a minor, died intestate in Ada County, Idaho, on March 29, 1967. His adoptive parents, who had separated sometime prior to his death, are the parties to this appeal. Approximately seven months after Richard's death, his mother, appellant Sally Reed, filed a petition in the Probate Court of Ada County, seeking appointment as administratrix of her son's estate. Prior to the date set for a hearing on the mother's petition, appellee Cecil Reed, the father of the decedent, filed a competing petition seeking to have himself appointed administrator of the son's estate. The probate court held a joint hearing on the two petitions and thereafter ordered that letters of administration be issued to appellee Cecil Reed upon his taking the oath and filing the bond required by law. The court treated § § 15–312 and 15–314 of the Idaho Code as the controlling statues and read those sections as compelling a preference for Cecil Reed because he was a male.

Section 15–312 designates the persons who are entitled to administer the estate of one who dies intestate. In making these designations, that section lists eleven classes of persons who are so entitled and provides, in substance, that the order in which those classes are listed in the section shall be determinative of the relative rights of competing applicants for letters of administration. One of the eleven classes so enumerated is "[t]he father or mother" of the person dying intestate. Under this section, then, appellant and appellee, being members of the same

From *Reed* v. *Reed*. 30 Lawyers' Edition 2nd 225.

entitlement class, would seem to have been equally entitled to administer their son's estate. Section 15–314 provides, however, that "[o]f several persons claiming and equally entitled [under § 15–314] to administer, males must be preferred to females, and relatives of the whole to those of the half blood."

. . .

. . . Having examined the record and considered the briefs and oral arguments of the parties, we have concluded that the arbitrary preference established in favor of males by § 15–314 of the Idaho Code cannot stand in the face of the Fourteenth Amendment's command that no State deny the equal protection of the laws to any person within its jurisdiction.

Idaho does not, of course, deny letters of administration to women altogether. Indeed, under § 15–312, a woman whose spouse dies intestate has a preference over a son, father, brother, or any other male relative of the decedent. Moreover, we can judicially notice that in this country, presumably due to the greater longevity of women, a large proportion of estates, both intestate and under wills of decedents, are administered by surviving widows.

Section 15–314 is restricted in its operation to those situations where competing applications for letters of administration have been filed by both male and female members of the same entitlement class established by § 15–312. In such situations, § 15–314 provides that different treatment be accorded to the applicants on the basis of their sex; it thus establishes a classification subject to scrutiny under the Equal Protection Clause.

In applying that clause, this Court has consistently recognized that the Fourteenth Amendment does not deny to states the power to treat different classes of persons in different ways. . . . The Equal Protection Clause of that amendment does, however, deny to states the power to legislate that different treatment be accorded to persons placed by a statute into different classes on the basis of criteria wholly unrelated to the objective of that statute. A classification "must be reasonable, not arbitrary, and must rest upon some ground of difference having a fair and substantial relation to the object of the legislation, so that all persons similarly circumstanced shall be treated alike". . . . The question presented by this case, then, is whether a difference in the sex of competing applicants for letters of administration bears a rational relationship to a state objective that is sought to be advanced by the operation of § § 15–312 and 15–314.

. . .

Clearly the objective of reducing the workload on probate courts by eliminating one class of contests is not without some legitimacy. The crucial question, however, is whether § 15–314 advances that objective in a manner consistent with the command of the Equal Protection Clause. We hold that it does not. To give a mandatory preference to members of either sex over members of the other, merely to accomplish the elimination of hearings on the merits, is to make the very kind of arbitrary legislative choice forbidden by the Equal Protection Clause of the Fourteenth Amendment; and whatever may be said as to the positive values of avoiding intrafamily controversy, the choice in this context may not lawfully be mandated solely on the basis of sex.

. . . By providing dissimilar treatment for men and women who are thus similarly situated, the challenged section violates the Equal Protection Clause. . . .

The judgment of the Idaho Supreme Court is reversed and the case remanded for further proceedings not inconsistent with this opinion.

Reversed and remanded.

One of the most compelling demands of the women's liberation movement is the right to control of the reproductive process. Male-dominated political and judicial institutions have established policies regulating sexual behavior and reproductive policies. Women today are challenging laws prohibiting dissemination of birth control information, forbidding the use of contraceptive devices or their dissemination to unmarried individuals, and forbidding abortions.

In the following case a lower federal court holds the Wisconsin abortion statute unconstitutional. The case is interesting for its exposition of a series of cases through which the courts have attempted to restrain political institutions from invading family relationships and substituting "public morality" for the dictates of private conscience.

Babbitz v. McCann

Before Kerner, Circuit Judge, and Reynolds and Gordon, District Judges.
Per Curiam.

The plaintiff is a physician who challenges the constitutionality of the Wisconsin abortion statute. He seeks an injunction restraining the defendants from enforcing a part of Wisconsin Statute § 940.04 and a judgment declaring it unconstitutional.

A temporary restraining order was denied by the order of a single-judge district court, . . . and the instant three-judge district court was convened to consider the other issues presented. We hold that portions of the statute are constitutionally invalid, but we decline to enjoin the pending state prosecution of the plaintiff.

The plaintiff is being prosecuted by the district attorney of Milwaukee county for allegedly having performed an abortion in violation of § 940.04, Wisconsin Statutes. The statute provides in part as follows:

1. Any person, other than the mother, who intentionally destroys the life of an unborn child may be fined not more than $5,000 or imprisoned not more than three years or both.
2. Any person, other than the mother, who does either of the following may be imprisoned not more than fifteen years:
    a. Intentionally destroys the life of an unborn quick child; or

* * *

5. This section does not apply to a therapeutic abortion which:
    a. Is performed by a physician; and
    b. Is necessary, or is advised by two other physicians as necessary, to save the life of the mother; and
    c. Unless an emergency prevents, is performed in a licensed maternity hospital.
6. In this section "unborn child" means a human being from the time of conception until it is born alive.

. . .

The plaintiff urges that § 940.04(5), Wisconsin Statutes, is vague and nebulous upon its face. That subsection, quoted above, excepts a therapeutic abortion when it is performed under specified terms. We have examined the challenged phraseology and are persuaded that it is not indefinite or vague. In our opinion, the word "necessary" and the expres-

From *Babbitz* v. *McCann*, 310 Federal Supplement 293.

sion "to save the life of the mother" are both reasonably comprehensible in their meaning.

The United States Supreme Court has ruled that a criminal statute must be definite enough to acquaint those who are subject to it with the conduct which will render them liable to its penalties. . . .

We believe that § 940.04(5) sets forth with reasonable clarity and sufficient particularity the kind of conduct which will constitute a violation. . . .

. . .

The plaintiff also charges that there is confusion in subsection 6, which provides that the words "unborn child" mean "a human being from the time of conception until it is born alive". The plaintiff may have medical or even practical justification for his disagreement with the correctness of this statutory definition of an unborn child, but he fails in his effort to convince us that the Wisconsin legislature was vague or indefinite in its choice of language. . . .

The plaintiff contends that the statute denies to him equal protection of the laws as guaranteed by the Fourteenth Amendment. It is urged that medical facilities are not constant throughout the state and that a doctor in a rural area in Wisconsin might be justified in performing a "necessary" abortion, whereas a doctor treating the same patient in Milwaukee would be unwarranted in performing the abortion because of the availability in Milwaukee of superior medical facilities.

We find more cogency in the argument that a wealthy woman, but not a poor one, is able, upon demand, to secure a safe and legal abortion in Japan or some other locale in which abortion is permitted. We take judicial notice of the fact that there are a number of places throughout the world where legal abortions are available. We have also considered the argument that an affluent woman, unlike the poor one, may enjoy a long-standing, personal relationship with a well-paid physician, who might more likely be willing or able to persuade his fellow doctors to authorize a therapeutic abortion. We are reluctant to equate these types of inequality with a denial of a protected right under the Fourteenth Amendment. We know of no analogous situation which goes as far as the plaintiff would have us go in applying the Fourteenth Amendment to the case at bar.

. . .

The Ninth Amendment to the United States Constitution provides:

The enumeration in the Constitution, of certain rights, shall not be construed to deny or disparage others retained by the people.

An examination of recent Supreme Court pronouncements regarding the Ninth Amendment compels our conclusion that the state of Wisconsin may not, in the manner set forth in § 940.04(1) and (5), Wisconsin Statutes, deprive a woman of her private decision whether to bear her unquickened child.

In terms of the Wisconsin statute, we do not purport to decide the question of a woman's aborting a fetus which has already quickened. We received into evidence the view of a gynecologist that a fetus normally becomes quick at about four and a half months after conception. . . .

While problems of overpopulation, ecology, and pollution have been brought to our attention, we deem them secondary as decisional factors in a judicial resolution of the issues at hand. So, too, we find it necessary to set aside arguments involving theological and ecclesiastical considerations.

Obviously, there is no topic more closely interwoven with the intimacy of the home and marriage than that which relates to the conception and bearing of progeny. Recent court cases have considered the sanctity of the right to privacy in home, sex, and marriage; however, the concept of private rights, with which the state may not interfere in the absence of a compelling state interest, is one of long standing.

· · ·

In *Meyer* v. *Nebraska* . . . (1923), the United States Supreme Court held that the private right "to marry, establish a home, and bring up children" was protected under the Fourteenth Amendment as an essential liberty. In *Prince* v. *Commonwealth of Massachusetts* . . . (1944), the Court spoke of the "private realm of family life which the state cannot enter".

In *Loving* v. *Virginia* . . . (1967), there was a challenge to the constitutionality of a state statute which purported to restrict marriages solely on the basis of race. While the Supreme Court observed, at page 7, . . . that "marriage is a social relation subject to the state's police power," the Court held, at page 12 . . . :

> The Fourteenth Amendment requires that the freedom of choice to marry not be restricted by invidious racial discriminations. Under our Constitution, the freedom to marry or not marry a person of another race resides with the individual and cannot be infringed by the state.

· · ·

Recent decisions have asserted a judicial application of the Ninth Amendment to the matter of privacy in marital relations and contraception. In *Griswold* v. *Connecticut* . . . (1965), the Court struck down the Connecticut statute which forbade the use of contraceptives. In so doing, the Court noted that the Bill of Rights contains both specific and penumbral guarantees which protect an individual from governmental invasion of the sanctity of his home and the privacies of his life. In the words of the Court, at page 485, . . . many decisions by the Supreme Court "bear witness that the right of privacy which presses for recognition here is a legitimate one." Three of the justices in a concurring opinion stated, at page 491 . . .:

> To hold that a right so basic and fundamental and so deep-rooted in our society as the right of privacy in marriage may be infringed because that right is not guaranteed in so many words by the first eight amendments to the Constitution is to ignore the Ninth Amendment and to give it no effect whatsoever.

                            .   .   .

In 2 Loyola University Law Review 1, 8 (April, 1969), former Supreme Court Justice Tom C. Clark concluded from a study of *Griswold* and its predecessor cases:

> The result of these decisions is the evolution of the concept that there is a certain zone of individual privacy which is protected by the Constitution. Unless the state has a compelling subordinating interest that outweighs the individual rights of human beings, it may not interfere with a person's marriage, home, children and day-to-day living habits. This is one of the most fundamental concepts that the Founding Fathers had in mind when they drafted the Constitution.

It is clear that in order to justify the regulation of such fundamental private rights, the state must show a compelling need. . . .

                            .   .   .

The defendants urge that the state's interest in protecting the embryo is a sufficient basis to sustain the statute. Upon a balancing of the relevant interests, we hold that a woman's right to refuse to carry an embryo during the early months of pregnancy may not be invaded by the state without a more compelling public necessity than is reflected in the statute in question. When measured against the claimed "rights" of an embryo of four months or less, we hold that the mother's right transcends that of such an embryo.

We also find no compelling state interest in a need to protect the mother's life. At common law, abortion was not a crime unless the mother was quick with child. . . . Today, many types of surgery, including abortion in the first trimester, are safe and routinely employed medical techniques. . . . Thus, the result of this court's decision that a mother has the right to determine whether to carry or reject an embryo that has not quickened is a return to the common law definition of abortion; this is not a position without well-established precedent in the common law.

We are persuaded that a medical abortion during early pregnancy is not inherently dangerous to the mother. Nor do we find a compelling state interest in connection with the discouragement of nonmarital sexual intercourse. The statute involved does not purport to distinguish between married and unmarried women.

We are invited to resolve the philosophical question, raised in some of the *amicus curiae* briefs, as to when an embryo becomes a child. For the purposes of this decision, we think it is sufficient to conclude that the mother's interests are superior to that of an unquickened embryo, whether the embryo is mere protoplasm, as the plaintiff contends, or a human being, as the Wisconsin statute declares.

There are a number of situations in which there are especially forceful reasons to support a woman's desire to reject an embryo. These include a rubella or thalidomide, pregnancy and one stemming from either rape or incest. The instant statute does not distinguish these special cases, but in our opinion, the state does not have a compelling interest even in the normal situation to require a woman to remain pregnant during the early months following her conception.

Under its police power, the state can regulate certain aspects of abortion. Thus, it is permissible for the state to require that abortions be conducted by qualified physicians. The police power of the state does not, however, entitle it to deny to a woman the basic right reserved to her under the Ninth Amendment to decide whether she should carry or reject an embryo which has not yet quickened. The challenged sections of the present Wisconsin statute suffer from an infirmity of fatal overbreadth.

5 GAY LIBERATION

The gay liberation movement began on June 28, 1969, in front of the Stonewall Inn, a popular gay bar in New York City's Greenwich Village. When police attempted to close the bar, gays fought the action. A new sense of pride, encapsuled in anger, developed in three successive nights of confrontation. That pride has become the motive force behind the activities of a new generation of homosexual activists.

The Gay Activists Alliance was formed to end discrimination against homosexuals. GAA estimates that there are twenty million homosexual Americans who are prevented from openly identifying themselves by a combination of social disapproval and economic and political sanctions. GAA is addressing itself to changing the narrowly defined images of homosexuals fostered by the heterosexual majority, to creating social and cultural alternatives to the gay bars (often run by criminal syndicates in collusion with local corrupt police), and to serving the psychological and religious needs of gays. Finally, GAA and approximately six hundred local organizations attempt through political action to secure civil rights and liberties guaranteed to Americans under the Constitution.

How are homosexuals oppressed? Forty-five states have statutes making it a crime to engage in consensual sodomy. Some have laws making it illegal for homosexuals to be served in bars or to rent apartments. Homosexuals may be given general discharges from the armed forces. They are discriminated against in public and private employment. They may be dismissed by employers if their sexual orientation becomes known.

Among the activities of the gay liberation movement is the attempt to change statutes and employment practices through militant action, lobbying, and litigation. With the help of the American Civil Liberties Union, homosexuals are challenging the constitutionality of sodomy statutes in the District of Columbia and the State of New York. The GAA is lobbying for civil rights bills in the City Councils of New York and other large cities. For the most part, however, the structure of discriminatory laws and practices remains unchanged; it may take years of effort before significant advances for the movement occur.

The movement has already produced many changes in social attitudes. The most important dynamic in the gay liberation movement is its effect within the homosexual community: there are hundreds of local groups fostering new pride in gays. New York University offers a course on homosexual behavior, and other major universities may follow that lead. Psychiatrists are reevaluating their analyses of homosexual behav-

124

ior, and at least one professional organization, the American Orthopsychiatric Association, has called for an end to discrimination against
homosexuals. In some cities liberal organizations affiliated with the
Democratic party have adopted similar positions. Civil rights measures
for homosexuals are being endorsed, albeit reluctantly, by elected
officials, labor, cultural, and religious leaders, and psychiatric organizations.

Within the gay community there are differences of opinion over tactics and strategy, and there is the factionalism to be expected in all
sociopolitical movements. But the gay liberation movement is not a
transitory phenomenon. Instead, it is a movement that will cause the
heterosexual majority to reassess its stereotypes about homosexuals.
Perhaps that reassessment will permit heterosexuals to become secure
in their own sexual orientations and will enable them to find the kindness and courage to welcome gays, with apologies for the past, into
the mainstream of American life.

The following article describes the diversity existing in the homosexual
world and the new social and political movements that have given the gay
liberation movement impetus in recent years.

New Styles in Homosexual Manliness

Laud Humphreys

Near the heart of a metropolis on the Eastern seaboard, there is a historic park where homosexuals have been cruising for at least a hundred years. An aging man told me:

> Back around 1930, when I was a very young man, I had sex with a really old fellow who was nearly 80. He told me that when he was a youngster—around the end of the Civil War—he would make spending money by hustling in that very park. Wealthy men would come down from the Hill in their carriages to pick up boys who waited in the shadows of the tree-lined walks at night.

In our motorized age, I have observed car drivers circling this park and adjoining residential blocks for the same sexual purposes. On a Friday night, unless the weather is bitter cold, a solid line of cars moves slowly along the one-way streets of this area, bumper to bumper, from 9:00 P.M. until 5:00 in the morning. The drivers pause in their rounds only long enough to exchange a few words with a young man on the sidewalk or to admit a willing passenger. There is no need to name this park. A knowledgeable person can find such pickup activity, both homosexual and heterosexual, in every major city of the Western world.

Cruising for "one-night-stands" is a major feature of the market economy in sex. In *The Wealth of Nations* Adam Smith postulated the ideal form of human relationship as being specific, depersonalized, short-term and contractual. This capitalist ideal is realized in the sex exchange of the homosexual underworld perhaps more fully than in any other social group, and the cruising scene of the gay world may continue for another hundred years or more. There are indications, however, that in the affluent, highly industrialized centers of our civilization the popularity of this sort of activity is declining. . . .

. . .

. . . The cruising scene, so familiar to those interested in the homosexual subculture, is yielding to attacks from two sides: it is not sufficiently impersonal and expedient for some, and too much so for others.

Published by permission of Transaction Inc. from *transaction*, Vol. 8 (March/April 1971). © 1971 Transaction Inc. Laud Humphreys is a social scientist who researches homosexual behavior.

Sexual exchanges in the gay underworld are experiencing a polarization, torn between a growing impersonalization on the one hand and increasing virilization on the other.

By virilization, I refer to the increasingly masculine image of the gay scene. Few gay bars are now distinguished by the presence of limp wrists and falsetto voices. Increasingly, these centers for the homosexual subculture are indistinguishable from other hangouts for youths of college age. Girls are now common among the patrons in gay bars. Beards, leather vests, letter jackets and boots have their place alongside the more traditional blue jeans and T-shirts. If any style predominates, it is that of the turned-on, hip generation.

As Tom Burke pointed out in *Esquire* a year ago, just when the public seemed ready to accept the sort of homosexual portrayed in *The Boys in the Band* that life style began to fade away: "That the public's information vis-a-vis the new deviate is now hopelessly outdated is not the public's fault. It cannot examine him on its own because, from a polite distance, he is indistinguishable from the heterosexual hippie." Although this "new homosexuality" is increasingly evident on both coasts, as well as on campuses across the country, it is just beginning to appear in the gay bars and coffeehouses of Denver, Omaha, and St. Louis. . . . Clearly, the youth counterculture with its attendant styles of dress and drug use has spawned a young, virile set to coexist with the effete martini sippers of the traditional gay world.

The new emphasis in the homosexual subculture, then, is upon virility: not the hypermasculinity of Muscle Beach and the motorcycle set, for these are part of the old gay world's parody on heterosexuality, but the youthful masculinity of bare chests and beads, long hair, mustaches, and hip-hugging pants. The new generation in gay society is more apt to sleep with a girl than to mock her speech or mannerisms. Many of these young men (along with the older ones who imitate their style) frown upon an exclusive orientation to homosexual or heterosexual activity. The idea is to be a "swinger," sensitive to ambisexual pleasures, capable of turning on sexually with both men and women.

In a crowded gay bar in Boston I recently watched this new facet of the subculture in action. Neither the young men nor the girls scattered throughout the room were at all distinguishable from any other college-age group in the taverns of that city. There were fewer women, to be sure, but the dress, appearance, and conversations were typical of any campus quadrangle. A handsome youth in a denim jacket and pants introduced an attractive young girl to a group standing at the bar as his fiancee. One man remarked, with a grin, that he was jealous. The young man, whom I shall call Jack, placed an arm around the shoulders of his fiancee, and, pulling her head toward his, explained: "Tom here is an old lover of mine." "Aren't we all!" another member of the party added, upon which all within earshot laughed.

After the bar closed, I was invited, along with the young couple, to join a number of patrons for "some group action" in a nearby apartment. A rather common, two-room pad with little furniture but many pillows and posters, the apartment was illuminated by only a single lightbulb suspended from the kitchen ceiling. Once our eyes had adjusted to the darkness of the other room, we could see about a dozen men, stretched in a number of stages of undress and sexual activity over the mattress and floor at the far end of the room. Excusing himself, Jack joined the orgy. In a few minutes, I could discern that he was necking with one man while being fellated by another.

Having explained my research purposes on the way to the apartment, I sought to explore the girl's reactions to her lover's apparent infidelity. I asked whether it bothered her. "Does it arouse me sexually, do you mean?" she replied. "No. Like, does Jack's behavior upset you?" With a laugh, she answered, "No, not at all. Like, I love Jack for what he is. You know, like, he swings both ways. If that's his thing, I groove on it. He could have left me home, you know—that's what some guys do. They leave their chicks home and, like, feed them a lot of shit so they can slip out and get their kicks. One of the things I dig most about Jack is that he shares everything with me. Having secrets just leads to hang-ups." "But don't you feel even a bit jealous?" I probed. "Like, wouldn't you rather be making love to him than standing here rapping with me?" "Why should I?" she said. "Like, Jack and I'll go home and ball after this is over. He's a beautiful person. Being able to share himself with so many different people makes him more beautiful!"

Later, Jack and his fiancee left those of us who were bound for an all-night restaurant. Arm in arm, they headed for the subway and a pad in Cambridge. Their story, I think, is an accurate reflection of the morality of the youth counterculture, both in its easy acceptance of a variety of sexual expressions and its nondefensive trust that the deeper, personal relationships are the more important ones. . . .

SUBCULTURAL DIVERSITY

. . . such norms of the counterculture have differing effects upon the sexual markets and life styles of the gay world, depending upon the permeability of various segments of the homosexual society. In order to outline and gauge these changes, it is necessary to construct a taxonomy of the homosexual community. Once we are able to consider its diverse segments in relation to each other, we can compare their reactions to some of the forces of contemporary society.

In my study of tearoom sex, I delineated four basic types of participants in these impersonal encounters: trade, ambisexuals, the gay, and closet queens. These men are differentiated most clearly by the relative autonomy afforded them by their marital and occupational statuses. When one engages in sexual behavior against which the society has erected strong negative sanctions, his resources for control of information carry a determining relationship to his life style, as well as to his self-image and the adaptations he makes to his own discreditable behavior. An example of this principle of classification would be that married men who are bound hand and foot to their jobs have more to fear—and less to enjoy—from their clandestine encounters because they have relatively fewer means of countering exposure than men of greater autonomy.

I have chosen the word "trade" from the argot of the homosexual community because it best describes that largest class of my respondents, the married men with little occupational autonomy. In its most inclusive sense in the gay vocabulary, this term refers to all men, married or single, who think they are heterosexual but who will take the insertor role in homosexual acts. Except for hustlers, who will be discussed later, most of these men are married. As participants in homosexual activity, they are nonsubcultural, lacking both the sources of information and the rationalization for their behavior that the gay circles provide. Generally, the trade are of lower-middle or upper-lower socioeconomic status. They are machinists, truck drivers, teachers, sales and clerical workers, invariably masculine in appearance, mannerisms, and self-image. Single men, I have found, are generally less stable in sexual identification. Once they begin to participate in homosexual relations, therefore, their straight self-image is threatened, and they tend to drift into the less heterosexual world of the closet queens or gay bar crowd. Apart from an exclusive concern with tearoom operations, however, I think it preferable to allow for the inclusion of some single men in the trade classification.

Moving into the upper strata of society, it is difficult to find participants in homosexual activity who think of themselves as strictly heterosexual. Americans with the higher educational level of the upper-middle and upper classes tend to find literary justification for their ventures into deviant sexual activity. The greater occupational autonomy of these men enables them to join in friendship networks with others who share their sexual interests. If these men are married, they tend to define themselves as "ambisexual," identifying with a distinguished company of men (Alexander the Great, Julius Caesar, Shakespeare, Walt Whitman, and a number of movie stars) who are said to have enjoyed the pleasures of both sexual worlds. In this classification are to be found business executives, salesmen with little direct supervision, doctors, lawyers, and interior decorators.

College students join with artists, the self-employed, and a few professional men to constitute the more autonomous, unmarried segment of the gay society. These men share enough resources for information control that they are unafraid to be active in the more visible portions of the homosexual subculture. In the tearoom study, I refer to them as "the gay," because they are the most clearly definable, in the sociological sense, as being homosexual. They are apt to have been labeled as such by their friends, associates, and even families. Their self-identification is strongly homosexual. Because their subcultural life centers in the gay bars, coffeehouses, and baths of the community, I will refer to them here as the "gay bar crowd."

The fourth type identified in my previous research are the "closet queens." In the homosexual argot this term has meanings with varying degrees of specificity. Occasionally, trade who fear their own homosexual tendencies are called closet queens. Again, the term may be used in referring to those in the subculture who feel that they are too good or proper to patronize the gay bars. In its most general sense, however, it is employed to designate those men who know they are gay but fear involvement in the more overt, bar-centered activities of the homosexual world. Because they avoid overt participation in the subculture, the married ambisexuals often receive the closet queen label from the gay bar crowd. I should like to maintain the distinctions I have outlined between ambisexuals and closet queens, however, because of the contrasting marital and socioeconomic statuses of the two groups. As I employ the term in my tearoom typology, the closet queens are unmarried teachers, clerks, salesmen, and factory workers. Living in fear that their deviance might be discovered, they tend to patterns of self-hatred, social isolation, and lone-wolf sexual forays.

There is a fifth type of man who is seldom found in tearooms, where money does not change hands, but who plays an important role in the homosexual markets. I mean the hustlers, homosexual prostitutes who operate from the streets, theaters, and certain bars, coffeehouses, and restaurants of the urban centers. The majority of these "midnight cowboys" share a heterosexual self-image. Indeed, since relatively few of them make a living from sexual activity, there is strong evidence that, for most hustlers, the exchange of money functions more to neutralize the societal norms, to justify the deviant sexual behavior, than to meet economic needs.

My observations suggest that there are at least three subdivisions among male prostitutes. One large, relatively amorphous group might properly be called "pseudo-hustlers." For them the amount of money received holds little importance, a pack of cigarettes or a handful of change sufficing to justify their involvement in the forbidden behavior, which is what they really wanted. Another large number of young men would be called "semiprofessionals." This type includes members of delinquent peer groups who hustle for money and thrills. Unlike the pseudo-hustlers, these young men receive support and training from other members of the hustling subculture. They are apt to frequent a particular set of bars and coffeehouses where a strict code of hustling standards is adhered to. Although a minority of these boys rely upon their earnings for support, the majority gain from their hustling only enough to supplement allowances, using their take to finance autos and heterosexual dates.

New to the sexual markets are the "call boys." Advertising in the underground papers of such cities as Los Angeles, San Francisco, and New York as "models," these young men charge an average fee of $100 for a night or $25 an hour. I have seen a catalogue distributed by one agency for such hustlers that provides frontal nude, full-page photographs of the "models," complete with telephone numbers. In general, the call boys share a gay or ambisexual identity and take pride in their professional status. The appearance of these handsome, masculine youngsters on the gay scene is an important manifestation of the virilization of the homosexual market.

. . .

POLARIZATION OF MARKET ACTIVITY

As the growing scarcity of time drives an increasing number of American males from every walk of life into one-night-stand sexuality, the impersonalized sex exchange thrives. Rest stops along the expressways, older tearooms in transportation terminals, subways, parks, and public buildings—all enjoy popularity as trysting places for "instant sex." The more expedient an encounter's structure and the greater the variety of participants, as is the case with tearoom sex, the less attractive are the time-demanding liaisons of the cruising grounds.

The trade and closet queens, in particular, find their needs met in the impersonal sex market of our consuming society. Here they can find sex without commitment, an activity sufficiently swift to fit into the lunch hour or a brief stop on the way home from work. The ambisexuals—many of them harried business executives—prefer the tearooms, not only for the speed and anonymity they offer, but also for the kicks they add to the daily routine.

Covert members of the gay society provide impetus to the impersonalization of the homosexual market. My study of tearoom participants
revealed that trade, closet queens, and ambisexuals share highly conservative social and political views, surrounding themselves with an
aura of respectability that I call the breastplate of righteousness. In
life style, they epitomize the consuming man of the affluent society. In
tearooms, they fill the role of sexual consumers, exchanging goods and
services in every spare moment they can wring from the demands of
computerized offices and automated homes. At the same time, however,
their conservatism makes them nearly impervious to the pressures of
the youth counterculture.

On the overt side of the gay world, the virile influence of hip culture
is having profound effects. Already poorly represented in the tearoom
scene, the gay bar crowd is preconditioned to embrace some of the
stronger norms of the flower people. At least in word, if not always in
deed, these overt leaders of the gay community espouse the deeper,
more personal type of relationship. . . .

. . .

The addition of the hip set with its virile, drug-using, ambisexual life
style has transformed the gay bar into a swinging, far less inhibited
setting for sexual contact. The old bar is familiar from gay novels: a
florid, clannish milieu for high-pitched flirtation. Patrons of the new
bars are justifiably suspicious of possible narcotics agents; but black,
white, lesbian, straight women, heterosexual couples, old, and young
mix with an abandon unknown a decade ago.

Gay bathhouses, once little more than shabby shelters for group sex,
although still active as sexual exchanges, are now becoming true centers for recreation. The underground press, along with homophile publications such as the *Los Angeles Advocate,* provide a medium for such
facilities to compete in advertising their expanding services. Such
advertisements, limited as they may be to underground newspapers, are
distinctive marks of the new virilized sex exchanges. By advertising,
bars, baths, and even hustlers proclaim their openness. It is as if this
overt portion of the homosexual community were announcing: "Look,
we're really men! Mod men, to be sure, children of the Age of Aquarius;
but we are real men, with all the proper equipment, looking for love."
In the 1970s it will be very difficult for a society to put that down as
deviant.

RADICALIZATION

The new generation's counterculture has also had its impact on the
homophile movement, a loose federation of civil rights organizations

that reached adolescence about the same time as the flower children. Beginning with the Mattachine Foundation, established around 1950 in Los Angeles, the homophile movement has produced a history remarkably parallel to that of the black freedom movement. Frightened by the spirit of McCarthyism, its first decade was devoted primarily to sponsoring educational forums and publications, along with mutual encouragement for members of an oppressed minority.

During the sixties, with the leadership of attorneys and other professional men, it began to enlist the support of the American Civil Liberties Union in using the courts to assure and defend the civil rights of homosexuals. About the time ministers marched in Selma, clergymen (inspired, perhaps, by the stand of the Church of England in support of homosexual law reform in that nation) began to join the movement as "concerned outsiders." The National Council on Religion and the Homosexual was formed, and, with clergy as sponsors and spokesmen, members of the movement entered into dialogues with straights.

With the proliferation of organizations for the homosexual, a variety of social services were initiated for the gay community: bulletins announcing social events; referral services to counselors, lawyers, and doctors; venereal disease clinics; legal guides for those who might suffer arrest; lonely hearts clubs. As they gained strength, the organizations began to foster changes in legislation and to organize gay bar owners for defense against pressures from both the police and organized crime.

In the mid-sixties, the first homosexual pickets began to appear, and the North American Conference of Homophile Organizations (NACHO) held its first national meeting. San Francisco's Society for Individual Rights (SIR), now the largest homophile group, was created and soon began to use picketing and techniques of applying political pressure. "Equal" signs in lavender and white appeared on lapels. But the new militancy began, significantly enough, with demonstrations by Columbia University's Student Homophile League in 1968. At that year's NACHO meetings, the movement's official slogan was adopted: "Gay is Good!"

Radicalization of the movement seems to have peaked in 1969. In that year, homosexuals rioted in New York, shouting "Gay Power!", and the Gay Liberation Front was organized. Student homophile organizations were recognized on half a dozen campuses. By the end of 1970, such groups were recognized on about thirty campuses.

THE BACKLASH—NORMALIZATION

Meanwhile, older leaders who had felt the sting of public sanctions recoiled in fear. Not only did the shouts of "Gay Power!" threaten to unleash a backlash of negative sentiment from a puritanical society, but the militants began to disrupt meetings, such as that of NACHO in San Francisco in the fall of 1970. As one homophile leader states: "The youngsters are demanding too much, too fast, and threatening to destroy all that has been gained over twenty painful years." Countless closet queens, who had joined when the movement was safer and more respectable, began to pressure the old militants to return to the early principles and activities of the movement.

An example of such reaction took place in St. Louis early in 1970. The campus-activist founders of the newly formed but thriving Mandrake Society were voted out of office and replaced by a conservative slate. Pages of the Mandrake newsletter, formerly occupied with items of national news interest, warnings about police activity, and exhortations for homosexuals to band together in self-defense, have since been filled with notices of forthcoming social events. A Gay Liberation front has been formed in that city during the past few months.

In his report to the membership on the year 1969, SIR's president criticized the "developing determined and very vocal viewpoint that the homosexual movement must be 'radicalized' " by aligning with the New Left on such issues as draft resistance, Vietnam, the Grape Boycott, student strikes and abortion. He replied to this demand: "SIR is a one-issue organization limiting itself to a concern for the welfare and rights of the homosexual as a homosexual. The SIR position has to be more like the American Civil Liberties Union than to be like a political club." While SIR's members recovered from the St. Valentine's Sweetheart Dance, the Gay Liberation Front at San Francisco State College threatened to take over all men's rooms on campus unless the administration grant them a charter.

As the process of normalization, with its emphasis on respectable causes, like social events and educational programs, asserts itself in established organizations of the gay world, more closet queens may be expected to join the movement. At the same time, gay liberation groups, cheered on by others of the New Left, should be expected to form on all the larger campuses of the nation. This marks a distinct rift in the homophile movement. At present, one finds an alignment of loyalties, chiefly along the dimensions of age and occupational status. Younger homophiles who enjoy relatively high autonomy follow a red banner with "Gay Power!" emblazoned upon it. (The motto of the recent Gay Liberation Conference was "Blatant Is Beautiful!") Older men—and those whose occupations require a style of covert behavior—sit beneath a lavender standard, neatly lettered "Gay Is Good!"

Sensitive to the need for unity, some leaders of the older homophile organizations plead for the changes needed to keep the young "Gayrevs" within the established groups. One such appeal is found in the April 1969, issue of *Vector:*

> It's time that we took some long, hard looks. If we want a retreat for middle-aged bitchery. A television room for tired cocksuckers. An eating club and community theatre—then let us admit it and work toward that.
>
> If we are, as we say we are, interested in social change—then let's get on the ball. Let's throw some youth into our midst. But I warn you . . . they don't want to live in 1956 (and neither do I).

UNITY IN ADVERSITY

In August of 1970, SIR began picketing Macy's in San Francisco to protest the arrest of forty men in that store's restrooms. Young men in sandals demonstrated alongside the middle-aged in business suits, together suffering the insults and threats of passersby. Recently, they have called for a nationwide boycott of the Macy's chain by homosexuals. Resulting internal struggle brought the resignation of Tom Maurer, SIR's conservative president. Present indications are that this large organization is successfully maintaining communication with both sides of the activist rift.

Meanwhile, New York's Gay Activists Alliance, dedicated to nonviolent protest, has provided youthful leadership for homophiles of varying ideological persuasions in the campaign to reform that state's sodomy, fair employment, and solicitation statutes. In both Albany and San Diego, organizations with reformist emphases have taken the name of Gay Liberation Front.

Although severe enough to confound social scientists who attempt to describe or analyze *the* homophile movement, the rift between homophile groups has yet to diminish their effectiveness. Much anger was generated when invading radicals disrupted the 1970 meetings of NACHO, but that organization has yet to enjoy what anyone would call a successful conference anyway. Meanwhile, the hotline maintained by the Homophile Union of Boston serves as a center of communication for the nine varied homophile groups that have developed in that city during the past eighteen months.

Three factors promote cooperation between the conservative, reform, and radical branches of the homophile movement. First, instances of police brutality in such widely scattered cities as New York, Los Angeles, San Francisco, and New Orleans have brought thousands of homosexuals together in protest marches during the past year. Nothing heals an ailing movement like martyrs, and the police seem pleased to provide them. Because a vice squad crusade is apt to strike baths and bars, parks and tearooms, all sectors of the homosexual market are subject to victimization in the form of arrests, extortion, assaults, and prosecution. There is a vice squad behind every active homophile group in America. With a common enemy in plain clothes, differences in ideology and life style become irrelevant.

Second, the *Los Angeles Advocate* has emerged as the homosexual grapevine in print. With up-to-date, thorough news coverage rivaling that of the *Christian Science Monitor* and a moderate-activist editorial policy, this biweekly is, as it claims, the "Newspaper of America's Homophile Community." With communication provided by the *Advocate* and inspiration gained from the successes of the women's liberation movement, the larger homophile organizations appear to be moving into a position best described as moderately activist.

Finally, a truly charismatic leader has appeared on the homophile scene. The Rev. Troy Perry, founder of the Metropolitan Community Church, a congregation for homosexuals in Los Angeles, was arrested during a fast in front of that city's Federal Building in June of 1970. The fast coincided with "Gay Liberation Day" marches of 2,000 persons in New York and 1,200 in Los Angeles. An articulate, moving speaker, Perry began to tour the nation for his cause. I have seen him honored by a standing ovation from an audience of a hundred main-line Protestant and Catholic clergy in Boston. Because he commands general respect from both gay libs and liberals in the movement, it is impossible not to draw a parallel between this minister and Martin Luther King. When I suggested that he was "the Martin Luther King of the homophile movement," he countered that "Martin Luther *Queen* might be more appropriate." As an evangelical religious movement spreads from the West Coast, replacing drugs as a source of enthusiasm for many in the youth counterculture, Perry's position of leadership should increase in importance.

Just as the world of female homosexuals should benefit from the trend towards liberation of women, so the male homosexual world of the 1970s should thrive. Divisions of the movement may provide the advantages of diversification. The new blood provided by the Gay Liberation Front, alarming as it may be to some traditionalists, is much healthier than the bad blood that has existed between a number of NACHO leaders.

Concurrently, the same social forces that are dividing and transforming the homophile movement have polarized and strengthened the homosexual markets. By now, the consuming American should know that diversification in places and styles of exchange is a healthy indicator in the market economy. Both virilization and impersonalization will attract more participants to the marketplaces of the gay world. At the same time, traditionalists will continue to cruise the streets and patronize the remaining sedate and elegant bars. When threatened by the forces of social control, however, even the closet queens should profit from the movement's newly found militance.

The selection below is an excerpt from a pamphlet distributed by the Gay Activists Alliance. It attempts to overcome myths about homosexuals and invites heterosexuals to join in the struggle for civil rights for homosexuals.

Sexuality and Justice

Gay Activists Alliance

You have a right to these facts:

1. For a large segment of humanity, heterosexuality is natural, healthy, and completely normal. For another large segment of humanity, homosexuality is natural, healthy, and completely normal. These are facts of natural history.

2. Many authority figures lie about homosexuality. They contradict themselves by saying that it is both uncommon and rampant. Some governments maintain that homosexual acts should be a crime. Some religions say "No, such acts are sins." Many psychiatrists say "No, such acts are signs of sickness." With the aid of these lies, some churches and psychiatrists become extremely rich.

3. School authorities and parents may repeat these and other lies out of simple ignorance or out of fear of seeming not to conform. One lie is that gay people are child-molesters. The fact is that gay people are no

Reprinted by permission of Richard Wandel, President of the Gay Activists Alliance.

more likely to molest children than straight people are; the vast number of both straight and gay people have no sexual interest in children.

4. Another lie is that gay people may convert straight people to homosexuality. The fact is that such conversion is impossible. Years of exposure to the System's antihomosexual propaganda cannot convert one gay man or woman to heterosexuality. And no gay man or woman is likely to convert anyone to homosexuality. There are countless gay people who pass as straight. When one of them finally comes out of his or her closet, it is hardly by "conversion."

5. It is alleged that gay people are unhappy because they are gay. The fact is that many gay men and women are happy and proud to feel sexually attracted to those of the same sex who represent values that are important to them.

6. It is alleged that homosexuality is wrong. A century ago it was alleged that all sexuality was wrong except in wedlock, and then only to breed offspring. According to that view, an individual existed, not to pursue happiness, but to breed. The fact is that living in harmony with one's sexual nature—straight, gay, or both—is not wrong. It is right.

Whether you are straight or gay—or both—

If truth and individual rights are important to you, here are specific things each of you can do in this struggle for rights and justice:

1. Understand that being a complete man or a complete woman has nothing to do with sexual preference. It has to do with courage, rationality, and concern for truth and justice.

2. Demand the facts about sexuality. You have a right to the facts, which are based in natural history and not in the assertions of unscrupulous psychiatric quacks. Insist that heterosexuality, bisexuality, and homosexuality be presented as equally valid and healthy forms of sexual expression. That is what they were, naturally and historically, until (in Western civilization) 1700 years ago. And that is what they are becoming again as more and more people begin to speak the truth.

3. Speak out against sexual bigotry. Point out that when people put down Gay Liberation, they may be putting down the freedom of some of your future children, or theirs.

4. Recognize that the freedom to indicate sexual interest can no longer be restricted to those who are (or who pretend to be) straight. Gay people are demanding their share in this freedom.

5. Encourage the formation of gay organizations in your school or college. *Do this if you are straight.* You will relate better to your friends if they are all real persons and not façades for something kept in a closet.

The American Orthopsychiatric Association, founded in 1924, is a professional association whose purposes are:

a. To unite and provide a common meeting ground for those engaged in the study and treatment of problems of human behavior;
b. To foster research and spread information concerning scientific work in the field of human behavior, including all forms of abnormal behavior.

The Board of Directors of the AOA issued a statement about the rights of homosexuals, which was approved at their meeting of October 16-17, 1971. The statement supports the goals of gay militants insofar as it calls for an end to the laws and regulations that discriminate against homosexuals.

Statement on Homosexuality

American Orthopsychiatric Association

The American Orthopsychiatric Association urges the end of repressive laws and regulations that interfere with the rights of homosexuals to live in our society. As a national membership association which embraces a variety of professional disciplines in the mental health field, we find no consistent body of scientific evidence to support the concept that homosexuals are necessarily harmful to others or incapable of responsible functioning. Laws, regulations, and prejudices that militate against individuals whose sexual preferences differ from those of the majority are essentially expressions of a moral judgment.

Sexual acts conducted in private by consenting adults consequently should not be subject to sanctions, legal or moral. They should in no way influence decisions as to the suitability of such persons for employment, housing, recreation, or any other human endeavor.

Reprinted by permission of the American Orthopsychiatric Association.

The First National Convention of Gay Activists was held in Chicago, Illinois, on February 11, 1972. Following is the 1972 gay rights platform adopted in Chicago.

1972 Gay Rights Platform in the United States

Gay Activists Convention

Millions of gay women and men in this country are subject to severe social, economic, legal, and psychological oppression because of their sexual orientation.

We affirm the right of all persons to define and express their own sexuality and emotionality and to choose their own life-style, so long as they do not infringe upon the rights of others. We pledge an end to all social, economic, legal, and psychological oppression of gay people.

We demand the repeal of all laws forbidding voluntary sex acts involving consenting gay American women and men in private.

Laws prohibiting loitering for the purpose of soliciting for a homosexual liaison are vague and unconstitutional. Nevertheless, they are frequently used as the legal cover for police entrapment of gay people.

We demand the repeal of all laws prohibiting the solicitation for a voluntary private sexual liaison.

Prejudice and myth have led to widespread discrimination against gay people.

We demand the enactment of civil rights legislation which will prohibit discrimination because of sexual orientation in employment, housing, public accommodation, and public services.

Transcribed for use in this volume by Morty Manford.

DEMANDS

Federal

1. Amend all federal civil rights acts, other legislation, and government controls to prohibit discrimination in employment, housing, public accommodation, and public services because of one's sexual orientation.
2. Issuance by the president of an executive order prohibiting the military from excluding persons who of their own volition desire entrance into the armed forces for reasons of their sexual orientation, and from issuing less-than-fully-honorable discharges for homosexuality, and the upgrading to fully honorable of all such discharges previously issued, with retroactive benefits.
3. Issuance by the president of an executive order prohibiting discrimination in the federal civil service because of sexual orientation, in hiring and promoting; and prohibiting discrimination against homosexuals in security clearances.
4. Elimination of tax inequities victimizing single persons and same-sex couples.
5. Elimination of bars to the entry, immigration, and naturalization of homosexual women and men aliens.
6. Federal encouragement and support for sex education courses prepared and taught by qualified gay women and men presenting homosexuality as a valid, healthy preference and life-style, and as a viable alternative to heterosexuality.
7. Appropriate executive orders, regulations, and legislation banning the compiling, maintenance, and dissemination of information on an individual's sexual preferences, behavior, and social and political activities for dossiers and data banks, and ordering the immediate destruction of all such existing data.
8. Federal funding of aid-projects by gay women's and men's organizations designed to alleviate the problems encountered by gay women and men which are engendered by an oppressive sexist society.
9. Immediate release of all gay women and men now incarcerated in detention centers, prisons, and mental hospitals because of sexual offense charges relating to victimless crimes or their sexual orientation, and that adequate compensation be made for the physical and mental duress encountered, and that all existing records relating to the incarceration be immediately expunged.

State

1. All federal legislation and programs enumerated in federal demands 1, 6, 7, 8, and 9 above should be implemented at the state level where applicable.

2. Repeal of all state laws prohibiting private sexual acts involving consenting persons; equalization for homosexuals and heterosexuals of
   the enforcement of all laws.
3. Repeal of all state laws prohibiting solicitation for private voluntary
   sexual liaisons and those laws prohibiting prostitution, both male and
   female.
4. Enactment of legislation prohibiting insurance companies and other
   state-regulated enterprises from discriminating because of sexual
   orientation, in insurance and in bonding or any other prerequisite to
   employment or control of one's personal demesne.
5. Enactment of legislation so that child custody, adoption, visitation
   rights, foster parenting, and the like shall not be denied because of
   sexual orientation or marital status.
6. Repeal of all laws prohibiting transvestitism and cross-dressing.
7. Repeal of all laws governing the age of sexual consent.
8. Repeal of all legislative provisions that restrict the sex or number of
   persons entering into a marriage unit, and the extension of legal benefits of marriage to all persons who cohabit regardless of sex or number.

(*Note:* It was not until after the convention that the inconsistency
between point 4 of federal demands and point 8 of state demands was
recognized. While [the latter] calls implicitly for tax privileges for gay
couples, [the former] calls for an end to tax privileges to couples. A
number of gays polled since the convention feel the federal demand
should preempt the clause in the state demand.)

––––––––––––––––––––

The judiciary becomes involved in the gay liberation movement when homosexual plaintiffs ask the courts to protect their constitutional rights. Gays have
challenged state laws prohibiting consensual sodomy, as well as laws or
administrative practices regulating employment of homosexuals.

McConnell v. Anderson involves a male homosexual, J. M. McConnell, who
"married" a student (also male) at the University of Minnesota. McConnell
thereupon was denied a promised position as a librarian at the university. The
student body then elected his lover, an avowed gay liberationist, as president
of the student body of the University. In spite of this electoral success, Mc-
Connell did not fare well in the courts. The lower federal district court affirmed
his right to employment, but the court of appeals (the intermediate federal
court) reversed the decision. On April 3, 1972, the Supreme Court let stand
the decision of the court of appeals upholding the right of the University of
Minnesota to refuse the job to McConnell. The Supreme Court did not offer
an opinion, but simply declined to review the case.

––––––––––––––––––––

McConnell v. Anderson (I)

Neville, District Judge.

Squarely presented to the court for decision is a case where the University of the State of Minnesota, acting through its Board of Regents, rejected as an employee an otherwise qualified male applicant because of his public profession that he is an homosexual. The question raised is whether under the 1871 Civil Rights Act, 42 USC. § 1983, the Board of Regents, acting "under color of any statute, ordinance, regulation, custom, or usage, of any state . . ." deprived plaintiff as an homosexual and as a citizen of the United States "of any rights, privileges, or immunities secured by the Constitution and laws," specifically the Due Process, Privileges and Immunities, and Equal Protection Clauses of the Fourteenth Amendment to the United States Constitution and collaterally the Freedom of Speech or "Expression" Clause of the First Amendment. . . .

The facts are largely undisputed. Plaintiff, twenty-eight years of age, is a librarian holding a Master's degree. He was last employed during the 1969–70 school year at the Park College Library in Missouri. In late December of 1969 he sent a number of letters of inquiry to prospective employers and received a favorable response from the librarian at the University of Minnesota. An interchange of correspondence and a personal interview followed, an employment application was submitted and by letter dated April 27, 1970 plaintiff was advised "This is to confirm the telephone conversation . . . in which we agreed to your appointment to the position of head of the cataloging division in our St. Paul campus library [carrying] an annual salary of $11,000 . . . to begin on or about July 1, 1970." Despite the language of this letter, it is acknowledged by plaintiff that no contract of employment was ever perfected, since the formal necessary approval by the Board of Regents was never forthcoming.

Plaintiff moved to Minneapolis and on or about May 18, 1970 publicly applied to the appropriate authority for a marriage license, seeking marriage to another man, one Jack Baker, a University of Minnesota law student. Both men freely admitted to the news media that they were and are homosexuals. This rather bizarre occurrence drew substantial publicity, including pictures in the newspapers of the two men, though no

From *McConnell* v. *Anderson*, 316 Federal Supplement 809.

reference was made to plaintiff's connection with or future employment by the university.

Plaintiff's appointment was scheduled to come routinely before the university board of regents for consideration at its July 1970 meeting. Prior thereto, a committee of the regents was appointed which met twice, the latter time on July 9, 1970 at which meeting eleven of the twelve regents were in attendance. The committee accorded plaintiff and his lawyers a personal interview and hearing. The following recommendation was thereinafter adopted unanimously:

> That the appointment of Mr. J. M. McConnell to the position of the Head of the cataloging division of the St. Paul campus library at the rank of instructor not be approved on the grounds that his personal conduct, as represented in the public and university news media, is not consistent with the best interest of the university.

Under the board's rules no appearance is permitted by anyone at its meetings but the committee's recommendation was duly adopted by the regents at its regular meeting the next day.

Plaintiff testified that he is presently receiving no earnings whatsoever; that he declined a tendered position elsewhere in reliance on his University of Minnesota employment, which position has now been filled; that he has approximately $200 total assets. He professes publicly his homosexuality. He is a member of an organization known as FREE, standing for "Fight Repression of Erotic Expression," though apparently its name recently has been changed. This organization is comprised of homosexuals and maintains headquarters in the University of Minnesota Student Union. Plaintiff is in no way clandestine about his homosexuality. On cross-examination he denied that he had ever practiced or committed the crime of sodomy within the State of Minnesota, though he is presently living at the same address as his intended "spouse" Jack Baker. He stated unequivocally that he has never advocated the practice of homosexuality by anyone else nor induced any other person to engage in its pursuits.

The chairman of the regents' aforesaid committee was a witness at the trial. Counsel for the university stated to the court that this is the first case in at least ten years where a rejection has occurred against the favorable recommendation of the academic staff. The regents' position, with no dissenting vote, is that even though plaintiff may be a very capable librarian, his professed homosexuality connotes to the public generally that he practices acts of sodomy, a crime under Minnesota law; that the regents have a right to presume that by his applying for a license to marry another man plaintiff intended, were the license to be granted, to engage in such sodomous criminal activities; that the regents cannot condone the commission of criminal acts by its employees and thus plaintiff has rendered himself unfit to be employed.

. . .

In the absence of any controlling statute, the question remains as to whether it is a violation of plaintiff's constitutional rights to refuse him public employment because he proclaims that he is an homosexual.

No case in the United States Supreme Court has been found where a person was either discharged or the prospective employer refused to hire him on the grounds that he was an homosexual or that specific acts of homosexuality were committed. In the circuit courts two cases have been found in the District of Columbia involving the same plaintiff. They hold that an admission that one is an homosexual, standing alone and without evidence of any practice thereof will not justify the Civil Service Commission in refusing to certify him as eligible for employment based on a determination of "immoral conduct". . . . These cases come as close as any to a refusal to hire for homosexuality as distinguished from a discharge from existing employment. There appear to be no circuit court cases where a government employee has been discharged for homosexuality per se. There are several cases where employees have been discharged for homosexual acts which are specified by the discharging agency and either clearly supported in the evidence before it, or simply not contested by the employee. . . .

. . .

The courts have abandoned the concept that public employment and the opportunity therefor is a mere privilege and not a constitutionally protected right. . . . More recently, however, this right-privilege distinction as a limitation on substantive or procedural due process affecting employment in the public sector has been seriously eroded if not virtually rejected. . . .

. . .

Though by current standards many persons characterize an homosexual as engaging in "immoral conduct," "indecent" and "disgraceful," it seems clear that to justify dismissal from public employment, or as the court finds in this case to reject an applicant for public employment, it must be shown that there is an observable and reasonable relationship between efficiency in the job and homosexuality. In the case at bar, of course, since plaintiff never has been permitted to enter on his duties, there is no history as to his performance or the possible claimed effect of his homosexuality. The regents are of necessity speculating and presuming. Plaintiff's position will not expose him to children of tender years who conceivably could be influenced or persuaded to his penchant. What he does in his private life, as with other employees, should not be his employer's concern unless it can be shown to affect in some degree his efficiency in the performance of his duties....

An homosexual is after all a human being, and a citizen of the United States despite the fact that he finds his sex gratification in what most consider to be an unconventional manner. He is as much entitled to the protection and benefits of the laws and due process fair treatment as are others, at least as to public employment in the absence of proof and not mere surmise that he has committed or will commit criminal acts or that his employment efficiency is impaired by his homosexuality. Further, the decided cases draw a distinction between homosexuality, i.e., sexual propensity for persons of one's own sex and the commission of homosexual criminal acts. Homosexuality is said to be a broad term involving all types of deviant sexual conduct with one of the same sex, but not necessarily criminal acts of sodomy.

Plaintiff does not have an inalienable right to be employed by the university but he has a right not to be discriminated against under the Fourteenth Amendment Due Process Clause. He has a constitutional right that the terms of his public employment which he must meet be "reasonable, lawful, and nondiscriminatory"....

The "purges" of the late 1940s and 1950s of homosexuals in the federal government service, particularly in the Department of State, are not authority in the case at bar. There clandestine homosexuals, when discovered, were claimed to have become the subject of possible blackmail.... Here plaintiff is very open about his deviation, and in any event is not dealing with classified or secret information important to the national security.

.   .   .

McConnell v. Anderson (II)

Stephenson, Circuit Judge....

On July 22, 1970, McConnell brought suit for injunctive relief in the United States District Court for the District of Minnesota, naming as defendants the individual members of the board of regents and Ralph H. Hopp, the University Librarian.... Judge Neville, after conducting an oral hearing at which evidence was taken, entered judgment for McConnell and enjoined the board from refusing to employ him "solely because, and on the grounds that he is a homosexual and that thereby 'his personal conduct, as presented in the public and university news media, is not consistent with the best interest of the university'".... Judge Neville stayed the judgment and suspended the injunction pending disposition of this appeal. We must reverse.

. . .

The board's primary demand for reversal is based upon a most fundamental contention. It is the board's claim that Judge Neville, in issuing the injunction, exceeded his proper function and authority by superimposing his own situational judgment upon legitimate board action supported by substantial and material factual data. The board also mounts a due process attack against the timeliness and sufficiency of service of process. It urges, too, that Judge Neville improperly prevented it from cross-examining McConnell at the oral hearing with reference to the nature of his past conduct.

We focus our initial attention upon our standard of review of the board's action. The Minnesota Supreme Court has had no less than five occasions to determine and review the proper role and function of the board of regents in the management, control and administration of the University of Minnesota. From these decisions we think it can be said generally that, insofar as Minnesota's highest court is concerned, the board is vested with plenary and exclusive authority to govern, control, and oversee the administration of the university and that the role of Minnesota courts in reviewing board action is limited to determining whether the board has kept within the scope of its constitutional powers. We think this is but another manner of saying that, at least with respect to matters purely administrative in nature, viz., the employment of university personnel and the like, the discretion of the

From *McConnell* v. *Anderson,* 451 Federal 2nd 193.

board necessarily is broad and subject only to such judicial review as normally is available to litigants allegedly aggrieved by administrative action generally. We think the attitude and approach to the board's role by Minnesota's court is sound and instructive and we adopt it as our own.

Without question, then, the board is on relevant and sound ground in asserting that the decision embodied in its resolution cannot be overturned in the absence of a clear and affirmative showing that it was premised upon arbitrary or capricious conduct. That a court is, in reviewing a determination of an administrative body, limited to deciding whether the administrative action was arbitrary, unreasonable, or capricious long has been settled. This particularly must be so, it seems to us, where, as here, the determination under challenge is one falling within the considerable discretion entrusted those charged with the heavy responsibility of supervising the administration of this nation's colleges and universities.

It is McConnell's position that the board's decision not to approve his employment application reflects "a clear example of the unreasoning prejudice and revulsion some people feel when confronted by a homosexual." That being so, he argues that the board's action was arbitrary and capricious and thus violative of his constitutional rights. We do not agree.

It is our conclusion that the board possessed ample specific factual information on the basis of which it reasonably could conclude that the appointment would not be consistent with the best interests of the university. We need only to observe that the board was given the unenviable task and duty of passing upon and judging McConnell's application against the background of his actual conduct. So postured, it is at once apparent that this is not a case involving mere homosexual propensities on the part of a prospective employee. Neither is it a case in which an applicant is excluded from employment because of a desire clandestinely to pursue homosexual conduct. It is, instead, a case in which something more than remunerative employment is sought; a case in which the applicant seeks employment on his own terms; a case in which the prospective employee demands, as shown both by the allegations of the complaint and by the marriage license incident as well, the right to pursue an activist role in *implementing* his unconventional ideas concerning the societal status to be accorded homosexuals and, thereby, to foist tacit approval of this socially repugnant concept upon his employer, who is, in this instance, an institution of higher learning. We know of no constitutional fiat or binding principle of decisional law which requires an employer to accede to such extravagant demands. We are therefore unable fairly to categorize the board's action here as arbitrary, unreasonable, or capricious.

. . .

Reversed, with directions to dissolve the injunction and to dismiss the action on the merits.

6 CORRECTIONS

Most judicial and congressional supervision of the criminal justice system in the 1960s focused on the rights of the accused, the rights of the defendant, and postconviction remedies. It was the adjudicatory process rather than the correctional system that received the most attention.

The Supreme Court took the initiative in supervising the customary police practices of interrogation. In *Escobedo* v. *Illinois* the right of the accused to the assistance of his counsel in the station house was affirmed. In *Miranda* v. *Arizona* the Court decided that a set of guarantees to the right to silence and the right to free counsel or chosen counsel would be applied by police as soon as the investigation focused on a particular person. Informing an individual of these rights became a part of the accusatory procedure.

Searches and seizures of evidence were also regulated. In *Mapp* v. *Ohio* the Supreme Court provided that evidence obtained unconstitutionally (in the particular case, without a search warrant) could be excluded from a state trial, thus applying the exclusionary rule developed in the federal court system to state judicial systems. In *Terry* v. *Ohio* the constitutionality of "stop and frisk" laws, permitting the police to make a limited search of a citizen for weapons under certain conditions, was upheld. Later cases also qualified the need to obtain a warrant prior to conducting a search and provided for a set of exceptions.

The right of the accused to counsel in trials conducted in state courts was affirmed in *Gideon* v. *Wainright*. Subsequent cases decided by the Supreme Court have broadened the rights of indigent defendants. These modifications include the right to a free transcript of the trial (if the case is appealed), the waiver of filing fees for the appeal, and the right to appointed counsel for the appeal.

Currently the Supreme Court is scrutinizing the "plea bargaining" process. Under this arrangement a defendant will plead guilty and, in return for this facilitating of the case, the prosecutor will recommend that the charge be reduced and a light sentence imposed.

Congress has reacted in mixed fashion to the expansion of constitutional rights in the criminal justice system. At times Congress has modified court decisions. For example, in the Omnibus Crime Control and Safe Streets Act of 1968 it provided that federal judges could admit confessions under conditions which were not as strict as those promulgated in *Miranda* v. *Arizona*. On the other hand, after the *Gideon* v. *Wainright* decision Congress provided funds for criminal representation for

150

indigents in all felony cases in the federal courts. But it also stipulated that the Legal Services Program cannot provide representation in state criminal proceedings, thus keeping state and local criminal defender agencies without adequate resources to provide effective (rather than minimal) representation in state proceedings.

State and local governments have taken little action to implement the decisions of the Supreme Court, and a realistic analysis of the criminal justice system must start with the understanding that these decisions represent *goals*, rather than accepted practices, for police and prosecutors. The police remain relatively unsupervised and free to ignore the spirit, if not the letter, of the *Miranda* warning and other decisions. Police brutality and illegal searches are often disregarded by state courts. The state legislatures do not provide the funds nor the supervisory apparatus to ensure that the police obey the decisions of the Supreme Court.

Yet as poor as the record of political leadership may be in regard to the criminal justice system in the adjudicatory stage, it is immeasurably worse when it comes to the correctional system. Courts have adopted the policy of judicial restraint and have been loath to attempt to supervise activities of state correctional officials. This attitude is slowly changing, but it has permitted conditions so inhumane and degrading that it is almost impossible to believe that they exist in the United States in the last third of the twentieth century.

Courts and legislative bodies have delegated most power to correctional officials. The prisoner has generally been held to have no rights, the idea being that he forfeited constitutional rights upon his conviction. Administrators determine, without due process or external checks, the classification of the prisoner, his placement in the cellblock, his work assignment, punishment such as solitary confinement or loss of privileges, and loss of "good behavior time" (that can reduce his sentence by one-fourth or one-third). Prison conditions may lead to cruel and unusual punishment by other inmates or by guards, and these can occasionally include electrical shocks applied to the genitals, splinters placed under nails, and confinement to "strip cells," where prisoners are kept naked and given only bread and water. Prisons are notorious for the practice of homosexual rape (which has nothing to do with consensual sodomy discussed elsewhere in this volume) and other perversions among inmates.

Usually prisons cannot provide adequate medical, psychiatric, educational, or vocational training facilities to inmates. The prison diet usually makes no allowance for the dietary needs of inmates such as Black Muslims, who refuse to eat pork. Prison libraries are small and materials are censored. Law books and legal assistance are rarely available. Personal mail is censored, and business communications are usually forbidden. The right of a prisoner to communicate with his lawyer is restricted. In the name of security, visits between prisoners and their families must take place under dehumanizing circumstances.

These conditions are now being scrutinized by courts and by state legislatures. Even in the period of judicial restraint, the Supreme Court in *Price* v. *Johnson* (1948) indicated that prison regulations should not exceed anything needed to maintain orderly administration and discipline. In 1949 the Supreme Court held that retribution was less important than rehabilitation, and in 1969, in *Johnson* v. *Avery* the Supreme Court invalidated a regulation in a state prison because it conflicted with the constitutional rights of prisoners.

Legislatures are scrutinizing conditions in prisons, and in some states legislation is providing for due process in prison proceedings. States are applying for federal funds to build different kinds of facilities and provide additional services to prisoners. Yet these "demonstration" programs should not obscure the fact that only a small start has been made on the fundamental reform of prisons so clearly required.

The reform movement of one generation creates problems for the next generation to solve. The following article by David J. Rothman discusses the development of state institutions as part of the reforming impulse of nineteenth-century America. It also indicates the reforms that a new generation concerned with the quality of correctional institutions will introduce in the 1970s.

Of Prisons, Asylums, and Other Decaying Institutions

David J. Rothman

Over the course of the past several decades, without clear theoretical justification or even a high degree of self-consciousness, we have been completing a revolution in the treatment of the insane, the criminal, the orphaned, the delinquent, and the poor. Whereas once we relied almost exclusively upon incarceration to treat or punish these classes of people, we now frame and administer many programs that maintain them within the community or at least remove them as quickly as possible from institutions. . . .

The basic statistics are, themselves, most striking. Since 1955 the annual number of inmates in the nation's mental hospitals has been falling. New York state institutions, for example, held 93,000 patients in 1955; in 1966, their number dropped to 82,765, and in 1970 to 64,239. A similar decline has occurred in correctional institutions. In 1940, 131.7 prisoners per 100,000 of the population served time in federal or state penitentiaries; in 1965, the number fell to 109.6 per 100,000, and this without a concomitant drop in the number of crimes committed or criminals convicted. Dramatic changes have also affected the young. The orphan asylum has almost disappeared, and the juvenile correction center has also declined in use. As for the poor, the almshouse or traditional poorhouse is no longer a specter in their lives.

Obviously, no one would be foolish enough to predict that within the next twenty or thirty years incarcerating institutions will disappear. Some 400,000 adults and juveniles remain in correctional institutions, and a similar number fill mental hospitals. Moreover, Attorney General Mitchell is insisting that money be spent on constructing new penitentiaries and refurbishing old ones, and the Justice Department's Law Enforcement Assistance Administration spends around $29 million annually in block grants to the states for these purposes. Nevertheless, when our current practices are viewed within historical perspective, the degree to which we have moved away from the incarcerative mode of coping with these social problems is clear enough. We are witnessing nothing less than the end of one era in social reform and the beginning of another.

From *The Public Interest,* 26 (Winter 1972), pp. 3–6, 8–16. Copyright © 1972 by National Affairs, Inc. Reprinted by permission of the author and the publisher. David J. Rothman is Professor of History at Columbia University.

THE MOVEMENT FOR INCARCERATION

Institutionalization of "problem people" in the United States originated in the opening decades of the nineteenth century. Prior to that, colonial communities, particularly the more settled ones along the seaboard, relied upon very different mechanisms of control. Their level of expectations was very low; they did not expect to eliminate poverty or to reform the criminal. Rather, the colonists devoted their energies to differentiating carefully between neighbor and stranger. Typically, they provided assistance to the resident within his household or that of a friend—and they banished the troublesome outsider. . . .

. . .

Beginning in the 1820s the perspective on both poverty and crime underwent a major shift. The relatively passive attitudes of the eighteenth century gave way to a new, energetic program, as Americans became convinced that poverty and crime, as well as insanity and delinquency, could be eliminated from the New World. Crime, it was decided, did not reflect the innate depravity of man but the temptations at loose in the society. Insanity was not the work of the devil, but the product of a deleterious environment. Poverty was not inevitable, but rather reflected the inadequacies of existing social arrangements. These interpretations revealed not only an Enlightenment optimism about the perfectibility of human nature, but a nagging fear that American society, with its unprecedented geographic and social mobility, was so open and fragmented that stability and cohesion could not be maintained unless reforms were instituted. An odd marriage of ideas occurred in the young republic. The optimism of an environmental doctrine joined a basic concern that American society was in a state of imbalance—though the majority were coping well enough, a minority seemed unable to confront the challenges of American life. The result was a widespread belief that insanity could be cured in the New World because its causes were rooted in a social order that encouraged limitless ambition and disrespect for traditional opinions and practices. The criminal, too, could be reformed, once he was removed from a setting in which gambling halls and dens of iniquity corrupted him. Poverty would also be eliminated as soon as the poor were taught to resist the temptations at loose in a free community.

Starting from these premises, reformers moved quickly and enthusiastically to a new program: the construction of asylums—new "environments"—for the deviant and dependent. Between 1820 and 1840 penitentiaries spread throughout the country, and the states constructed insane asylums. Concomitantly, they built orphan asylums, houses of refuge (for juvenile delinquents), and almshouses. The walls that surrounded these structures were intended not only to confine the deviant and dependent but also to exclude the community—for, in origin, incarceration was a semiutopian venture. Superintendents aimed to establish a corruption-free environment which would compensate for the irregularities and temptations existing in the larger, more turbulent society....

In fact, the initial organization of the asylums closely approximated the reformers' designs. The institutions consistently isolated the inmates from the community. Wardens sharply limited the number of letters and visits a prisoner could receive and prohibited the circulation of periodicals and newspapers. Insane asylum superintendents instructed relatives to remove the sick patient from the family and bring him to the institution as soon after the onset of the disease as possible, and then not to visit or to write him frequently. Many child-care institutions insisted that the parents abdicate all rights to their children.

The asylums' internal organization put a premium on bell-ringing punctuality and a precise routine. Regimentation became the standard style of prison life in the popular Auburn plan, where the inmates remained isolated in individual cells during the night and worked in congregate shops during the day. Convicts did not walk from place to place, but went in lock step, a curious American invention that combined a march and shuffle. A military precision marked other aspects of their lives. At the sound of a morning bell, keepers opened the cells, prisoners stepped onto the deck, lock-stepped into the yard, washed their pails and utensils, marched to breakfast, and then, when the bell rang, stood, and marched to the workshops where they remained till the next signal....

.   .   .

The Progressive era marked a dividing point in public policy, giving the initial thrust to new, noninstitutional programs. Change was uneven and selective, affecting some areas more quickly than others. Nevertheless, between 1890 and 1920 care and correction of the deviant and dependent began to shift away from incarceration. The changes were most popular and complete where citizens' suspicions and fears were least intense. The first caretaker institutions to decline in importance were orphan asylums, replaced by foster homes and liberalized adoption proceedings. Public and private benevolent societies that in the nineteenth century had devoted their funds to administering child-care institutions transformed themselves into placing-out and adoption agencies. Simultaneously, innovations in public welfare programs decreased reliance on the almshouses, at least for some groups. State aid that allowed widowed mothers to care for their dependent children at home was first enacted in Illinois in 1911 and then spread quickly through densely populated and industrial states. No longer would these women be dispatched to an almshouse and their dependents to an orphan asylum.

New Deal legislation furthered these trends. The Social Security Act of 1935 eliminated incarceration for other segments of the poor, keeping the aged and the able-bodied unemployed out of the almshouse. The law expressly prohibited federal grants to states to expand their alms-houses, and refused to match state funds that went to the support of persons institutionalized. Incarceration had been the mainstay of public relief for over one hundred years, and the abolition of this policy was no mean feat.

. . .

Although prison walls still impose themselves massively upon the public eye, in this field too we have decreased our reliance upon incar-ceration. Correctional institutions have lost their nineteenth-century monopoly. Since 1961 the percentage of the population in prisons has declined annually. The most important procedure effecting this change is probation. In 1965, 53 per cent of all offenders were out in the community under the periodic supervision of a probation officer. By 1975, according to the estimates of an advisory committee to the President's Commission on Law Enforcement and the Administration of Justice, the proportion will rise to 58 per cent. The most dramatic increases have been among juvenile offenders. In 1965 only 18 per cent of convicted delinquents served in correctional institutions, while 64 per cent were on probation. Among adult offenders, 39 per cent of those convicted of a crime were institutionalized, while 49 per cent (including, to be sure, misdemeanants) were on probation.

The other major alternative to prolonged incarceration is parole, whereby a convict having completed some fraction of his sentence is discharged from prison and obliged to report regularly to a corrections officer. Although the idea of parole is not new—it was advocated by many prison experts as early as the 1870s—it has been extensively used only in the post-1930 period. . . . Among all convicts serving in American prisons in 1964, fully 65 per cent won release under this program.

Several states are also experimenting with new programs to de-crease the distance between correction programs and the community. The publicity given these procedures to date outweighs their actual importance, but they all look to the same anti-institutional goal. One such effort is work release, whereby the offender leaves the prison in the morning, works at his job in the community, and then returns to confinement at night. One warden regards this innovation as "revolu-tionary, not evolutionary. It's going to change," he predicts, "about all of penology." For the moment, however, work release has been authorized in some twenty-four states and for the federal corrections systems. . . . But the scope of work release is limited, typically not covering those convicted of crimes of violence or of a morals charge, or those believed to be part of an organized crime syndicate. Some preliminary evaluations also suggest that the arrangement is expensive and cumbersome to administer. Nevertheless, some states are trying to extend the program to cover felons, and they also report a significant drop in such incarceration-related costs as welfare payments to convicts' families. . . .

These developments have stimulated and in turn been furthered by an important series of legal actions intended to reduce dependence on incarceration. The most notable advances have occurred in the field of juvenile detention. In the *Gault* decision (1967) the Supreme Court brought some of the protections of "due process" to the juvenile courts. While the requirements that the Court insisted upon were by no means negligible—notification of charges and the right to confront witnesses—it is not only for procedural reasons that the case stands out; for the *Gault* decision was premised upon a disillusionment with incarceration. Underlying the majority opinion, written by Justice Fortas, was the belief that the juvenile institution was totally inadequate to the job of reformation. As Justice Black insisted in a concurring opinion, "It is in all but name a penitentiary." And since the disposition of a juvenile case might well result in confining the offender to an essentially penal institution, the justices wanted the trial proceedings to protect the defendants' rights. A similar reason appeared in the Court's decision in the *Winship* case. In an earlier day, magistrates assumed that a reformatory would accomplish some good and were therefore content to incarcerate delinquents on the basis of the "preponderance of the evidence." Now, far less enthusiastic about these institutions, the Court ruled that juvenile convictions had to meet the standard of "beyond a reasonable doubt."

Public interest law firms and reform organizations have also launched major campaigns to extend legal protections to prison inmates and to reduce the disabilities convicts suffer after release. As a result of these efforts, lower courts have ruled that solitary confinement for juveniles violates their constitutional right against cruel and unusual punishment. They have also extended this reasoning to prohibit the use of "strip cells," in which the convict must crouch naked in a space so designed that he can neither stand nor sit down. Recent state penal codes have begun to expand convicts' procedural rights, and the courts, most notably and recently in the *Landman* decision, have also insisted on expanding the prerogatives and protection due to convict. In *Landman*, the federal district court forbade the Virginia state penitentiary system from any longer imposing a bread and water diet, from using chains or tape or tear gas except in an immediate emergency, from using physical force as a punishment; it also demanded minimum due process protections before a convict lost "good time" (that would shorten his sentence), or suffered any deprivation of his normal prison privileges (such as loss of exercise or communication with other inmates). Suits now pending are also contesting the constitutionality of prohibiting ex-convicts from obtaining trucker's or chauffeur's licenses and the restrictions on parolees' rights of association and travel. Thus, one detects not only a closing of the gap between the legal rights of citizens and those of inmates, but the beginnings of a series of changes that will make the prison system as we know it increasingly unworkable.

. . .

Thus, over the past several decades public officials and private organizations have energetically and successfully attempted to reduce reliance upon incarceration. They have done so with considerable enthusiasm—one doesn't achieve sweeping reforms of this kind without enthusiasm. However, there is the danger that this enthusiasm could lead to exaggerated expectations and, eventually, public disillusionment.

. . . We do not yet know whether the anti-incarceration movement will be any more effective than the original pro-incarceration movement—equally idealistic and enthusiastic—in effecting "cures." But there are other and very powerful arguments in its favor.

To begin with, there is the fact that many of the institutions functioning today, particularly correctional ones, are simply a national scandal, a shame to the society. They brutalize the inmates, humiliate them, and educate them in the ways of crime. Moreover, an impressive sociological literature, exemplified in the writings of Erving Goffman and Gresham Sykes, convincingly demonstrates that these characteristics are inherent in institutions, which by their very nature are infantilizing or corrupting. Moreover, while incarceration does exclude the deviant from the community for a period of time, eventually he is released; so unless one is prepared to lock up the criminal and throw away the key, institutionalization does not offer permanent security. And while public opinion may be growing tougher on the offender, we have not yet reached, and in all likelihood we are not going to reach, the point where life sentences for robbers, burglars, car thieves, and embezzlers will seem like an equitable solution.

Institutionalization is also incredibly expensive. To confine 201,220 criminals in state institutions in 1965 cost $384,980,648; to administer probation programs for slightly more than twice that number of people cost $60 million. Somehow, it would seem, the vast sums expended on institutionalization could be better spent.

But perhaps the most compelling reason for experimenting with anti-institutional programs is that the penitentiary has actually lost much, if not all, of its legitimacy in our society. It is not just academic students of criminal incarceration who despair of the penal system. Those in charge of the prisons, from wardens and corrections commissioners to state legislators, also share an incredibly high degree of self-doubt, ambivalence, dismay, and even guilt over prison operations. They are no longer secure in what they are doing. The depth and impact of these attitudes emerged with striking clarity and force in the recent events at Attica. Given the history of prison administration in this country, what is surprising and unusual about this revolt is not that it was suppressed harshly, but that several days were spent in negotiation. Attica was not our first prison riot; all through the 1920s and 1930s bloody revolts broke out, only to be repressed immediately, even at the cost of some hostages' lives. Why was Attica different? Why were negotiators flown in, an ad hoc committee formed, proposals and counterproposals exchanged? Why did this prison riot come to resemble so closely the student uprising and the university administration's response at Columbia in 1968?

The most obvious answer, that many hostages' lives were at stake, is altogether inadequate. It is a clear rule of prison guard life, one that is conveyed immediately to recruits, that guards are not ransomable. Should one or more of them be taken hostage, no bargain will be struck for their release. The maxim is not as coldhearted as one might first think. On the contrary, it assumes that once convicts understand that guards are not ransomable, they will have no reason—except for pure revenge—to take them as hostages. And, in fact, events have usually borne out the shrewdness of this calculation: for all the brutality of the prison system, guards have not often been the victims of the prisoners' anger or desperation. Then why did not officials in New York stand by this rule, move in quickly at Attica to regain control, and rationalize the entire operation as necessary to protect guards' live everywhere?

The failure to act immediately and with confidence points directly to the prison's loss of legitimacy. Both the inmates and their keepers shared an attitude that Attica was in a fundamental way out of step with American society. Most of the convicts' demands were not obviously unreasonable in the light of public opinion today: better pay for their work, better communication with their families, rights to law books and counsel. Most citizens were probably surprised to learn that these privileges were not already established. Commissioner Oswald himself had promised Attica inmates just before the riot that these changes were long overdue and would soon be enacted. How could he then act with sure and fast resolve to repress harshly a revolt when many of its aims were conceded to be sensible and appropriate and long overdue? It is one thing to sacrifice guards' lives for a system that has a sense of its own purpose; it is quite another to sacrifice them when the system is full of self-doubts. So Oswald negotiated, brought in outsiders, and tried to bargain. In the end it did not work, perhaps because not enough time was allowed, perhaps because compromise is impossible in such a charged situation. The revolt was suppressed, with a rage and force that in part reflects the urge to obliterate the questions and the ambivalence. Still, from Attica we have learned that we cannot administer penal institutions that we no longer believe in.

From Attica we have also learned how impossible it is to administer existing prisons when inmates withhold their compliance. The internal organization of penitentiaries today is an irrational mix of old rules, some relaxed, others enforced. Whereas once all prisoners spent their time isolated in a cell, now they mingle freely in the yard, communicate with each other, and move about. As a result, the cooperation of hundreds of prisoners is necessary to the smooth running of the institution. The ratio of guards to inmates is generally low; officers are able to prevent mass breakouts but are not able to prevent takeovers. As events at Attica demonstrated clearly, a group acting in concert has great power to disrupt the normal routine. Moreover, the likelihood of similar actions recurring seems very high. For one, prisoners are certain to sense the steady loss of legitimacy of incarcerating institutions in our society. For another, the convicts in state institutions are bound to be more homogeneous in terms of class (lower), color (black), crime (violent), and politics (radical). As white embezzlers or blacks guilty of property offenses increasingly go out on probation or enter minimum-security prison farms, the possibilities for uprisings by those remaining in penitentiaries increases. To be sure, the state might respond to this crisis by building bigger and internally more secure prisons; we do have the managerial ability to structure settings where twenty guards can keep 1,000 men captive. But this response will probably not get very far. The courts, given their due process inclinations, will not allow such prisons, and wardens do not seem to have the inclination to administer them. . . .

The implication of this state of affairs makes clear that we must experiment with alternatives. Incarceration is at once inhumane by current standards, destructive of inmates, incredibly expensive, and increasingly losing its legitimacy. Our institutions of incarceration are nineteenth-century anachronisms, out of step with the other American institutions of the 1970s. This marked discrepancy among our social institutions cannot continue for very long without provoking crises more disastrous than Attica. It is time for a new calculus and a new strategy.

The correctional system is increasingly a place for the poor and the black. The following article discusses the victimization of black prisoners.

The Black Prisoner As Victim

Haywood Burns

... Coast to coast, with too few exceptions, America's jails and prisons are crumbling, inadequate structures, understaffed, overcrowded, unfit for human habitation. They are, in fact, a national disgrace.

There are, of course, reasons why individuals are still being housed in jails built at the time of the American Revolution, thrown with two other persons into cells built for one person, subjected to indignities and humiliations from insufficiently trained, insensitive prison guards. These reasons basically add up to a lack of caring on the part of the public. Prisoners are part of America's invisible population. They are shunted off behind the gray stone walls where they can be more readily forgotten or ignored, making it easier to pretend that many of the serious social problems they represent do not exist. But beyond apathy, there is vengeance. For those who are apt to think about prisoners at all are more apt to have a negative or antagonistic attitude toward them, often with the hostility born of the vindictive desire to punish other human beings because they are evil, and because of their "crimes against society."[1] It is the prevalence of attitudes such as these that is largely responsible for the pittance of our national wealth that is allocated to corrections. Perhaps even more telling, however, is the way in which the money that is available is spent. Ninety-five per cent of the country's entire correction effort is spent on holding people in (and

[1] See Karl Menninger, *The Crime of Punishment* (Viking, Compass ed., 1969), pp. 3–15.

From *The Black Law Journal*, 1, No. 2, Summer 1971, pp. 120–24. Reprinted by permission. Haywood Burns is the Executive Director of the National Conference of Black Lawyers.

down)—on custodial costs: walls, bars, guards—with only the remaining meager 5 per cent to cover rehabilitation efforts: education, job training, and health services.[2]

From penal institutions of every size and description across the country come reports of corrections officers who overstep their authority, misuse their power, and often in the most vicious and wanton fashion inflict summary punishment upon inmates who are in their charge.[3]

These problems—inadequate facilities, inequitable bail, unfair administrative procedures, physical and psychological brutality—make up the lot of thousands of men and women caged behind American bars. For the black prisoner, however, there is a peculiar racial dimension to these problems. To understand the black prisoner's plight, it is necessary to look beyond the general surveys and critiques of American prison conditions and view his situation through the prism of race.

In the first instance it is important to note that nonwhites make up a disproportionate number of the nation's prison population. In California over 40 per cent.[4] In New York, more than 70 per cent.[5] Thus the described burdens of an oppressive prison system are disproportionately borne by nonwhites. This is likewise true of the victims of the money-bail system. Under this system it is the poor who are sentenced by their poverty to long terms in jail awaiting trial though convicted of no crime. Again, a disproportionate number of the poor are nonwhite.

[2] Ramsey Clark, *Crime in America* (1970), p. 213. See also President's Commission on Law Enforcement and the Administration of Justice, *The Challenge of Crime in a Free Society* (1968).

[3] See George Jackson, *Soledad Brother* (1970); Etherilge Knight, *Black Voices from Prison* (1970); Prisoners Solidarity Day Committee, *Prisoners Call Out: Freedom* (1971), detailing the experiences of black inmates in Auburn (New York) Prison who charge that they have been the victims of a campaign of systematic brutality following their participation in a Black Solidarity Day demonstration within the prison on November 1970. Former Attorney General Ramsey Clark details an extreme example as revealed by the 1966 investigations of the Cummins and Tucker prison farms in Arkansas: "Allegations, at least partially verified and largely credible, included the murder of inmates, brutal beatings, and shootings. Shallow graves with broken bodies were uncovered. Food unfit to eat was regularly served. Forced homosexuality was openly tolerated. Extortion of money by wardens and sexual favors from families of inmates to protect their helpless prisoner relatives from physical injury or death were alleged. Torture devices included such bizarre items as the 'Tucker telephone,' components of which were an old telephone, wiring, and a heavy battery. After an inmate was stripped, one wire was fastened to his penis, the other to a wrist or ankle, and electric shocks were sent through his body until he was unconscious." Clark, *Crime in America*, p. 213.

[4] Ridenour, "Who Is A Political Prisoner?," *Black Law Journal*, 1 (1971), p. 17.

[5] *Sostre* v. *McGinnis*, 319 F. Supp. 863 at 876–77.

On the other hand, those who administer the prison system, who are responsible for the custody, care, and rehabilitation of inmates are disproportionately white. In New York, for example, it is reported that despite the fact that close to some three-fourths of the prisoners are nonwhite, some 98 per cent of the corrections officials over them are white.[6]

For the black prisoner the general problems of lack of administrative fairness and brutality are compounded by the racism rampant in many penal institutions. Complete racial segregation within prison systems is less widespread than it used to be,[7] but reports of systematic discrimination persist—especially with regard to exclusion of blacks from certain preferred prison work assignments and programs. Further, the personal racism—conscious or unconscious—of prison authorities works to the distinct disadvantage of blacks enmeshed in prison administrative proceedings. This is particularly true where the decision maker is not required to articulate the grounds of his decision or is free to exercise a series of options without close detailed standards as to their exercise. Much racism can be cloaked behind the rubric of "administrative discretion." It is particularly hard for black inmates who are outspoken and who refuse to adopt the proper degree of servility expected of them when they are placed in the position of having prison officials make decisions about them that will ultimately affect their lives. The indeterminate sentence especially as employed in California is supposed to be a progressive bit of penology. It is often in fact a dangerous weapon in the hands of hostile guards who are always capable of imagining, provoking, or exaggerating some or other prison infraction until the incident becomes the basis in whole or in part for the prolongation of a one-year to life sentence, on the ground that the inmate is "not ready" yet. It is all the more dangerous when the guard in question is actuated by racial animus.[8]

The brutality problem has racial vectors, not only because of the extent to which a guard's racism may stimulate him to act out his antipathy to blacks violently, but because the racism can become so pervasive that racist guards and racist white prisoners team up in their attacks upon the nonwhite prisoners. The fact that one is guard and the other is prisoner makes no difference. They have found common ground; in a microcosm of much in the larger society, they are

[6] *Idem.*
[7] See *Washington* v. *Lee,* 263 F. Supp. 327, 331 (M.D. Ala. 1966).
[8] See Mitford, "Kind and Usual Punishment in California," *The Atlantic,* March 1971.

bound together only by the whiteness of their skin and the depth of their antiblack feeling. That is enough. They attack.[9]

Apart from the racism that he finds in the prisons, the situation of the black prisoner must be viewed differently from that of others because of the role that racism has played in getting so many blacks into jail in the first place. The Kerner Commission told the nation something most blacks have known for a long time—America is a country permeated by racism.[10] The law like other institutions has not been able to escape this racism. Rather than transcend the racism of the society, the law, like other institutions, often reflects it. In fact, the law has been the vehicle by which the generalized racism in the society has been made particular, and converted into the policies and standards of social control that govern our lives. In this kind of social context "antisocial" acts by blacks otherwise denominated as criminal may be signs of health or at least signs of life. They may be acts of self-preservation, evidences of a refusal to acquiesce in a system which by calculation and design is bent on the destruction of nonwhite peoples, and which, daily, accomplishes that mission. This is not to over-romanticize black prisoners to say that every black man and woman in prison is necessarily a race hero—but many are. That there are not even more blacks behind bars may often be no more than an indication of lives of "getting by," made up of a string of bitter accommodations and stale compromises with oppression. Our American history begins with our capture and imprisonment in the bacaroons—the fetid slave pens erected on the coast of West Africa to hold blacks until their imprisonment as cargo in the dark holds of the slave ships which would carry them (those who lived) to imprisonment in the American social system of slavery. Our struggle through slavery, Jim Crow, discrimination, and modern racism has been for liberation from these prisons. Every major social indicator reflects that we still have not made it. Regardless of which side of the bars you are on, if you are black and American you are, as Malcolm said, in prison—the prison of racism, the prison of exploitation, the prison of governmental repression. Some victims are just more obvious than others. We are all victims.

A significant development in recent times has been the increased awareness on the part of black prisoners of the nature and extent of their victimization. A growing political awareness in the prisons has fomented acute social analysis that is often unrivaled among so-called

[9] See Jackson, *Soledad Brother.* For a varied and provocative description of black prison life as seen through the eyes of several black prisoners, see *The Black Scholar*, April-May 1971.

[10] *Report of the National Advisory Commission on Civil Disorder* (Bantam ed., 1968), p. 10.

"free" blacks walking around outside the prison walls. Though a great number of black prisoners have arrived at their political conclusions through independent study and informal group discussion, the politicalization of the black prisoner has also been aided greatly by the organized efforts of the Nation of Islam (Black Muslims) and, more recently, the Black Panther Party. As prisoners become more and more conscious of the social and political ramifications of their situation and are able to exchange destructive negative self images for new senses of dignity and pride, they become less willing to accept passively the dehumanizing conditions of American prisons as an immutable given. Responses have come in various forms. In the past year major jail or prison rebellions have flared in almost every part of the country. There has been as well an upsurge in litigation on prison conditions and prisoners' rights, as inmates, sometimes on their own and sometimes through efforts of civil rights and civil liberties organizations, turn to the courts seeking vindication.[11]

Great attempts at self-help are being made through the organization of black groups within the prisons. Afro-American Societies springing up at various institutions engage in a wide range of programs from studying black history and culture to carrying out political activity directed at their grievances. A survey of activity within the nation's prisons reveals that black prisoners are not only men and women on the move, but increasingly they are moving from a basis of group solidarity with concerted action.

Prisoners are being aided now by support groups on the outside which, through a variety of techniques, address different aspects of the prisoner's dilemma. There are those, for example, who concentrate on alleviating the prolonged pretrial incarceration by providing bail for the indigent accused from a revolving bail fund. A pool of money is raised from which bail for individual prisoners is posted. When the bail is returned, the money goes back into the pool to bail other prisoners out. Simultaneously attempts are constantly being made to increase the size of the pool. The revolving bail fund approach has been pioneered by the Women's Bail Fund of New York City in efforts to assist inmates in New York's Women's House of Detention—most of whom are black and Puerto Rican.[12]

Other outside groups concentrate on helping inmates who are serving

[11] Though many organizations have taken an interest in litigating questions of prisoners' rights, some of the most important work in this field is currently being done by lawyers in the Corrections Project of the NAACP Legal Defense and Educational Fund, under the direction of Stanley Bass, Esq., 10 Columbus Circle, New York, N.Y. 10019.

[12] The Women's Bail Fund may be contacted at Box 637, Cooper Station, New York, N.Y. 10003.

sentences. They may even form an outside organization which becomes an adjunct of a group already existing in the prison. These outside support groups are limited according to the latitude permitted them by the various prison authorities, but they attempt to form a communications link with those on the inside. They visit the inmates, hold classes for them, contact and assist inmates' families, carry out tasks for inmates in the outside world that imprisonment makes impossible, and attempt to inform others about the realities of prison life. One group that has achieved a notable degree of success in using this approach is a black organization in Rhode Island, affiliated with the Afro-American Society in the Rhode Island state prison.[13]

Still other groups focus their energies on assisting the man or woman just coming out of prison. For many ex-prisoners this is a critical period. If he or she can be assured of some assistance in finding a job, food, clothes, shelter as well as sensitive, sympathetic, supportive people the adjustment to the outside world is less difficult and the chances of returning to prison less great. This has been one of the major thrusts of the Fortune Society, an East-Coast-based group that has been in operation for a little more than three years. The work of the Fortune Society is directed and carried out largely by ex-inmates.[14]

Present outside efforts in assisting the imprisoned are far from adequate—especially the black prisoner, whose problems are, after all, special. The black community cannot afford to share the distance and the hostility which much of the dominant society reserves for those in prison. We must not be in a position of having others define for us who our friends and who our enemies are, which *persona* is *non grata*. Some of the finest talent of an oppressed people is always to be found in the prisons of the oppressor. For the strength of our community we must redeem from human waste as many of our imprisoned brothers and sisters as possible. We must address the problems of the American penal system because of the historic threat it has represented and continues to represent to significant portions of our youth. The fight for the humanity and dignity of those of us who are behind bars is part and parcel of our overall fight for liberation. For we—those on both sides of the wall—are the common victims of a social system that demands of us to be less than we are. Any quest for black justice is incomplete that does not include within its scheme the black prisoner. We must not take the judgment of a criminal society as to who the real criminals are. Black voices from within the prison walls are grow-

[13] The External Committee of the Afro-American Society of the Adult Correctional Institution may be contacted c/o Rev. Benny Smith, 53 Cypress Street, Providence, R.I. 02906.
[14] The Fortune Society may be contacted at 1545 Broadway, New York, N.Y. 10036.

ing louder now, as brothers and sisters, despite cruel hands that would twist and maim, are straightening themselves out, wending their way to health, strength, and, eventually, power—power with which to confront the afflictions of prison life and beyond, the larger injustices of America. The voices are calling to us for help. It is a call which, in this uncivilized land, must not go unheeded.

Federal funds are being provided by the Law Enforcement Assistance Administration to improve the correctional systems of the states. But the innovative "demonstration" programs are few, and funds sufficient to revamp the prisons completely will not be allocated, according to the official of the LEAA who wrote the following article.

Correcting Corrections

Richard W. Velde

INTRODUCTION

The inhuman neglect we show human beings in our corrections system carries with it in rising crime the high cost of that crime.

Some four out of every five felonies are committed by repeaters, people who have already been in contact with the criminal justice system and who were not corrected. The recidivism rate is about 65 per cent or higher, and closer to 75 per cent where younger prisoners are concerned.[1]

[1] *Uniform Crime Reports,* 1969.

From *The Black Law Journal,* 1, No. 2, Summer 1971, pp. 125–30. Reprinted by permission. Richard W. Velde is the Assistant Administrator of the Law Enforcement Assistance Administration.

Presumably if we could cut recidivism in half—and this should certainly be a practical goal—we could cut serious crime by at least a third, and perhaps more. This was noted in the recent report of the Senate Judiciary Committee on the Omnibus Crime Control Act of 1970, which said in part:

> Of all the activities within the criminal justice process, corrections appears to offer the greatest potential for significantly reducing crime.

The report then continues:

> Ironically, it has been the most neglected component of the system, principally because of the very high cost of building or renovating prisons and other correctional facilities.[2]

And that leads me to the basis of this article, how much it will cost to build a modern correctional system, how long it will require, and most important, what direction the change and improvement should take.

IMPROVING THE SYSTEM

There are presently some 400,000 prisoners in lockups, detention centers, jails, and state and federal prisons. Of the approximately $7.5 billion spent by local, state, and federal governments on the entire criminal justice system each year, perhaps $1.5 billion goes for corrections.[3] That average is about $3,000 per prisoner—enough to maintain each of them above the poverty line, if handed over in cash.

I am not suggesting that.

We could embark on a massive building progrom to construct adequate prisons to hold this population of half a million prisoners.

Modern prison construction cost comes to about $15,000 to $20,000 per prisoner. If you assume, and it is a reasonable assumption, that between 50 and 75 per cent of prison accommodations are unfit and should be replaced, you are talking about a prison building program of between 3.75 and 7.5 billion dollars, and that makes no allowance for additional personnel needed for adequate administration. In other words, it could cost more to build adequate cell blocks than we now spend annually for the entire criminal justice system.

[2] S. Sep. No. 91-1253 91st Cong., 2nd Sess., 27 (1971).

[3] *Expenditure and Employment Data for the Criminal Justice System,* 1968-69, Law Enforcement Assistance Administration, U.S. Department of Justice (1970), Table 3, p. 11.

But I am not suggesting we do that, either.

Some knowledgeable experts have suggested that only between 10 and 25 per cent of those now in jails and prisons really belong there— these are the so-called "hard-core" prisoners. At least 75 per cent or more of those in jails and prisons make up people awaiting trial, or drug addicts and alcoholics who would be far better off in rehabilitation and control programs, or prisoners who should be in properly supervised probation or parole situations.

In other words, we have enough cells now. Certainly most prisons and jails need improvement. There are few model jails—we know; we tried to find them. There are some that must simply be torn down and replaced, they are unfit for any kind of human habitation, if they ever were. But the need is not for more cells. It is for more community-based corrections programs, more probation and parole systems that really work, more work-release programs, more regional centers designed for rehabilitation, not pure punishment.

Many judges will tell you that they sentence offenders to jail simply because the only alternative is to turn them loose—the judges are well aware that the probation and parole systems which provide adequate and workable alternatives to incarceration could cost as much as $15 billion, including staff and programs. About $12 billion of this would be required for construction of regional detention centers, community-based correction centers, and modern prisons.

George J. Beto, the President of the American Correctional Association, summed up the situation in a recent issue of the *Journal of the American Correctional Association.*

> If we are honest with ourselves, we will admit that our massive prison buildings, the expensive jail paraphernalia with which they are equipped, the time-honored, elaborate, and almost ritualistic security measures which we practice, are actually designed for a small percentage of our prisoners— 25 per cent at the most. The best interests of the majority of our inmates, as well as those of society, would be better served by intelligently supervised probation and parole rather than by the artificially contrived rehabilitation programs found in the stultifying atmosphere of most prisons.[4]

WHAT CONGRESS IS DOING

Senator Roman Hruska of Nebraska has long had a keen appreciation of the problem of corrections, as have other members of the Congress. He was the moving force in winning passage of the Nixon administra-

[4] George J. Beto, "Presidential Address," *American Journal of Corrections,* 32 (November-December, 1970), p. 7.

tion's bill to create Part E of the Omnibus Crime Control Act of 1970[5] which the President signed into law this year. This provides approximately $50 million this year, $100 million next year, and greater amounts in later years to fund new corrections programs, particularly community-based corrections.

. . .

In order to obtain the block grant funds the states would have to provide certain assurances:

That the comprehensive state plan sets forth a statewide program for the construction, acquisition, or renovation of correctional institutions and facilities in the state and the improvement of correctional programs and practices throughout the state.

That there is satisfactory emphasis on the development and operation of community-based correctional facilities and programs, including diagnostic services, halfway houses, probation, and other supervisory release programs for preadjudication and postadjudication referral of delinquents, youthful offenders, and first offenders, and community-oriented programs for the supervision of parolees.

That advanced techniques in the design of institutions and facilities are used.

That where feasible and desirable there be a sharing of correctional institutions on a regional basis.

That the personnel standards and programs of the institutions and facilities will reflect advance practices.

That the state is engaging in projects and programs to improve the recruiting, organization, training, and education of personnel employed in correctional activities, including those of probation, parole, and rehabilitation.[6]

Part E also authorized LEAA, after consultation with the Bureau of Prisons, to prescribe by regulation, basic criteria for the administration and use of Federal funds. This provision will enable LEAA to insure that the money will not go into the kind of jails, prisons and programs that will merely perpetuate the past, but into substantial and significant improvements.

. . .

WHAT LEAA IS DOING

Two years ago LEAA set improvement in corrections as a major goal. The result was that the total of LEAA funds spent for corrections and

[5] 42 U.S.C. 3732 (1971).
[6] U.S.C. 3732 (1971).

corrections-related programs rose from about $2 million in fiscal 1969 to $58 million last year to an estimated $178 million this year. Next year it could go as high as $250 million.

Under the comprehensive law enforcement plans submitted to LEAA by the states, due provision was made for legal services for offenders involved in the criminal justice process, for the revision of penal codes, and for statutory reforms which would pave the way for the sharing of facilities among geographical groupings of counties and communities, for multijurisdictional arrangements for the care and treatment of special types of offenders, and for improvements in the organization and administration of correctional systems.

The National Institute of Law Enforcement and Criminal Justice, the research arm of LEAA, made a grant to the University of Arizona to produce a casebook on postconviction legal practices. The casebook will deal with the legal problems in prisoner representation, and will be designed as a text for law school seminars and as a reference work for state attorneys general and public and legal aid offices. This effort should not only bring about an improved respect for the rights of prisoners but also reduce frivolous litigation.

The Institute also made a grant to the South Carolina Department of Corrections which, with the help of the University of South Carolina's School of Law, will study the various court decisions which have been made in the field of law with the objective of formulating the principles which underlie these decisions. The product is intended to provide correctional administrators, legislators, and the courts with a resource to guide their future decisions, and in the case of the administrators, to avoid litigation. The project workers have so far identified approximately a thousand such decisions.

A third grant has been made by the Institute to the College of Law of the University of Nebraska to develop a Handbook on Correctional Law Reform. Under the terms of the project the university will analyze the correctional laws of the fifty states, provide a critique, and outline the needs, goals, and procedures for reform efforts. On the basis of this effort it will also formulate a model correctional code.

In conjunction with the foregoing, the Office of Criminal Justice Assistance, the action arm of LEAA, has approved a discretionary grant for a national conference on correctional law reform, which would involve the participation of state attorneys general, law enforcement planners, and legislators. The conference will be co-sponsored by the University of Nebraska, the American Correctional Association, and the American Bar Association's Commission on Correctional Facilities and Services.

THE FUTURE OF CORRECTIONS

We can expect that the needed legal reforms can be accomplished within the next four or five years, at least if it is possible for money and efforts of the ABA Commission to bring this result about.

We can also expect, with the priority being exercised by LEAA and the states, substantial expansion and improvement of probation and parole. It will be feasible within available funding to establish probation departments where they do not now exist and to strengthen them and to provide significant resources where they do exist.

The projections of the states and the priorities of LEAA also suggest that the good start made in 1970 on the establishment of community-based programs will result in the proliferation and common establishment of such programs over the next five-year period. The communities should end up well endowed with such resources as halfway houses, group homes, court diversion projects, and community programs for the education, training, guidance, and employment of probationers, parolees, and other ex-offenders.

The jails present a different kind of problem. They are the shame of almost every community and county in which they are located. But considering the amount of money required for their replacement and the long lean times involved in any new construction, we should see only a start made on this problem within the next five years.

LEAA is funding the preparation of technical assistance materials in the planning and design of community and regional correctional facilities. These will replace the jails with community centers which will provide rehabilitative services to misdemeanants. LEAA is also funding the development of specific projects of this kind in a number of communities. But a recent survey by the Bureau of the Census under an LEAA contract suggests that a great many jails need to be either replaced outright or substantially rebuilt for rehabilitative purposes. The task will require at least a generation, and probably more.

Until LEAA's jail survey, information in this area was totally lacking. Few state law enforcement officials could even tell you how many jails exist in their state.

The jail survey shows:

There are 4,021 locally administered jails with 48-hour retention authority, and they house about 153,000 adults and 7,800 juveniles.

About 550 of these were constructed during the nineteenth century and six in the eighteenth century.

Jail authorities report they anticipate spending a total of $170 million on construction and renovation this year.

Some 130 jails were built to house 300 or more prisoners, and of these, about one-third are overcrowded, almost all of them large jails in big cities.

A facilities survey was made of the 3,300 jails located in cities or counties of more than 25,000 population. This showed:

More than 85 per cent had no recreational or educational facilities of any kind.
About 50 per cent had no medical facilities.
About 25 per cent had no visiting facilities.
Of the 97,500 cells in the 3,300 jails, almost 25,000 were more than 50 years old, including 5,400 more than 100 years old.[7]

The prison also presents a unique problem and many of the considerations that apply to the jails also apply to them. Also, there are no prison programs that have really proved to have achieved significantly efficient results in rehabilitating offenders. Until we have valid findings identifying such programs, we have no basis upon which to plan new facilities. Furthermore, the costs of a national broad-scale effort to replace our prisons is prohibitive, and is likely to remain so under any foreseeable level of federal funding.

There are some experts in the correctional field, and some outside it, who feel that the realization of widespread community-based services and the strengthening of probation and parole, particularly for juvenile delinquents and youths, will minimize the need for new prisons and major state institutions. The dictates of reality will provide an opportunity to find out whether they are right.

In any event, it can be forecast that the next five years will see an abrupt shift in emphasis in the field of corrections from the traditional reliance on custodially-oriented institutions to rehabilitation-oriented community-based programs. The prisons will remain, hopefully with reduced populations, but those who are incarcerated should experience a more humane and legally supervised regime. Meanwhile, LEAA will continue to commit adequate funds for experimentation in the search for methods and techniques of salvaging the hard-core offenders for whom the prisons are really intended.

Lawyers, bar associations, and even judges have an important part to play on this twofold attack on the problems of the corrections system.

[7] Law Enforcement Assistance Administration, U.S. Department of Justice, *1970 National Jail Census* (1971), Table 7, p. 17; Table 8, pp. 18–19.

During the next several years, they can help substantially as their states attempt to establish and improve probation and parole programs.

For all practical purposes, probation has never been tried in the United States. The cost of probation supervision is now about $250 a year, and it should be raised to at least $1,000 or more, but even at this it is far cheaper than the $4,000 to $5,000 estimated annual cost of keeping a man in prison.

Lawyers—and judges as well—should be as active as possible in taking part in the criminal justice planning activity in their state, and they can use their influence in the community to promote not only attitudes about the changing face of corrections, but programs as well. If they take the trouble to familiarize themselves with jail and prison facilities and problems they will find the general lack of information so widespread they will become experts in the field without realizing it.

Bar associations can appoint committees to look into local and state problems and programs and make recommendations. State and regional criminal justice councils will welcome their interest and support.

Lawyers, bar associations, and judges will also have an important role in urging greater use of probation and parole systems once they are operating, as well as encouraging work-release programs, and helping to coordinate them with the community, and win public and employer acceptance so they operate successfully.

Finally, during the years it will take to rebuild or replace the broken-down jail system, lawyers, bar associations, judges, and the courts can play a more active role in seeing to it these facilities are maintained in as humane a manner as possible. This means not only court concern— since the court sends a prisoner to prison in the first place—but informal supervision of conditions by lawyers and bar associations, to bring matters to court attention where necessary, and to improve them without legal action where possible.

Two years ago, President Nixon directed the Attorney General to marshal federal resources in an all-out effort to improve corrections.[8] LEAA and the Bureau of Prisons and other concerned agencies have responded, with the result that we now have the first comprehensive national effort to improve our corrections system in our history.

How urgently the states respond, how promptly and effectively they move, how soon probation and parole systems can be set up and the long-haul business of construction planning begun, will depend a great deal on how much attention courts, judges, lawyers, and bar associations focus on corrections.

[8] Presidential Directive to Attorney General Mitchell on Corrections, November 13, 1969.

On October 31, 1971, a federal district judge ordered major changes in the prison system of Virginia in Landman v. Royster. Should this case, presented here, be sustained by the Supreme Court, it will become an important precedent for changing practices in other state prison systems.

Landman v. Royster

District Judge Merhige.

Defendants named in the complaint, or their successors, are the Director of the Department of Welfare and Institutions, the Director of the Division of Corrections, the Superintendent of the State Penitentiary, and the Superintendent of the State Farm.

Plaintiffs, who are representative of the class they purport to represent, mount their attack upon the administration of discipline within the prisons: the reasons for invoking sanctions, the adjudication process, and the various penalties imposed. The evidence adduced has disclosed as to each of these points a disregard of constitutional guaranties of so grave a nature as to violate the most common notions of due process and humane treatment by certain of the defendants, their agents, servants, and employees.

One of the principal issues before the Court has to do with lack of appropriate due process prior to punishing members of the class for supposed infraction of rules. As the Court has already indicated, it finds that in many instances punishment has been of such a nature as to be abusive and violative of the most generic elements of due process and humane treatment.

. . .

The rule for years has been that, absent claims of gross violations of fundamental rights, federal courts will make no inquiry into the

From *Landman* v. *Royster,* 333 Federal Supplement 621 (1971).

manner in which state prison officials manage their charges. . . . It is not difficult to discern the principal rationales for this doctrine. A prisoner after all is presumed to have been justly convicted and sentenced; that presumptively valid judgment imposed a punishment of confinement under certain contemplated conditions. "Lawful incarceration brings about the necessary withdrawal or limitation of many privileges and rights, a retraction justified by the considerations underlying our penal system". . . . This is not to say that prisoners possess no further rights to be infringed or liberties to be taken. However, while confined, their fate is by law in the hands of administrators whose acts, like those of most administrative decision makers, may be presumed legal.

Furthermore, courts have, perhaps implicitly, honored the theory of criminal punishment that holds that men who have been found guilty of violations of criminal laws may be utilized, so to speak, by society for ends related to the general welfare, such as the deterrence of similar acts by others and the alteration of their own patterns of behavior. Criminal activity, it is thought, once proved by legal procedures, fairly works a forfeiture of any rights the curtailment of which may be necessary in pursuit of these ends, such as the right of privacy, association, travel, and choice of occupation. Because federal courts have considered themselves both lacking in the authority to dictate those uses to which society may put convicts and without the specialized knowledge to test the necessity of losing certain liberties to accomplish various goals, they have not generally questioned such deprivations. Even now no court has required that states adapt their penal system to the goal of rehabilitation.

Moreover, in a society concededly subject to increasing legal regulations, prisoners more than any others are subjected to state control. State officials govern inmates' lives by a series of decisions on an hourly, indeed continual, basis. Many of their decisions may be subject to more than colorable constitutional attack. If each is to be subject for federal examination of a plenary sort, the energy and time of the federal judiciary and of state penal officials would be diverted to an inordinate extent. Even if the law permitted many such matters to be determined without the taking of testimony, little if any saving in time would be accomplished. Concerns of judicial efficiency must be among the reasons which cause courts to pause in considering whether Congress intended federal civil rights jurisdiction to extend over such claims. . . .

Nevertheless, whether detention should be imposed at all has always been matter for federal review. . . .

Recent caselaw too supports inquiry into prison administrators' restriction of constitutional rights other than that of liberty itself.

> There is no doubt that discipline and administration of state detention facilities are state functions. They are subject to federal authority only where paramount federal constitutional or statutory rights supervene. It is clear, however, that in instances where state regulations applicable to inmates of prison facilities conflict with such rights, the regulations may be invalidated. (*Johnson* v. *Avery*)

Prior to *Johnson* and since, federal courts have directed state and federal penal officials to honor convicts' claims to religious freedom, and freedom from racial classification. . . . The reasoning supporting such intervention must be that the prison authorities have shown no compelling need to suppress these rights. Plainly stated, they have not shown such remarkable success in achieving any conceivable valid penological end by means which entail the abridgment of these constitutional guarantees as might make their denial seem worthwhile. . . .

Courts have also intervened when sentences are administered in a manner that seems unintended and unauthorized by the convicting court. Relief is justifiable in some cases on the fairly basic rationale that to extend or augment punishment beyond that imposed by a state court is to penalize without due process. A valid state judgment affords no license to exceed its terms. . . .

. . .

Finally, penal authorities have been constrained to refrain from punishment deemed cruel and unusual in situations where some other penalty might legally be imposed. Some courts have, further, held that any penalty at all for an act which could not legally be a violation amounts to cruel and unusual punishment. . . .

. . . Reasons of security may justify restrictive confinement, but that is not to say that such needs may be determined arbitrarily or without appropriate procedures. In an obvious sense, too, any treatment to which a prisoner is exposed is a form of punishment and subject to Eighth Amendment standards. This is not to say, though, that prison officials may not treat their charges as individuals. Deprivations of benefits of various sorts may be used so long as they are related to some valid penal objective and substantial deprivations are administered with due process. "Security" or "rehabilitation" are not shibboleths to justify any treatment. Still courts must keep in mind that a recognized valid object of imprisonment is not just to separate and house prisoners but to change them. When it is asserted that certain disabilities must be imposed to these ends, courts may still inquire as to the actuality of a relation between means and end. The test of necessity will, as mentioned above, be more stringent when a deprivation of a fundamental constitutional right is involved. When officials assert lack of funds needed to achieve their goals by means which would not infringe constitutional rights, moreover, the attempted justification will usually fail. . . .

Extensive evidence was presented and detailed factfindings have been made for the reason that the plaintiffs contend, and the Court has concluded, that the constitutional violations of which they complain are not isolated deviations from normal practice but rather indicated traditional procedures in the state penal system. When such a showing is made it is the Court's duty not solely to amend so far as possible the defaults of the past but to prevent their likely recurrence in the future.

. . .

The proof shows three general classes of constitutional deprivation, each a subject for injunctive relief. Discipline has been imposed for the wrong reasons. It has been imposed in cases of what may have been validly punishable misconduct, but without the requisites of procedural due process. And, punishment of a sort that the Constitution bars in any event has been imposed.

. . .

Bread and water provides a daily intake of only 700 calories, whereas sedentary men on the average need 2,000 calories or more to maintain continued health. Evidence is not presented on the other nutritional shortcomings of a bread diet, but it does no violence to doctrine of judicial notice to remark that vitamin, protein, and mineral content is probably deficient as well. The purpose and intended effect of such a diet is to discipline a recalcitrant by debilitating him physically. Without food, his strength and mental alertness begin to decline immediately. It is a telling reminder too that prison authorities enjoy complete control over all sources of pleasure, comfort, and basic needs. Moreover, the pains of hunger constitute a dull, prolonged sort of corporal punishment. That marked physical effects ensue is evident from the numerous instances of substantial weight loss during solitary confinement.

. . . A current manual on prison practices strongly disapproves any disciplinary diet which impairs health (American Correctional Association, Manual of Correctional Standards). . . .

The practice is therefore both generally disapproved and obsolescent even within this penal system. It is not seriously defended as essential to security. It amounts therefore to an unnecessary infliction of pain. Furthermore, as a technique designed to break a man's spirit not just by denial of physical comforts but of necessities, to the end that his powers of resistance diminish, the bread and water diet is inconsistent with current minimum standards of respect for human dignity. The Court has no difficulty in determining that it is a violation of the Eighth Amendment. . . .

Likewise, to restrain or control misbehavior by placing an inmate in chains or handcuffs in his cell is unconstitutionally excessive. . . .

. . .

The practices of taking inmates' clothing while in solitary and keeping them in unheated cells with open windows in the winter have been disapproved. . . . Such penalties, which work to degrade an inmate by denying him any of the sources of human dignity and imperil his health as well, are cruel and unusual. The Court recognizes, as pointed out by the prison authorities, that recalcitrant inmates may well, and undoubtedly do, break windows deliberately—nevertheless this conduct can surely be punished by a method less likely to endanger the health of the inmate. . . . The Court will permit an inmate to be kept nude in his cell only when a doctor states in writing that the inmate's health will not thereby be affected and that the inmate presents a substantial risk of injuring himself if given garments.

. . .

On occasion prisoners in solitary confinement have been deprived of their mattresses and blankets as punishment for misconduct. . . . In the past this has been done for such offenses as noisemaking. . . . The penalty is undoubtedly harsh, but the Court is not persuaded that it is cruel and unusual. There is no evidence that it had a substantial effect upon anyone's health. If the cell is otherwise clean, and well heated, and the prisoner keeps his clothing, it should not be detrimental. Other cases holding solitary confinement, which included a denial of bedding, cruel and unusual generally included the element of unsanitary conditions. . . .

The practice of crowding several men into a single "solitary" cell, however, must be condemned. . . . Clearly if a number of men had earned a term in meditation, the authorities had the capacity to distribute them among various penal units. The crowding is thus shown unnecessary and takes on a vindictive aspect.

Cases involving overcrowding in prison cells have generally included aggravating conditions such as denial of clothing, unhygienic conditions, and other abuses. . . . Four men here were penned like animals in a small cell, designed for one, for fourteen days without respite. Lack of space made sleeping very difficult. If confined men retain any claim at all to human dignity, they cannot be needlessly so dealt with for such long periods of time. . . .

Tear gas has been used to silence noisy, misbehaving men while confined to their cells. . . . The problem of dealing with convicts who persist in disturbing entire cell blocks and inciting others to join in the disorder is a real one. The Court has not found any instances of gassing men in cells who were not currently disruptive. Yet the use of gas to disable a man physically who poses no present physical threat constitutes a form of corporal punishment, the use of which in such a situation is generally disapproved. Undoubtedly it is effective, but it is painful, and its abuse is difficult to forestall. The problem appears to arise because there appears to be no way to isolate a misbehaving inmate to an area where his rantings will not disturb anyone. This difficulty is, however, one of the system's own creation. If chaining a man to his bars, punishing him with a strap, and other corporal punishment should be enjoined, . . . this Court cannot make a principled distinction which would permit the use of tear gas to punish or control the nonthreatening inmate.

There was evidence, furthermore, that some inmates were not permitted to shower during extended stays in solitary. Relief on this score will be denied because there is no proof that at such times they were also denied the necessary sanitary items so that they might wash in their cells.

The Court would not enter upon a review of the procedural aspects of prison discipline were there a lack of evidence in this case that discipline had been imposed upon men guilty of no infraction. Unfortunately, there is credible evidence to the contra. Many of the prisoner witnesses, who testified that they were placed in solitary cells or lost certain privileges, readily admitted that they had disrupted legitimate prison functions. Others, however, just as plainly were penalized for communicating with courts or lawyers in a fashion that might not be punished, for protected litigation activities, for offenses that simply had not occurred, or on the basis of unfounded suspicion. In other cases the reasons men were punished cannot be determined with certainty; had more explicit procedural directions been followed in such cases there might well be no question now. . . .

. . .

In these adjudicatory proceedings the Court concludes that certain due process rights are both necessary and will not unduly impede legitimate prison functions.

First, the decision to punish must be made by an impartial tribunal. This bars any official who reported a violation from ruling. . . . There appears to be no reason to require that the disciplinary board be composed of any specific number of individuals. Each member of a panel must, however, be free of prior involvement with the incident under examination so that he may settle the case on the basis of the evidence at the hearing.

Second, there shall be a hearing. Disposition of charges on the basis of written reports is insufficient. Prisoners are not as a class highly educated men nor is assistance readily available. If they are forced to present their evidence in writing, moreover, they will be in many cases unable to anticipate the evidence adduced against them. . . . Necessarily a hearing encompasses the right to present evidence in defense, including the testimony of voluntary witnesses.

A hearing must be preceded by notice in writing of the substance of the factual charge of misconduct. Only with written notice can a prisoner prepare to meet claims and insist that the hearing be kept within bounds. . . . A reasonable interval to prepare a defense must be allowed as well, but the Court declines to fix any definite period. Rather whether a trial has been too speedy must be determined on a case-by-case basis.

Cross-examination of adverse witnesses likewise is necessary. The Court appreciates the concern of prison officials that interrogation by prisoner of the guard force may be at variance with their ordinary respective positions in the penal hierarchy. Because most disciplinary cases will turn on issues of fact, however, the right to confront and cross-examine witnesses is essential. . . . It is, however, well within the power of the disciplinary official or tribunal to restrict questioning to relevant matters, to preserve decorum, and to limit repetition.

Fundamental to due process is that the ultimate decision be based upon evidence presented at the hearing, which the prisoner has the opportunity to refute. . . . To permit punishment to be imposed for reasons not presented and aired would invite arbitrariness and nullify the right to notice and hearing.

. . .

In addition, for the reason that the evidence shows that some inmates are unfortunately intellectually unable to represent themselves in discipline hearings, the tribunal should permit a prisoner to select a lay adviser to present his case. This may be either a member of the non-custodial staff or another inmate, serving on a voluntary basis. . . .

In other instances where proceedings may result in the loss of substantial rights, the right to representation by counsel has been considered an essential element of due process. . . . Therefore a prisoner who desires to secure counsel for hearing may be required to notify the committee of that fact, and postponement of the hearing to secure counsel may reasonably be limited to four days.

These minimum due process standards are necessary when solitary confinement, transfer to maximum security confinement, or loss of good time are imposed, or a prisoner is held in padlock confinement more than ten days.

The imposition of the minor fines disclosed by the evidence, for example, or, hypothetically, loss of commissary rights, restriction of individual recreational privileges, or padlocking for less than ten days, do not require this panoply of guaranties. The right to be represented by another may be omitted. Written notice may be dispensed with, and appellate review need not be formally conducted. The Court will only require verbal notice and the opportunity for a hearing before an impartial decision maker, with a chance to cross-examine the complaining officer and to present testimony in defense. As always, however, procedural formality may not shield arbitrary action. Impartiality and a chance to air the facts may be expected to prevent arbitrary action as well as the good faith factual errors which the Court has observed in the record.

. . .

Rehabilitative treatment, to repeat, constitutes no talismanic state interest which will justify any exactions from individual prisoners. In this case the state officials have candidly not attempted to make it so; the word rarely was spoken in the course of the trial. Partly because they failed to assert the necessity for current disciplinary procedures for the sake of rehabilitation, the Court has presumed to intrude as it has into the workings of the system.

For the time may come in the future when substantial reasons for depriving men of various liberties, to the end that their behavior may be amended, may be presented. "Prison authorities have a legitimate interest in the rehabilitation of prisoners, and may legitimately restrict freedoms in order to further this interest, where a coherent, consistently applied program of rehabilitation exists". . . . At such time the best justification for the hands-off doctrine will appear. While courts by definition are expert in the field of quasi-criminal procedures, their knowledge of the administration of programs that educate and change men may rightly be questioned. Likewise, it may be imagined that judicial intervention or formal administrative procedures might be positively harmful to some rehabilitative efforts.

This is not to say, of course, that courts should then abandon the individual. However, where the state supports its interest in certain practices by demonstrating a substantial hope of success, deference may be owing, and courts may tend to find certain rights, now protected by conventional procedures, implicitly limited while a man is incarcerated.

7 SURVEILLANCE

Who should have the right to conduct surveillance of domestic organizations? When should such surveillance be conducted, and with what safeguards? As surveillance activities of local police forces, state police intelligence units, the Federal Bureau of Investigation, and the armed services increased in the 1960s, these questions assumed new urgency for civil libertarians, congressional investigating committees, and members of the executive branch.

Such surveillance is conducted because law enforcement agencies and the military wish to prevent espionage, sabotage, and conspiracies to engage in illegal acts such as bombing and rioting. Local police forces infiltrate organizations involved in antiwar or civil rights activities. Their agents testify at trials involving members of the Black Panthers (none of whom has yet been convicted, and many of whom have been acquitted after trials involving testimony by police agents). The intelligence units of a number of states have developed computerized file systems on political organizations and their members. The FBI operates an extensive informer system supervised by permanent agents, and the Interdivisional Information Unit of the Department of Justice coordinates intelligence activities of federal agencies and receives information reports from state and local police units. The Army, for a number of years, also engaged in surveillance of domestic political organizations.

Political surveillance is often conducted with the knowledge of the legislative and judicial branches. The FBI and Justice Department, for example, conduct much surveillance under statutory authority and through court orders. Congress at times has appropriated additional funds for surveillance or has provided statutory authority that expands surveillance activities.

On the other hand, much surveillance occurs without the knowledge or prior approval of Congress or the Judiciary. Congressional committees have expressed strong disapproval of domestic intelligence activities conducted by the Department of the Army—activities about which they were not informed in advance. Congressmen and senators have charged that the FBI has spied on members of Congress. In a number of court cases the prosecuting attorneys for the United States Government admitted to having had wiretapping done without obtaining prior court order.

The surveillance activities of the executive branch have provoked a clash between the executive branch of the national government and a number of lower federal courts. The key point of contention is over the requirement imposed by the courts that all wiretapping be authorized by a magistrate, be for a limited time, and be conducted only when there is cause to believe that a crime has been or is about to be committed. If such rules are violated, the courts intend to impose three kinds of penalties on the government: first, criminal penalties against law enforcement officials engaging in illegal tapping; second, exclusion of evidence so obtained from criminal trials prosecuted by the government; and third, a full disclosure of the transcripts of all such surveillance to the defense in the criminal prosecution.

The Justice Department, on the other hand, has taken the position that it should be able to decide unilaterally when and how to conduct surveillance in cases involving national security. Former Assistant Attorney General (now Supreme Court Justice) William Rehnquist argued the case before the Senate Subcommittee on Constitutional Rights, when he said:

> Self discipline on the part of the executive branch will provide an answer to virtually all of the legitimate complaints against excesses of information gathering.

Specifically rejecting supervision by Congress or the Judiciary, he added that the Department of Justice would:

> . . . vigorously oppose any legislation which, by opening the door to unnecessary and unmanageable judicial supervision . . . would effectively impair this extraordinarily important function of the federal government.

On June 19, 1972, in *United States* v. *United States Federal District Court,* the Supreme Court decided, in a unanimous opinion (Justice Rehnquist abstaining), that judicial approval was required for domestic wiretapping under provisions of the Omnibus Crime Control and Safe Streets Act of 1968. It was probable that legislation would be introduced in Congress to overturn that decision, but in the interim civil libertarians had won a victory of major proportions.

The articles in this chapter explore some of the dimensions of the surveillance controversy. The testimony offered by Christopher Pyle indicates that Army surveillance of civilian politics was extensive in the 1960s. The judicial decision reprinted here demonstrates that the judiciary did not believe that this practice constituted any danger. The article by Alan Dershowitz takes the view that wiretapping by the Justice Department has exceeded constitutional limits—a position upheld by the Supreme Court in excerpts from the decision by Justice Powell.

The following selection is taken from testimony offered by former Army Captain Christopher Pyle, one of the leading authorities in the United States on surveillance agencies, to the Senate Subcommittee on Constitutional Rights. As a result of this testimony, a number of articles appearing in opinion magazines, and a series of court challenges, the U.S. Army decided to end surveillance of civilian political movements. Its activities have subsequently been transferred to other agencies mentioned in the testimony.

The Coming Police State?

Christopher H. Pyle

Mr. Chairman and members of the subcommittee, I wish to thank you for this opportunity to discuss what I believe to be the alarming growth of political data banks and the surveillance of lawful political activity within the United States.

. . .

DOMESTIC INTELLIGENCE

Plainly stated, my thesis is that the United States today possesses the intelligence apparatus of a police state. This apparatus is not something of the future; it exists today as a loose coalition of federal, state, municipal, and military agencies. Together, these law enforcement, counter-intelligence, and internal security agencies have developed to the point where authoritarian government is now an operational possibility.

I do not mean to suggest that the emergency of this domestic intelligence community has turned the United States into a police state. On the contrary, I find it somewhat paradoxical that as this apparatus has

From *Federal Data Banks, Computers, and the Bill of Rights*, Hearings before the Subcommittee on Constitutional Rights, Committee on the Judiciary, United States Senate, 92nd Congress, 1st Session, Part I, pp. 169–83. Reprinted by permission of the author. Christopher Pyle is a graduate student, Department of Political Science, Columbia University.

proliferated, the civil liberties of most Americans have also grown. The reason for this apparent contradiction may be that the men who have developed these agencies are, by and large, decent and well-intentioned men. However, the fact that we may trust them is no guarantee that the apparatus which they have created will not someday come under the control of others for whom the investigatory power is a weapon to be wielded against political and personal foes. As Mr. Justice Brandeis once wrote: "Experience should teach us to be most on our guard to protect liberty when the government's purposes are beneficient. . . . The greatest dangers to liberty lurk in the insidious encroachment by men of zeal, well-meaning, but without understanding."

Accordingly, without questioning the motives of the officials who make up the domestic intelligence community, it makes sense to see what they have been up to, and to contemplate what might come of their endeavors.

DOMESTIC INTELLIGENCE OPERATIONS

What they have done in their eagerness to protect us from subversion, espionage, and civil disorder is to impose a blanket surveillance upon nearly all political dissent throughout the United States. Today, it is almost impossible for a private citizen to sign a newspaper ad protesting the war or to speak at a peaceful demonstration of any kind without being subjected to the government's surveillance. The fact that he signed the ad will be noted by the state subversive activities control board, some legislative committees, and the U.S. Civil Service Commission. If the demonstration is large, or relates to a controversial topic, the citizen can expect to be photographed by the local police intelligence unit, the Federal Bureau of Investigation, and, until recently, the U.S. Army. In many instances, the photography will involve both still pictures and videotapes, and the photographers will be posing as members of the press. Later they will get together with their counterparts in other agencies to identify the dissenters and to swap pictures. Eventually some of these will find their way into personality and organizational files, civil disturbance estimates, and mug books on dissenters.

But this is not all. If the local paper writes an article describing the demonstration and the citizen's role in it, the article is likely to become a permanent part of one or more data banks. Political archives are now kept by municipal police, state police, the National Guard, subversive activities control boards, internal security committees, each of the armed services, the Civil Service Commission, the Secret Service, the FBI, the Passport Office, and the Justice Department. In addition, information from the article may be recorded in card indexes, computer indexes, personality files, organizational files, and mug books.

Like their counterparts in foreign intelligence, the domestic intelligence agencies depend upon the press and each other for most of their information. On occasion, however, they find it necessary to conduct their own covert operations. Sometimes these are justified, as when an agent of New York City's Bureau of Special Services successfully infiltrated the Revolutionary Action Movement and foiled a plot to blow up the Statue of Liberty. But sometimes covert operations are not justified.

An especially outrageous covert operation came to light recently in upstate New York when an inquiry into the destruction of an ROTC building on the Hobart College campus disclosed that an agent from the Ontario County sheriff's office had posed as an organizer for the Students for a Democratic Society and had incited campus violence by offering students bombs, guns, and lessons in guerrilla tactics. In New York City last May, defense counsel for thirteen Black Panthers charged with conspiracy to bomb public places alleged that an agent or informer for the FBI had given one of the defendants an unsolicited gift of sixty sticks of dynamite. The FBI's use of wiretaps to collect information pertaining to what it alleges to be the sexual liaisons of the late Rev. Martin Luther King also is well known.

Less sinister, but no less violative of the rights of law-abiding dissenters is the conduct of surveillances that intimidate and harass. Examples include:

1. The detention, by Army agents, of a busload of demonstrators preparing to leave Dupont Circle in Washington, D.C. for Wilmington, Delaware, following the counterinaugural of January 1969.

2. FBI and Army inquiries at banks and bus companies concerning the identity and finances of persons and groups chartering buses to carry demonstrators to Washington, D.C., to participate in the November 1969 moratorium. Lawsuits filed in New York allege that these investigations led to the cancellation of some charters, thus depriving some citizens of their right to petition their government for redress of grievances.

3. Close-in surveillance and photography of law-abiding demonstrators that serves no peacekeeping function, but lets the demonstrators know that the price of dissent is the recording of their activities in political data banks. For example, when approximately 100 demonstrators marked the twenty-fifth anniversary of the destruction of Hiroshima last August by planting a locust tree near the laboratory in which the bomb was built, they were watched by undercover agents and filmed by thirteen government cameramen. Harassing photography is now the subject of

suits for injunctions against the police in New York City, Buffalo, Richmond, Virginia, and New Orleans, while data banks are being challenged in Los Angeles, New Jersey, and Oklahoma. The New Jersey police intelligence system seeks not only the identity of law-abiding demonstrators, but the identity of their employers as well.

THE DOMESTIC INTELLIGENCE COMMUNITY

The domestic intelligence community within the United States is composed principally of police intelligence units, military counterintelligence units, subversive activities control boards, internal security committees of legislatures, National Guard intelligence units, the FBI, the Secret Service, the Civil Service Commission, the Passport Office, and the Justice Department's interdivisional intelligence unit. Associate members of the community include a host of organizations in the fields of industrial security, campus security, preemployment reporting and retail credit.

Police Intelligence Units

Most metropolitan police departments and almost every major state has a bureau engaged in the collection of political intelligence. Some of these date back to the First World War, when they hunted anarchists, Communists, and aliens. Others have been established more recently in response to the growth of mass demonstrations and the occurrence of urban riots. The National Advisory Commission on Civil Disorders urged their establishment:

> An intelligence unit staffed with full-time personnel should be established to gather, evaluate, analyze, and disseminate information on potential as well as actual civil disorders. . . . It should use undercover police personnel and informants, but it should also draw on community leaders, agencies, and organizations in the ghetto.

Some of these units are surprisingly large. New York City's Bureau of Special Services, for example, employs over 120 agents and has an annual budget in excess of $1 million. Chicago's is not quite as large.

Because their operations are rarely limited by city hall, these units sometimes carry their investigations beyond the territorial bounds of their jurisdiction. New York police undercover agents, for example, went to Chicago during the 1968 Democratic National Convention.

Similarly, their curiosity can be quite broad. Frank Rizzo, Philadelphia police chief, boasted to NBC-TV last April:

> We know everything about the people who are going to cause problems in our city . . . no police department could be successful without the information we glean from our intelligence squad. We know, generally, who's going to do what before they do it. We know who comes into the town, we know who's going to leave it, when they're to leave it.

State subversive activities units, unlike police intelligence units, function primarily as clearinghouses for data collected by municipal and state police. The subversive activities division of the Massachusetts State Police is typical of many of the older units. It employs five men, operates on an annual budget of $43,000, and spends much of its time conducting "security name checks." In 1967, 2,194 were run, and in 1968, 4,034. The division's annual report for 1969 describes the extent of its information swapping: "the files in this division have grown to such an extent that the FBI, the Immigration and Naturalization Service, Department of Defense, U.S. Army Intelligence, Federal Civil Service Commission, Treasury Department, several departments of the Commonwealth, industrial plants and educational institutions now clear with this division on security checks."

The Oklahoma Office of Inter-Agency Coordination represents a newer breed of agency which is principally concerned with civil disorders. Established in 1968 as part of the state's military department, it coordinates the intelligence activities of municipal and state police and issues regular intelligence reports on protests, marches, demonstrations. It employs a staff of two professionals and has set aside a portion of its $45,808 budget to hire part-time investigators and informants. It exists to inform the governor, police, and National Guard about political activists in Oklahoma but has been forced by a lack of activism in that state to devote much of its regular intelligence reports to events occurring elsewhere in the country. The report for June 30, 1970, for example, alerted Oklahoma authorities to a pop festival in Atlanta, a Black Panther convention in Philadelphia, and antiwar demonstrations planned for numerous cities in the fall. In addition, it called attention to the activities of a candidate for Congress, a group called Oklahomans for Indian Opportunity founded by the wife of Senator Fred Harris, and the Coalition for Civic Leadership of Oklahoma City. The agency was established without legislative authorization by the governor through the disbursement of funds appropriated for the state's military department. Since then it has received a grant of $18,347 from the U.S. Department of Justice's Law Enforcement Assistance Administration. Like its Massachusetts counterpart, it also swaps information with a variety of agencies including the FBI, the National Guard, and the Army.

The National Guard

The part-time nature of most National Guard units makes the sustained collection of domestic intelligence difficult. Those units with the most extensive files depend heavily on state agencies like the Oklahoma Office of Inter-Agency Coordination. A zealous intelligence officer, however, can make a difference. In 1968, a Major C. Allen March, the G-2 (intelligence officer) of the California National Guard, made headlines by regularly publishing an intelligence summary of protest politics inside and outside of California. March's summaries appeared to be drawn primarily from newspapers and police reports, but were written from an ultra-right-wing point of view. They eventually became the subject of controversy in the state legislature and were discontinued.

Stateside Military Units

The commander of each military unit, installation, base, or activity in the United States has an understandable curiosity about protest politics in the surrounding civilian community. This curiosity is heightened if the protests threaten to undermine the morale, discipline, or security of the post. The antiwar, antidraft, and soldiers' rights movements, not surprisingly, have been perceived to pose such a threat. Accordingly, installation and unit intelligence offices have for many years collected information on persons and organizations supporting these causes. This activity is separate from, and in addition to the very extensive collection efforts of the U.S. Army Intelligence Command, which I will describe in detail later in this statement.

One of the main foci of stateside military intelligence, then, has been the "RITA Program." RITA is short for Resistance in the Army, and takes its name from a group of deserters in Europe who first organized under that name to encourage other soldiers to follow their example. The activities of the American Servicemans Union and the antiwar coffeehouses have been primary objects of RITA surveillance, which frequently make use of informants and undercover agents drawn from military intelligence, military police, the Criminal Investigation Division, and the barracks.

A secondary focus of the domestic intelligence activities of stateside military units is race relations. In Europe, Vietnam, and the United States, military posts have been the scene of serious racial violence, and reporting systems have been set up to keep field commanders and the Pentagon informed of racial tensions. Like the civil disturbance and RITA intelligence efforts, this system also has an inherent tendency to probe into the private beliefs and associations of individuals both inside and outside the Armed Forces.

In addition, a number of stateside units—particularly those with riot control duties—have taken an active interest in civil disturbances which they suspect might grow into riots. Chief among these is the Continental Army Command (CONARC), which is the holding company for most stateside Army units, installations, and activities. It would seem that CONARC, which is responsible for defending the United States against invasion, should also defend it against insurrections and riots. But this is not the case. CONARC was deprived of this responsibility in 1968 by the creation of the Directorate for Civil Disturbance Planning and Operations.[1] This is the 150-man unit which runs the Pentagon's domestic war room. Three years earlier, CONARC also had lost much of its capacity to set up a civil disturbance early warning system when six counterintelligence groups (occupying some thirty offices coast to coast) were taken away from the major Army commands under its jurisdiction and reassembled to make the U.S. Army Intelligence Command. The main purpose for this shift of personnel to an independent support command was to facilitate the conduct of personnel security investigations. But during the Newark riots of 1967, the Intelligence Command also got the assignment to accelerate its occasional monitoring of potential civil disturbances into a full-fledged early warning system, complete with a nationwide teletype hookup and a computerized storage system. Miffed by this turn of events, CONARC resolved to create its own civil disturbance reporting system. It did so by giving domestic intelligence assignments to combat intelligence units in training and to post intelligence staffs. Eventually, it even installed its own computerized civil disturbance data bank at its headquarters at Fort Monroe, Virginia. All of this preparation was to be a hedge against the day when command of its own troops in time of riot might be returned.

In the summer and fall of 1969 it was one of CONARC's units (the Fifth Military Intelligence Detachment of the Fifth Mechanized Infantry Division, Fort Carson, Colorado) that infiltrated the Colorado Springs peace movement, sent agents to peace vigils in the chapel of Colorado State College, and placed both an agent and an informant in the Colorado Springs young adult project, a coalition of church youth groups which ran a recreation center for emotionally disturbed young people.

At Fort Hood, Texas, another CONARC unit computerized its files on civil disturbances and civilian politics.

To a lesser extent, the Marines, Air Force, and Navy also have been involved in similar domestic intelligence activities. The Marine Corps, like the Army, has been plagued by serious internal racial strife. Accordingly, to keep commanders, the Commandant, and the Pentagon informed

---

[1] The name of this unit has recently been changed to the Directorate of Military Support (DOMS).

of these matters, the Corps has set up an internal reporting system not unlike CONARC's. The Air Force has followed suit. In a memorandum dated May 25, 1970, entitled "Subversive Activities," the commander of Sheppard Air Force Base in Texas called upon his subordinates to report:

Personnel making conversation about the overthrow of the U.S. Government;

Personnel making statements which indicate disloyalty;

Personnel making threats against the president of the United States, or other high government officials, or high-ranking military personnel;

Congregations of unauthorized persons;

Persons attempting to spread antiwar sentiment in public places on Sheppard Air Force Base;

Persons making statements with racial overtones.

This memorandum led to a protest by Senator Sam J. Ervin, Jr., chairman of the Senate Subcommittee on Constitutional Rights. The Air Force replied that such reporting systems were not department policy, and ordered the memorandum rewritten. But the revised text, published on August 7, 1970, was also conspicuously overboard. It extended the monitoring of supposedly "disloyal" statements to the civilian dependents of Air Force personnel, and continued to require reports on all persons who "unlawfully make provoking statements with racial overtones," or who make threats against the president or other high government or military officials. What constituted "disloyal," "unlawfully provoking," or "threatening" statements was not spelled out. Further protests from Congress persuaded the Air Force to rescind the revised text, but similar directives remain in force.

The Navy, like the Air Force, is mostly concerned with antiwar, anti-military sentiment. Its curiosity with these matters has sometimes been excessive. For example, when Naval Investigative Service sought to find a way of dealing with Roger Priest, a young seaman who published an antiwar newspaper with a Pentagon address, it assigned twenty-five agents to monitor his every move. When Priest spoke at an antiwar workshop in Cleveland while on leave and out of uniform, six of the fifteen persons in his civilian audience were NIS agents. In Chicago at the time of the Democratic National Convention, a civilian employee of NIS tape recorded speeches by demonstrators in Grant Park. He later testified against some of them at the Chicago Eight (minus one) trial. But neither he nor the Navy has ever satisfactorily explained what a naval intelligence agent was doing monitoring the political activities of civilians wholly unassociated with the Navy.

Internal Security Agencies

Wherever state secrets need protection, domestic intelligence units have undertaken security checks of personnel assigned to sensitive positions. These checks are required by Executive Order 10450 and delve into matters of "loyalty" and "suitability." All of the military departments, the FBI, CIA, Civil Service Commission, Atomic Energy Commission, as well as other agencies, are involved in this kind of inquiry which, like the civil disturbance, RITA, and racial inquiries, has a great potential for invading privacy and inhibiting people in their beliefs, expressions, and associations.

Typical of these personnel security agencies is the U.S. Army Intelligence Command, which investigates most of the Army's military and civilian personnel, as well as persons holding sensitive jobs with firms doing work on classified Army contracts. (It was the Intelligence Command's future agents whom I taught at Fort Holabird.)

The Intelligence Command has never been sensitive to the constitutional implications of its conduct. This was demonstrated by the excessive zeal with which it established its civil disturbance early warning system and political computer, and it is no less true for its conduct of personnel security investigations.

Part of the problem undoubtedly lies in the imprecise wording of Executive Order 10450 and the corresponding Army regulation (604–10) which permit the denial of a security clearance—and the job that goes with it—on less evidence than would support a magistrate's finding of "probable cause." In other words, it is not a question of whether reliable evidence indicates that the individual cannot be trusted with state secrets, but of whether the granting of the clearance would be "clearly consistent with the interests of national security." No one knows what this ambiguous phrase means.

In an attempt to clarify it for the entire Department of Defense, Walter T. Skallerup, Jr., Deputy Assistant Secretary of Defense (Security Police), wrote a memorandum on November 26, 1962, addressed to the undersecretaries of each of the services. He said:

> Persons conducting security investigations and inquiries normally have broad latitude in performing these essential and vital functions. This places a high premium upon the exercise of good judgment and common sense.
>
> . . .
>
> . . . For example, religious beliefs and affiliations or beliefs and opinions regarding racial matters, political beliefs and affiliations of a nonsubversive nature, opinions regarding the constitutionality of legislative policies, and affiliations with labor unions are not proper subjects for such inquiries.
>
> Inquiries which have no relevance to a security determination should not be made. Questions regarding personal and domestic affairs, financial mat-

ters, and the status of physical health, fall into this category unless evidence clearly indicates a reasonable basis for believing there may be illegal or subversive activities, personal or moral irresponsibility, or mental or emotional instability involved. The probing of a person's thoughts or beliefs and questions about his conduct, which have no security implications, are unwarranted. Department of Defense representatives always should be prepared to explain the relevance of their inquiries upon request. Adverse inferences cannot properly be drawn from the refusal of a person to answer questions the relevance of which has not been established.

As a direct result of Skallerup's memorandum and accompanying inquiry into the training of the Army's personnel security investigators, the thirty-hour course in "Investigative Legal Principles" which I taught at the Intelligence School was instituted. The Skallerup memorandum was part of the curriculum.

Unfortunately, much of what he said and what the legal instructors at the Intelligence School have taught has been countermanded by the colonels and lieutenant colonels who command the military intelligence groups which do the actual investigations. Sometimes the orders come from the Army personnel security group and related offices inside the Intelligence Command headquarters at Fort Holabird. Typical of the questions which they have required agents in the field to ask are the following, which were written last March by officials in the Intelligence Command's headquarters and given to an agent of the 109th MI Group to ask a young officer:

Q. Have you ever read the *Berkeley Barb*?
Q. Have you ever read the *Los Angeles Free Press*?
Q. What is your attitude toward publications of this sort?
Q. What are the names of all publications to which you are a subscriber?
Q. What is your attitude toward the war in Vietnam?
Q. Why did you display on the rear of your car the two inverted United States flags?
Q. . . . the Department of the Army desires an explanation concerning the display of the two inverted United States flags because your association with a vehicle displaying these symbols might lead to the conclusion that you are disloyal to the United States . . .
Q. Why did you display the "peace" symbol on your car?

Interrogations of this sort are among the papers used by security clearance adjudicators to reach a decision regarding the individual's loyalty and suitability. The adjudicators themselves have no legal training, and receive a minimal education at the Intelligence School before undertaking their sensitive tasks. The most highly trained—civilian adjudicators employed by the stateside army command—receive only nine days of job instruction on loyalty determinations. They receive no training on the subject of suitability whatever. The least trained adjudicators—intelligence officers assigned to field commands—receive exactly two classroom hours on loyalty and two on suitability. Because of this extremely brief training, it is not unusual for an adjudicator to conclude that a person arrested in connection with a political protest is not suited for a security clearance, regardless of the circumstances of his arrest, the legality of his detention, or his innocence of the charges.

Thus the right to due process when applying for a security clearance is tenuous at best. It has been made even more precarious by the use to which newspaper clippings and other often reliable sources of information are put. For example, until recently, the Army has made a practice of taking "spot reports" on demonstrations, protests, and various kinds of civil disorders, which happen to mention someone whose security clearance dossier is on file, and filing them in that dossier. (The Army has between seven and nine million of these dossiers.) Then, whenever that person's loyalty and suitability is reconsidered by the Army or any other federal agency the adjudicator gets to see the unsubstantiated report and to take it into account.

The Civil Service Commission has a different practice. According to its chairman, the Commission maintains a "security file" of some 2,120,000 index cards containing "lead information relating to possible questions . . . involving loyalty or subversive activity. The lead information contained in these files has been developed from published hearings of congressional committees, state legislative committees, public investigative bodies, reports of investigation, publications of subversive organizations, and various other newspapers and periodicals."

On the face of it, this file might seem like a sensible way to focus investigations. It probably is. But at the same time it poses a substantial threat to individual liberties because there are no criteria for determining what is evidence of "disloyalty" or "subversive activity." The decision is a wholly personal one which the Commission's security staff makes on the basis of its own judgment as to what is proper politics and what is subversive. Asked by a newspaper reporter for an example of someone with questionable politics, Ed Knazik, one of the Commission's evaluators, responded: "An extreme example would be Linus Pauling." Pauling is the Nobel prizewinning chemist who revealed the structure of complex protein molecules in the early 1950s and who has more recently been an outspoken critic of American strategic policy, the atomic bomb, and recent wars.

The Federal Bureau of Investigation

The FBI has been the chief domestic intelligence agency of the United States almost since its inception. Its authority for intelligence gathering is drawn from:

1. Formal and informal presidential directives dating back to 1936 order-ing it to gather information "concerning subversive activities being conducted in the United States by . . . organizations or groups advo-cating the overthrow or replacement of the government of the United States by illegal means."
2. Criminal statutes, such as the espionage, sedition, selective service, and anti-riot acts, which authorize the Bureau to investigate political activities which may involve violations of federal law.
3. The Emergency Detention Act of 1950 under which the FBI has author-ity to assemble lists of persons to be rounded up and confined in detention camps should the president declare an "Internal Security Emergency."
4. The Internal Security Act of 1950 which authorizes the FBI to gather information to be used by the attorney general or the Subversive Activities Control Board in designating "subversive" groups.
5. Executive Order 10450 authorizing federal agencies to investigate the loyalty and suitability of persons being considered for sensitive gov-ernment positions.
6. Presidential requests for investigations into the backgrounds of per-sons being considered for political appointment to high government positions.

Unlike the Army, which established its civil disturbance early warning with little thought to its legal basis, the FBI usually has been careful to tie its domestic intelligence activities to some statutory or executive authorization. Thus the main focus of its intelligence efforts has been on possible threats to national security or threats of violence. The activities of foreign intelligence agencies, the American Communist party, its fronts, and affiliates, the Weathermen, Minutemen, and Black Panthers currently receive its closest attention. Surveillance of New Left groups is predicated on the hypothesis of Communist infiltration, exploitation, or support, or the expectation of large-scale civil disorder.

The Bureau's principal sources of domestic intelligence include news-papers and periodicals and the files of state and local police. Its reliance on the police has at times been heavy. Until recently, one official con-fided to the *New York Times*, 80 per cent of the FBI's information about the Black Panthers came from the subversive units of local police departments.

Nonetheless, resort is made to covert operations—so much so that agents are rated on their skill in developing informants. Wiretapping is also used on domestic political groups when the attorney general is persuaded that the group, or individuals in it, pose a threat to national security. Groups tapped during recent years include the Black Muslims, the Southern Christian Leadership Conference, and the Black Panthers; individuals include the late Rev. Martin Luther King, Cassius Clay, and David Dellinger.

While other domestic intelligence agencies have moved towards computerization of their files, the FBI's Domestic Intelligence Division keeps its data in "raw" form. However, its reports do go to the Justice Department's Interdivisional Intelligence Unit where they are fed to a computer.

To the extent that political dissidents are also criminal suspects, records concerning them will be found in the Bureau's new computerized National Crime Information Center (NCIC). The Center's computer provides 40,000 instant, automatic teletype printouts each day on wanted persons and stolen property to forty-nine states and Canada; it also "talks" to twenty-four other computers maintained by local and state police departments for themselves and about 2,500 police jurisdictions. Other NCIC clients include the Immigration and Naturalization Service, the Internal Revenue Service, and the Federal Narcotics Bureau. The FBI says that its information is based wholly on federal and local warrants, complaints, arrests and convictions, but the potential of this system for noncriminal intelligence is virtually unlimited.

Plans for the new FBI headquarters on Pennsylvania Avenue suggest the priority now assigned to domestic intelligence. Of the space set aside, 35,000 square feet is for the domestic intelligence staff—as opposed to 23,000 square feet for criminal and other investigations.

The Justice Department

The principal consumer of FBI reports on political activists is the Justice Department's Interdivisional Intelligence Unit. Other recipients include the Criminal, Internal Security, and Civil Rights Divisions, the Community Relations Service, and the so-called Black Panther task force set up in 1969 to monitor the activities of all radicals.

The Interdivisional Intelligence Unit operates on a budget of $274,000, employs twelve intelligence analysts, and works in a domestic war room in the Justice Department on the sixth floor. Its director is James T. Devine who works directly under Deputy Attorney General Richard G. Kleindienst. Since the November 1969 moratorium in Washington, D.C., it has supplanted the Army's counterintelligence analysis detachment as the government's headquarters for civil disturbance and political protest information.

To fulfill this duty the Unit maintains a political computer larger than the one at Fort Holabird which the Army shut down. Most of the information in this computer comes from the FBI. The rest is supplied by ninety-three U.S. attorneys around the country and by other government agencies, such as the Treasury Department's Alcohol and Tobacco Division (which enforce federal firearms laws), the Secret Service, and the Army.

Each week the Justice Department's computer disgorges a huge printout which describes coming events on the protest circuit. It is divided into four volumes, each about two inches thick, and is bound in brown cardboard covers. Each book covers a region of the country and presents a city-by-city assessment of the potential for civil disorder. It details what marches, rallies, or meetings are scheduled, the organizations and individuals sponsoring them, and the city's history of civil disturbances.

The books are then culled by analysts in the Interdivisional Intelligence Unit who abstract and forward data of interest to the Attorney General and various divisions of the department. For example, the Community Relations Service receives information on potential racial problems which it might be called upon to conciliate. The Civil Rights Division is alerted to possible violations of the laws it enforces while the Criminal Division gets data on such offenses as draft card burning and the crossing of state lines with intent to incite a riot.

In addition to the weekly civil disturbance estimate, the computer can produce a rundown on almost any past or coming demonstration of size which will include all stored information on the membership, ideology, and plans of the sponsors. This was done, for example, prior to the November 15, 1969 antiwar demonstration in Washington organized by the Vietnam Moratorium Committee and the New Mobilization Committee to End the War. Special printouts have also been done on the Black Panthers.

The Secret Service

In its zeal to protect the president and other high government officials from assassins, the Secret Service has developed one of the most versatile—and constitutionally offensive—political data systems in the government. Built around a Honeywell 2200 computer, this system is capable of sorting and retrieving by name, alias, method of operation, affiliation, and physical appearance. As a result the Secret Service is able to detect, investigate, and, if necessary, detain in advance persons whom it suspects might try to harass, harm, or embarrass officials under its protection.

Starting with computer-printed lists of persons of "protective interest" grouped geographically, analysts in the Protective Intelligence

Division can assemble descriptions and photographs for the teams of Secret Service Service agents who travel in advance of the presidential party. A spokesman for the Service explained to the *New York Times* how the system works:

> You take a waiter in a hotel dining room where the boss is going to speak. Let's say the computer turns up his name and we investigate and decide it would be better for him to be assigned to some other duties. No one has a constitutional right to wait on the president, you know. That's how it works.

Guided by a more sophisticated computer program, the same machine can also produce lists of individuals by their characteristics—such as all of the long-haired, skinny campus radicals in Walla Walla, Washington. No other government computer has this capability.

The data base now covers more than 50,000 persons. It is drawn from many sources, including the FBI, state and municipal police, military intelligence, the Internal Revenue Service, federal building guards, the White House (which keeps a record of all abusive telephone calls and letters), and individual informants. Thus, to anyone concerned about the intimidating effect which this computer could have on the exercise of political rights, the criteria that determine who is worthy of space in the computer becomes critical.

The Secret Service contends that its analysts apply relatively sophisticated and realistic standards. But the guidelines it has issued to govern the reporting of information go far beyond the recommendations of the Warren Commission and leave much to be clarified. They call for:

A. Information pertaining to a threat, plan or attempt by an individual, a group, or an organization to physically harm or embarrass the persons protected by the U.S. Secret Service, or any other high U.S. government official at home or abroad.

B. Information pertaining to individuals, groups, or organizations who have plotted, attempted, or carried out assassinations of senior officials of domestic or foreign governments.

C. Information concerning the use of bodily harm or assassination as a political weapon. This should include training and techniques used to carry out the act.

D. Information on persons who insist upon personally contacting high government officials for the purpose of redress of imaginary grievances, etc.

E. Information on any person who makes oral or written statements about high government officials in the following categories: (1) threatening statements, (2) irrational statements, and (3) abusive statements.

F. Information on professional gate crashers.

G. Information pertaining to "terrorist" bombings.

H. Information pertaining to the ownership or concealment by individuals or groups of caches of firearms, explosives, or other implements of war.

I. Information regarding anti-American or anti-U.S. government demonstrations in the United States or overseas.

J. Information regarding civil disturbances.

The breadth and vagueness of these guidelines has prompted Senator Ervin to observe in a Senate speech: "Although I am not a 'professional gate crasher,' I am a 'malcontent' on many issues. I have written the President and other high officials complaining of grievances that some may consider 'imaginary.' And on occasion, I may also have 'embarrassed high government officials.'" Accordingly, he concluded, he was probably qualified for listing in the computer.

Private Organizations

Associate members of the domestic intelligence community today include a host of individuals and organizations in such fields as preemployment reporting, industrial security, campus security, private detection, and retail credit.

One of the more chilling is a seemingly innocuous group called the Laymans Church League of America—a preemployment firm based in Wheaton, Illinois. The sort of services it provides are described in a letter written in December 1968 by Andrew W. Hunter, a field director, to the president of one of the nation's leading department stores.

> American businessmen are faced with a grave problem. . . . Our working forces include more than a few radicals, socialists, revolutionaries, communists, and troublemakers of all sorts. The colleges and schools are educating and training thousands more who will soon be seeking employment.
>
> The hiring and training costs to industry for individual workers run into many thousands of dollars. Before they are employed, their educational and professional backgrounds are screened most carefully. On the other hand, little if anything is done to determine their philosophy of life. In many cases this is of paramount importance.
>
> The Church League of America is non-denominational, non-political, and tax exempt. For thirty-two years we have been intensively researching the activities of troublesome individuals, groups, and publications, about which management would be well advised to be aware. Our files are the most reliable, comprehensive and complete, and second only to those of the FBI, which, of course, are not available to you.
>
> . . .

We can supply you with all the data regarding your people that you may deem advisable. . . . In return, we seek cooperation to the end that we may modernize and keep abreast of what appears to be an ever-growing need.

My office will be glad to send a representative, at your request, to go into this delicate matter at greater length.

Like preemployment reporting, the industrial security business has drawn heavily upon the internal securities agencies for policy guidance, training, and manpower. In fact, it is a common practice for lieutenant colonels who cannot make the grade in the combat arms to transfer to military intelligence about two years prior to retirement in the hope that their experience as commanders of stateside MI groups will qualify them for postretirement jobs in industrial security.

Campus security, on the other hand, has been a haven for retired policemen and FBI agents. With the advent of student radicalism, many campus security chiefs have assembled extensive files on the political and social views of students. They also have hired photographers and recruited networks of informers. Some surveillance obviously makes sense, particularly where bombing, burning, and assault have been employed as expressions of dissent. But all too often, these departments have been insensitive to the rights of law-abiding students. Two years ago Yale University was shocked to discover that its security chief had amassed a huge file on the politics and associations of students, many of whom had never participated in campus demonstrations. As recently as last fall, security personnel at the University of Minnesota actively encouraged military and police agents to photograph demonstrations of all kinds on campus. They also helped to identify demonstrators in Army photographs and gave Army agents pictures they had taken.

The automation of civilian records has made banks, airlines, credit companies, hotels, car rental firms, and telephone companies easy sources of information about the activities, habits, and associations of the government's critics. FBI inquiries into bank accounts, for example, have been widely publicized. Less well known is the investigative use which military commands—including the Army Intelligence Command— have made of onpost credit unions.

THE IMPACT OF POLITICAL SURVEILLANCE

When most people hear of improper political surveillances, they think first of police states and military dictatorships. To start with this perception, however, may be to misperceive the problem.

The most immediate threats posed by political surveillance in the United States are more mundane. They exist in all data systems and involve such abuses as blackmail, defamation, release of information to unauthorized persons, blacklisting, and other forms of economic coercion and reprisal. These are the hard, tangible, everyday misuses of political data systems. Proof of their occurrence is irrefutable.

Less tangible, but no less real, is the "chilling effect" which knowledge of political surveillance can have upon the willingness of persons to participate in politics or otherwise exercise their constitutional freedoms of expression and association, and their right to petition the government for redress of grievances. The chilling effect is easiest to demonstrate where police deliberately conduct harassing surveillance in order to deter political expression and association. But it can also result from the creation of large political centers. In *Anderson* v. *Sills*, a suit filed by the American Civil Liberties Union on behalf of the Jersey City branch of the NAACP, the lower court held: "The secret files that would be maintained as a result of this (police) intelligence system are inherently dangerous, and by their very existence tend to restrict those who would advocate . . . social and political change."

The dynamics of the chilling effect are not well known, but research that has been done attributes great influence to the political tolerance level of society. My own experience confirms this finding. Thus far, most of the former intelligence agents whom I have asked to speak out against the Army's surveillance are less worried about official reprisals than they are about the reactions of their neighbors, friends, families, and employers. While nearly all are convinced that the surveillance is wrong, many are hesitant to make their views public. Their most frequent explanations are: "I live in a conservative community. . . . The people here wouldn't understand. . . . I could lose my job." Some worry that their criticism of unauthorized intelligence activities could cost them security clearances later in life, even though their criticism would in no way touch on classified matters.

Beyond the chilling effect, I believe, there is a real danger of the outright repression of unpopular political minorities by state and local police. We already have ample evidence of unwarranted and vindictive violence directed against Negroes and students by poorly trained and undisciplined policemen. However, this is nothing compared to the harassment and brutality which could result if the disciplining of police departments does not keep pace with the growth of political intelligence about provocative dissenters. The record of local "red squads" has always been a shameful one, but it could become substantially worse if the new interstate and intrastate criminal intelligence systems become a vehicle for noncriminal information.

The unregulated spread of covert intelligence techniques to police investigations poses similar dangers. While it may make sense to allow the police limited covert powers (such as court-authorized wiretaps and informers) to deal with campus bombers and organized crime, it makes no sense whatever to permit the same tools to be used for the surveillance of nonviolent protesters. Such techniques not only raise grave constitutional problems: they also force moderates to resort to criminal means to express their dissent.

Finally, we must face the fact that police statism—especially at the local level—is now a clear, if not present danger. National and local members of the domestic intelligence community are no longer fragmented by narrow conceptions of jurisdiction, limited resources, or the boundaries of federalism. Computer and teletype technology has brought them together into a variety of regional and national galaxies, and it has made the political files of one the potential resource of others. Before we allow this process to go much further, we would do well to remind ourselves that a country may be able to survive the centralization of domestic intelligence without becoming authoritarian, but it almost certainly cannot become authoritarian without centralized domestic intelligence.

Several suits were brought in federal district courts by civil libertarians challenging the Army surveillance of civilian groups. On April 22, 1970, in Tatum v. Laird, a federal district judge in Washington, D.C., dismissed a suit brought by Arlo Tatum, Director of the Central Committee for Conscientious Objectors, which would have enjoined the Army from conducting surveillance against him and fourteen domestic organizations. The district judge refused to hear testimony in the case, holding that Army surveillance did not violate the Constitution or any statute. On April 27, 1970, the Court of Appeals of the District of Columbia ruled that a trial must be held on the assertions of the plaintiffs. The government appealed that decision, and the Supreme Court will decide sometime in the spring of 1973 whether a trial must be held by a lower court.

The case reprinted here, American Civil Liberties Union v. Westmoreland (January 1971), represents a defeat for civil libertarians. The district judge rejected the argument that the existence of surveillance apparatus had a "chilling effect" on the exercise of First Amendment rights. Instead, the judge held that the competence of the Army agents was so low that it could not "chill" the freedom of expression of any political group.

The Supreme Court, in cases decided in the 1960s, had developed two standards for evaluating the effect of executive action on First Amendment rights. In the case Dombrowski v. Pfister (1966) the Court seemed to say that the existence of certain statutes, orders, or actions could "chill" the First Amendment rights of groups. In the case Cameron v. Johnson, decided in 1968, the Supreme Court held that the performance of the agency could determine whether its action had "chilled" First Amendment rights. With two separate lines of development, the district judge in American Civil Liberties Union **v.** Westmoreland **chose to rely on the second case and used performance of the Army (or lack of it) to justify, in part, its surveillance activities.**

American Civil Liberties Union v. Westmoreland

Austin, District Judge.

There has been a cliché, or an accepted statement from the past that a certain profession is known as the world's oldest profession. I question that. I think the world's oldest profession is spying, and it started in the Garden of Eden when somebody was looking and saw Eve eat the apple. And then Cain started spying on Abel.

Spying goes back to antiquity, and according to the Old Testament, all the way back to the Garden of Eden.

. . .

There is no question that the administration has a right to use all the facilities available to the administration to try and fulfill the oath that was taken to protect and defend the Constitution and to preserve the Constitution from all enemies foreign and domestic, and I, at this time, strive as I have endeavored to, have great difficulty in determining that there has been any violation of anybody's constitutional rights.

The Fourth, Fifth and Ninth have been abandoned. We are now down to the First Amendment, the chilling effect of this activity on someone's freedom of speech.

If there has been anything disclosed by what we have heard here for the past week, if we must rely on Army Intelligence, that there will be

From *American Civil Liberties Union* v. *Westmoreland* 323 Federal Supplement 1153 (1971).

no seven days in May in this country, a man on a white horse will never arrive.

This evidence indicates that typical, gigantic Washington bureaucratic boondoggle. Military intelligence is the Army's WPA, its leaf-rakers, its shovel-leaners, and paper-shufflers. It has revealed that there are too many Colonel Throttlebottoms, Major Ashtired—regional Special Operations Officer Fumbles and uncontrollable special agents Bumbles seducing unwitting bartenders to assist in this threatening, menacing assemblage of Keystone Cops.

The chief beneficiary of military intelligence has been newspaper circulation.

The chief menace has been the increase in air pollution from burning newspapers from which has been extracted, for dossiers, valuable secretive bits of common knowledge available to all who can read.

I think unquestionably the first appointment of all ancient pharaohs was a papyrus clipper, and that has gone down from that day to this through all of the bureaucratic assemblages on the local, state, and national level.

I hope that those who have testified and swore that they were chilled by the Army surveillance have been warmed by the revelations in this hearing. I am still confused and bemused and puzzled as to why one of the witnesses, Mr. Miller, who admitted reading the same clippings in his file in the sanctity of his office, why doing this there had no effect on his thermometer. I think perhaps he read and reread them because they tended to warm the cockles of his heart.

This clipping business is a national pastime of all of those who have some desire to see themselves in print.

I find that while there is no violation proved by a preponderance of the evidence of the violation of any constitutional rights, there has been a tremendous waste of taxpayers' money in hiring people to perform the duties that were performed as revealed by the evidence in this case, and this is not limited merely to one branch of the federal government, it is not limited, based on my experience, to all branches of the federal government, all of whom have papyrus paper clippers to preserve for posterity and their grandchildren their importance while they occupied the federal scene.

. . .

The Court denies the request for a declaratory judgment.

The Court finds that the Army, for whatever reason, has sought to eliminate from their files this mountain of paper. I feel unable to restrain any agency whose job it is to preserve and protect the Constitution to limit their activities. Only the thin-skinned, and I have had no thin-skinned witnesses testify before me in this case, could have any chill as a result of the evidence that has been disclosed in this courtroom.

Foot surveillance—I don't know whether that is done in three-quarter time or how it is done, but it is ridiculous, but it is a term that tends to glamorize a spy who has been looking at too many statues, statues of Nathan Hale.

The request for a preliminary and a permanent injunction to limit that surveillance is denied.

The request to destroy the remnants of whatever files still remain is denied.

I think Shakespeare, at the time that he wrote some of his yarns, may have contemplated that this case might come up and named two of them, in regard to the evidence that has been disclosed here: one was "A Comedy of Errors" and the other was "Much Ado About Nothing."

That is the finding of the Court; that is the decision of the Court. We will stand adjourned, Mr. Marshal.

Wiretapping was used extensively by federal authorities during Prohibition in order to gather information against bootleggers. In the case of Olmstead v. United States in 1928 the Supreme Court ruled five to four that a wiretap by federal agents on a bootlegger's phone did not constitute unreasonable search and seizure, as forbidden under the Fourth Amendment. As a result of that decision, Congress in 1934 passed a statute with the following provision:

> No person not being authorized by the sender shall intercept any communication and divulge or publish the existence, contents, substance, purport, effect, or meaning of such intercepted communication to any person. (47 USC 605)

Yet the provision was full of loopholes. First, the caller could authorize a tap on his call. Second, the statute could be read to forbid divulging information, but not necessarily forbidding interception per se. Third, the statute did not forbid the use in judicial proceedings of illegally obtained evidence gained by wiretapping. Finally, the statute restricted itself to "communication" and hence did not prohibit "bugging" an apartment to intercept conversation between occupants of a room.

In 1937, in Nardone v. United States the Supreme Court held that while the Constitution did not bar wiretapping (Olmstead), the Congress, by statute, could bar it. Hence, section 605 was upheld. A few years later, in Goldman v. United States (1942) the Supreme Court upheld the use of a wall microphone to "bug" an apartment. While a "spike mike" that intruded into another apartment could not be used (Silverman v. United States, 1961), the Supreme Court did uphold the use of a "thumbtack mike" under court order (Wong Sun v. United States, **1964**).

In the late 1960s, the Supreme Court in two decisions virtually invited Congress and the states to legalize wiretaps. In June 1967 the Supreme Court struck down, in Berger v. New York, a state statute passed in 1966 permitting police to wiretap without a court order and without probable cause. Yet in that decision Justice Tom Clark invited Congress and the states to pass statutes that would permit courts to authorize wiretaps. In Katz v. United States in 1967, the Supreme Court indicated that federal agents might be permitted to tap public telephones if they obtained a judicial warrant, provided Congress passed a statute permitting such interception and divulgence.

Congress responded to the invitation, and in 1968 authorized wiretapping in the Omnibus Crime Control and Safe Streets Act. The act provided in Title III that federal agents, upon obtaining a warrant based on probable cause, could wiretap to secure evidence that could be used in courts. Yet the act contained two provisions that could circumvent judicial supervision. First, an "emergency clause" provided that federal or state officials could intercept communications for forty-eight hours without a court order if they "reasonably determined" that "an emergency situation exists with respect to conspiratorial activities threatening the national security interest." Second, Title III contained a "national security" clause stating that nothing in the act or in section 605 (of the 1934 act) limits the constitutional power of the president to tap during a time of actual or potential attack by a foreign power or to obain foreign intelligence for national security. This clause was designed to protect the president's practice of tapping selected embassies maintained by foreign governments. Furthermore, the provision added:

> Nor shall anything in this chapter be deemed to limit the constitutional power of the president to take such measures as he deems necessary to protect the United States against the overthrow of the government by force or other unlawful means, or against any clear and present danger to the structure of the government.

No order was needed for these taps. Unlike the taps in criminal cases, national security taps need not be disclosed in annual reports of the Department of Justice, except as the president might provide. And these taps could be used as evidence in hearings, grand jury proceedings, and trials.

Some civil libertarians opposed the use of wiretaps in criminal cases, believing them to be an expensive and ineffective means of obtaining evidence, as well as an unconstitutional unreasonable search and invasion of privacy, prohibited by the Fourth and Ninth Amendments, respectively, and a means of self-incrimination prohibited by the Fifth Amendment. Other civil libertarians believed that with proper judicial safeguards, the use of wiretaps in criminal cases was a "reasonable search" not prohibited by the Fourth Amendment. Yet most civil libertarians, no matter what their feeling about the criminal cases, were aghast at the Title III provisions involving the national security. For one thing, the language was vague. It did not include tapping only if there was probable cause to believe that treason, sabotage, espionage, or criminal activities were being committed or about to be committed. Moreover, in the floor debate, senators introduced amendments that would limit the president's authority to "foreign threats." These amendments were rejected, leaving the president free to tap domestic organizations.

In fact, ever since President Truman's time, wiretapping against domestic political organizations had occurred under executive orders without benefit of Congressional statute. The effect of Title III was to provide legislative history and a statute to ratify the status quo ante.

Civil liberties organizations attacked the statute and the executive branch practice of wiretapping against domestic political organizations. These cases are some of the most important ones being decided in the 1970s. In some cases, federal district courts have sharply attacked the practice of tapping without a court order. In the case United States v. Smith, decided January 11, 1971, Judge Warren Ferguson rejected the argument of the Justice Department that national security considerations could permit it to tap without a warrant. Instead, Judge Ferguson declared:

> The government cannot act in this manner when only domestic political organizations are involved, even if these organizations espouse views which are inconsistent with our present form of government. To do so is to ride roughshod over numerous political freedoms which have long received constitutional protection.

The case is being appealed by the Justice Department.

The most important case that was decided by the Supreme Court is that of Plamondon v. United States. At first the Department of Justice prepared a legal argument that it had "inherent power" to wiretap in national security cases. On January 24, 1971, Federal District Court Judge Damon Keith rejected the argument of the Justice Department. Keith ordered the government to make a full disclosure to the defendant of all transcripts of tapped conversations. If the government did not wish to make the disclosure, Keith suggested it could drop the case or appeal it to a higher court.

On April 9, 1971, the Sixth Circuit Court of Appeals again rejected the inherent power argument of the Justice Department. The Justice Department appealed the case to the Supreme Court, but has dropped the notion of inherent executive power. The department argues that Title III grants it authority to tap domestic organizations such as the "White Panthers," involved in Plamondon v. United States, without obtaining a judicial warrant. On October 1, 1971, the Supreme Court announced that it would hear arguments on Plamondon, now renamed United States v. U.S. District Court. The article that follows explains the significance of that case and others involving national security. The decision by Justice Powell, handed down on June 19, 1972, follows.

———————————————

Wiretaps and National Security

Alan M. Dershowitz

During its current term, the Supreme Court will be hearing argument on whether warrantless "national security" wiretaps are constitutional. The phrase "national security" conjures up the image of spies, sabotage, and invasion, but a considerable number of such taps are conducted against domestic organizations or individuals who are suspected of activities deemed contrary to the national interest. It was recently learned, for example, that such persons as Martin Luther King and Elijah Muhammad and such organizations as the Jewish Defense League and the Black Panther party have been the subject of extended national security taps. These taps are authorized exclusively by the prosecutorial arm of the government—by the attorney general—without the need for a judicial warrant based on probable cause. How many national security taps and "bugs"[1] are currently in operation, and against what sorts of persons, is a well-guarded secret, but bits of information that are slowly emerging raise some disturbing questions.

The case presenting the issue of the constitutionality of warrantless national security taps involves "Pun" Plamondon, an alleged "White Panther" standing trial for conspiracy to blow up a CIA office in Ann Arbor, Michigan. Plamondon's lawyer, William Kunstler, filed a pretrial motion asking the government to disclose whether any of the defendant's conversations had been monitored. Motions of this kind are made rather routinely these days in so-called political cases, and—not infrequently—they strike paydirt, as Kunstler's motion did. It elicited an

[1] A "bug" is a monitoring device concealed anywhere and capable of picking up conversations as well as other sounds; a wiretap picks up only phone conversations. Some confusion has resulted from the fact that "bugs" are sometimes installed in the mechanism of a telephone. The government is fond of citing statistics purporting to demonstrate that the number of "national security surveillances"—a phrase that includes both bugs and taps—has "significantly declined" over the past few years. These statistics are fallacious for two obvious reasons: (1) they include figures only on the number of warrantless taps, not bugs; and (2) they show a decline around the time the Supreme Court implicitly authorized the use of taps with a warrant. (Prior to that decision, all taps involving national security were warrantless, and were therefore included in the government statistics; now warrants are secured for some of these taps, and only the warrantless ones are listed by the government.)

From *Commentary*, 53 (January 1972), pp. 56–61. Copyright © 1972 by the American Jewish Committee. Reprinted by permission of the author and *Commentary*. Alan M. Dershowitz is Professor of Law at Harvard University.

affidavit from the attorney general himself, acknowledging that "Plamondon has participated in conversations which were overheard by government agents," and that no warrant had been obtained. But Mitchell vigorously asserted that the tap—which was on some unnamed person's phone, not on Plamondon's—was legal, since it was "employed to gather intelligence information deemed necessary to protect the nation from attempts of domestic organizations to attack and subvert the existing structure of the government."

The lower court disagreed. It described the "sweep of the assertion of the presidential power" to tap without a warrant as "both eloquent and breathtaking," but it declined to "suspend an important principle of the Constitution." It held that "in dealing with the threat of domestic subversion," the warrant requirement of the Fourth Amendment could not be dispensed with. (The lower court did not decide whether a warrantless tap could be authorized to protect the country from "attack, espionage or sabotage by foes or agents of a *foreign* power," since the government had conceded that the Plamondon tap was not installed for any such "foreign intelligence" purpose.)[2] The court ordered the government to disclose to Plamondon the transcripts of each of his monitored conversations. If this ruling is upheld, Plamondon could be tried and convicted only if the government can prove that neither the indictment nor any of the trial evidence emanated from the tainted tap.

The issue thus presented for the Supreme Court to resolve is a fundamental one, going to the heart of the "separation of powers" on which our government is based. For the executive branch is asserting the power to dispense with an important judicial "check" on its action, namely the requirement that a judicial officer determine whether there is probable cause on which to issue a warrant. It is somewhat surprising that the Supreme Court has never decided—or even intimated how it would decide—whether national security wiretaps constitute an exception to the warrant requirement, especially since the practice of warrantless national security taps is now more than thirty years old.

---

[2] The American Bar Association Project on Minimum Standards for Criminal Justice "considered and rejected [a proposal] which would have recognized a . . . power in the president not subject to prior judicial review to deal with purely domestic subversive groups." Instead, it recognized a power limited to "foreign intelligence activities." Thus, it is precisely the power rejected by the ABA committee—certainly no radical organization—that the government is asserting in the *Plamondon* case. In its brief before the Supreme Court, the government argues that no real distinction can be drawn between foreign and domestic subversion (though in prior cases it had argued in favor of such a distinction). Moreover, if no distinction can be drawn between foreign and domestic subversion, it would seem to follow that warrants should be required in both cases. Finally, a real distinction can be drawn between foreign intelligence gathering and domestic subversion.

It was on May 21, 1940 that President Franklin Roosevelt sent to his attorney general the confidential memorandum that is regarded as the baptismal certificate of the national security wiretap (though, significantly, the term "national security" was not used).[3] Roosevelt began by expressing his agreement with an early Supreme Court decision that "under ordinary and normal circumstances wiretapping by government agents should not be carried on for the excellent reason that it is almost bound to lead to abuse of civil rights." But these were not ordinary and normal times: America was preparing to enter the war; German and Japanese spy rings were operating on both coasts; and "certain other nations" had been engaged "in preparation for sabotage." Concluding that the Supreme Court had never intended its prohibition on wiretapping to extend "to grave matters involving the defense of the nation," Roosevelt informed the FBI that they were "at liberty to secure information by listening devices direct[ed] to the conversations . . . of persons suspected of subversive activities against the government . . . , including suspected spies."[4] The President cautioned, however, that these investigations must be limited "to a minimum" and "insofar as possible to aliens."

But governments grow comfortable with special war powers, even when peace returns. And so, after the cessation of hostilities, Attorney General Tom Clark convinced President Truman that "the present troubled period in international affairs, accompanied as it is by an increase in subversive activity here at home," required a continuation of the "investigative measures" authorized by Roosevelt. Nor was Clark content merely with retaining the status quo. Warning that "the country is threatened by a very substantial increase in crime"—an exaggeration typically made by attorneys general requesting additional powers or appropriations—he "reluctantly" requested the president to approve the power to tap "in cases vitally affecting the domestic security" (for that high-sounding phrase, read "organized crime") or "where human life is in jeopardy" (for that, read "murder, kidnapping, robbery, arson, burglary, and the sale of narcotics"). With Truman's quick concurrence, the narrow exception virtually became the rule. It was President Johnson who—at the urging of another Clark (this one more sensitive to

---

[3] The baptismal rather than the birth certificate, because it is acknowledged that J. Edgar Hoover was widely engaged in such wiretaps well before obtaining the president's formal authority to do so.

[4] Since the McCarthy era the word "subversive" has taken on an extremely broad meaning. At the time Roosevelt used it in his 1940 memorandum, it still retained its somewhat narrower (thought still imprecise) dictionary meaning: "intended to bring about the overthrow of the government by unlawful means."

civil liberties)[5]—again narrowed the exception. In doing so, he introduced the current phrase "national security" which falls somewhere
between Roosevelt's national "defense" and Truman's "domestic
security."

It is not entirely clear why the government needs a national security
exception to the ordinary rules now governing wiretaps. When the
exception was first created, there was an absolute prohibition against
all wiretapping by federal officials—*with or without a warrant.* (The
rule was not technically framed in terms of a prohibition on tapping,
but rather in terms of a prohibition on all use of such evidence—and
its fruits—in federal criminal prosecutions.) Thus, if national security
wiretaps were to be conducted at all, they would have to be authorized
under an exception to the ordinary rules. In 1967, however, the Supreme
Court said that wiretaps could be conducted—where any kind of
criminal conduct was suspected—provided that the government secured
a warrant based on probable cause and narrowly limited in time and
scope. Under that decision, the FBI may lawfully conduct wiretaps in
national security cases if they secure a warrant. Unwilling to comply
with this requirement, the federal government claims that national
security taps are still an exception to the ordinary rules, even though
the ordinary rules which gave rise to the national security exception
have now been dramatically changed.

The government, arguing in support of this position before the lower
courts, invoked "the inherent power of the president to safeguard the
security of the nation"—the "historical power of the sovereign to
preserve itself." The government was saying, in effect, that there is no
separation of powers—no checks or balances on the executive by the
other branches—when the president decides that the security of the
nation is involved. The president must be trusted to exercise his powers
in a constitutional manner, since "the occupant of that office, like the
members of this Court, takes a solemn oath to protect and defend the
Constitution," and this "carries with it the weightiest presumption that
those powers will not be abused." (The attorney general—to whom the
president has delegated all authority in these matters—also takes such
an oath; but it is not without relevance that the attorney general is the
country's top prosecutor; nor is it immaterial that two of the holders
of this office during the past ten years have also been presidential campaign managers, intensely involved in partisan politics.) If by some
chance these powers were to be abused by the president or his depu-
ties, the argument continues, then the "final significant restraint" lies

---

[5] In fairness to Justice Clark, it should be noted that subsequently he became
quite critical of wiretapping.

not with the courts, but with the "electorate" which "can reflect its dissatisfaction with the exercise of the power."

This argument—which entirely neglects the countermajoritarian purpose of the Bill of Rights and the anticentralist thrust of the Constitution itself—has been rejected by the Supreme Court over and over again. The classic response was formulated in a case growing out of Lincoln's attempt to limit the judicial power during the Civil War:

> This nation, as experience has proved . . . , has no right to expect that it will always have wise and humane rulers, sincerely attached to the Constitution. Wicked men, ambitious of power, with hatred of liberty and contempt of law, may fill the place once occupied by Washington and Lincoln. . . . If our fathers had failed to provide for just such a contingency, they would have been false to the trust reposed in them. They knew—the history of the world had told them—that unlimited power, wherever lodged at such a time, was especially hazardous to freemen.

More recently, the Supreme Court rejected a similar assertion of executive power in the Pentagon Papers case, and it was probably this rejection that led the government to play down the "inherent power" argument in its wiretap brief recently filed in the Supreme Court. Instead, the government is now claiming that warrantless national security taps were authorized by Congress in the Omnibus Crime Control and Safe Streets Act of 1968.

That act actually provides three separate national security exceptions to its otherwise absolute requirement of a warrant before any tap. The first authorizes a forty-eight-hour tap if "an emergency situation exists" with respect to "conspiratorial activities threatening the national security interests," provided that a warrant is immediately sought at the expiration of that period. The government did not act pursuant to that emergency exception in the *Plamondon* case. Nor is it relying on the second exception, which is limited to the prevention of attack by a foreign enemy or the gathering of foreign intelligence information. The "exception" which is being relied on by the government provides as follows: "Nor shall anything contained in this chapter be deemed to limit the constitutional power of the president to take such measures as he deems necessary to protect the United States against the overthrow of the government by force or other unlawful means, or against any other clear and present danger to the structure or existence of the government." That provision, however, begs the critical question: "What precisely is 'the constitutional power of the president' in dealing with domestic threats to the structure and existence of the government?" As the lower court observed, the 1968 act was "clearly designed to place Congress in a completely neutral position in the very controversy with which this case is concerned." Moreover, even if Congress had explicitly

exempted domestic national security wiretaps from the warrant requirement of the Fourth Amendment, the constitutionality of that exemption
would still have to be decided by the Supreme Court.[6]

In passing on that difficult constitutional question, the Supreme Court
might well ponder why the government is so vigorously asserting its
right to dispense with warrants in national security cases. Is it interested merely in preserving its convictions in the few pending cases that
might be reversed if warrantless taps, conducted years ago, were held
unconstitutional? Or does it have a real—and legitimate—need to tap
phones without judicial intervention in this category of cases? There
is little doubt that it could secure a warrant in any case in which there
were a plausible—even a weak—claim that the national security
required a tap. After all, the government may seek its warrant from the
magistrate or judge of its choice. In the unlikely event that it were to
fail on the first (or even the second) attempt, it could continue until
it succeeded.[7]

The government explains its unwillingness to comply with the warrant
requirement by suggesting that compliance would pose problems of
security, presumably because an indiscreet or corruptible judge or court
employee might betray the tap or disclose the identity of a secret informant whose information was used in the warrant application. But the
government's wide discretion in selecting the judge before whom it
will make the application diminishes the force of this argument. Surely
there are some judges whose patriotism and discretion are beyond
question in the view of the government. In an extremely delicate case,
for example, the government could present its application to the chief
justice without even the clerk being made privy to its contents. Moreover, under existing law, the government need not disclose the name
of its informant—even to the judge in secret—in order to secure a
warrant. Finally, the government concedes that in the event of a prosecution against anyone whose conversation was overheard, it must dis-

---

[6] The Fourth Amendment does not unambiguously require a warrant for all
searches. It provides for the right to be secure "against unreasonable searches,"
and it also specifies that "no warrant shall issue, but upon probable cause. . . ."
The court, however, has interpreted the amendment to require a warrant for all
searches, except in a narrow class of emergencies—for example, where there
is imminent danger that the evidence will be destroyed. In such cases, the
search must be justified, after the fact, as "reasonable" if its fruits are to be
employed. But the government has taken the position that the usual standard
of reasonableness is inapplicable to a national-security wiretap, even in an after-
the-fact judicial evaluation. It argues that "great deference must be given to
the attorney general's judgment" and that the range of review is "extremely
limited."

[7] Of the 217 wiretap-warrant applications during the last two years, only one was
denied.

close the entire record of the tap to a judge in a secret proceeding (as it did in the *Plamondon* case). Now, if the government is willing to trust the discretion of a judge (selected at random) not to disclose the contents of a tap after it has occurred, why is it not willing to trust the discretion of a judge (chosen by the government) not to reveal the existence of a tap before it has occurred? The "indiscreet judge" argument, though vigorously pressed by the government, is obviously a makeweight.

There is a weightier argument against requiring a warrant in national security cases, but the government has been reluctant to articulate it. A warrant, after all, must be based on probable cause that a crime has been, is being, or is about to be committed. The government would like to be free, however, to conduct certain wiretaps even when probable cause is lacking. For example, the Soviet ambassador engages in no crime when he discusses his country's negotiating position on the Mideast or the SALT talks, but our government would like to—and surely will try to—monitor such conversations (as the Soviet government just as surely tries to monitor similar conversations by our diplomats). If a warrant, based on ordinary probable cause, were required, the monitoring of this kind of conversation would become legally impossible.[8]

But this argument, which has considerable force in the context of foreign intelligence wiretapping, is wholly inapplicable to the kind of tapping at issue in the case now before the Supreme Court. For the tap in the *Plamondon* case was not installed for purposes of gathering foreign intelligence; it was installed, in the words of the government, "to protect the national security against the threat posed by individuals and groups within the United States." Put most generously to the government, this means that the tap was directed against American citizens and organizations suspected of engaging in and planning bombings, riots, and other violent activities. All such activities are, of course, illegal, and anyone who is planning them—or even talking about planning them—is, under present government thinking, guilty of conspiracy (witness the Berrigan indictment). Surely, in any such case there would be little difficulty in obtaining a warrant. Yet the government insists that it must—and that it will—continue to tap phones without securing the judicial approval that it could so readily get in any plausible case.

If it is true that warrants in national security cases would be so easy to obtain, then another question—really the converse of the question

[8] A warrant requirement would not necessarily prevent the continuation of all warrantless taps. It would merely prevent prosecution in the small number of cases where a defendant's conversations were overheard. Recently, however, an affirmative suit was filed on behalf of the Jewish Defense League seeking monetary damages for the warrantless tapping of their telephones.

previously posed—is suggested: Why do civil libertarians press so hard for what appears to be the hollow protection of a warrant secured from a government-selected magistrate? Or to put it another way, why is the warrant issue viewed as so crucial by both sides?

To understand why civil libertarians feel the way they do about warrants in national security cases requires a bit of background on the way they view wiretaps in general. To begin with, a great many civil libertarians oppose all wiretapping, even when authorized by warrant. They single out that technique of law enforcement because of its tendency to be indiscriminately overinclusive. As Ramsey Clark has put it: "No technique of law enforcement casts a wider net than electronic surveillance. Blind, it catches everything in the sea of sound but cannot discriminate between fish and fowl." Of course, no technique of law enforcement casts a perfectly narrow net. We do, after all, convict some innocent people; we shoot some fleeing "felons" who turn out to be guiltless bystanders; we preventively detain some defendants who are ultimately acquitted. But we do insist, as we should, that these deprivations be imposed mostly on people who are guilty, and only rarely on those who are innocent.

Wiretapping is different. It is a deprivation that falls mostly on the innocent. The ratio of "innocent" monitored conversations to "guilty" monitored conversations is extremely high, especially in national security cases. This is so for a number of reasons. National security taps are often installed on the phones of persons who are conceded to be innocent of any wrongdoing. And even taps installed on the phones of persons who are themselves guilty succeed in picking up the conversations of many innocent callers and recipients of calls. Finally, most of the monitored conversations, even between two guilty persons, involve matters unrelated to any wrongdoing. Moreover, because wiretapping is a clandestine "deprivation," its precise effects are difficult to assess. The behavior of some persons whose conversations are not, in fact, being monitored is significantly affected by the *fear* that their phones are tapped (witness the "debugging" operations recently conducted by various senators and congressmen), while others, whose phones are being tapped, but who do not—and never will—know that their conversations were monitored, are entirely unaffected. Yet despite the pervasiveness of the wiretap, and its obvious chilling effect, the government blandly asserts in its brief that "[t]he overhearing of a telephone conversation involves a lesser invasion of privacy than a physical search of a man's home or his person." (This assertion sharply raises the question of whether an administration that values the privacy of conversation and thought less than the privacy of property is the appropriate authority to decide, without any judicial check, that a phone must be tapped for national security purposes.)

Making national security taps conditional on a warrant, some civil libertarians argue, would reduce the ratio of innocent to guilty conversations overheard because warrants must be narrowly circumscribed, limited in time and scope, and related to criminal conduct. While recognizing that most magistrates issue wiretap warrants as if they were presents at Christmastime, the civil libertarians contend that there might be some reluctance to issue them in instances where it was plain that the primary motivation was political and that the national security concern was a pretext. For it is widely assumed by civil libertarians today that a considerable number of domestic national security wiretaps are conducted primarily for reasons unrelated to genuine national security concerns. They are thought to be directed against political dissidents—both inside and outside the government—and general troublemakers who could be adequately, and lawfully, dealt with by the ordinary process of the criminal law. This is not to say that a plausible national security concern—broadly defined—is lacking in each instance of a tap. It is to say that this concern frequently serves as an *excuse* for a broad surveillance whose primary purpose is either political or conventional law enforcement.

Whether or not the civil libertarians are correct in their assessment of the value of warrants in curbing abuse, their claim that domestic national security wiretaps have been authorized in highly questionable cases is supported by the evidence currently available. Consider, for example, the tapping of Martin Luther King's telephone (and the electronic "bugging" of his hotel rooms). These warrantless invasions of King's privacy—and the privacy of countless others who conversed with him—have been defended as necessary for the national security. But in what specific sense did the security of this nation depend on the FBI's overhearing King's telephone conversations and eavesdropping on his hotel room activities? A number of justifications have been offered by those close to Robert Kennedy, who, as attorney general, acceded to J. Edgar Hoover's request to authorize the tap. (No authorization was ever given for the bug in the hotel rooms.)

The Kennedy version goes something like this: two of King's close associates—one a New York lawyer, the other a member of the SCLC staff—were thought to be either Communist agents, party members, or sympathizers. After receiving warnings from the Justice Department that associating with these persons might damage the civil rights movement, King dismissed the tainted staff member and initially severed his relationship with the suspected lawyer. But after a while, contact with the lawyer was gradually reestablished. It was this that led Kennedy to authorize Hoover to tap King's home phones and those in his Atlanta and New York offices.

Burke Marshall—Kennedy's respected and civil-liberties-minded assistant attorney general—has made the shocking statement that his boss may have "refused too long" to authorize the King national security tap. "I can't tell you who the man was or what the allegations were," he says, "but I can tell you I think it would not be responsible for an attorney general—in view of the characterizations of what that man was doing and who he was working for—for the attorney general to refuse a tap." He continues, suggestively but mysteriously: "If you take it as being true that there has been an espionage system and that the Bureau has an obligation to do things about that—if you put that all together, I would say you could say he refused too long."

Very well, then, let us "take" all that as "being true." Let us assume the very worst: that the New York lawyer was a real Russian spy, working for, and being paid by, the KGB. Assume further that his sole job was to influence King in directions favored by the Soviet Union. Assume even further that he was succeeding. Would this justify a national security tap on King's phone? There is surely no claim that King was being used to further espionage or sabotage activities. He was, after all, engaged primarily in entirely lawful and constitutionally protected activity (even if that activity could hypothetically be shown to have favored the interests of the Soviet Union). He made and received thousands of calls to and from concerned, patriotic, and law-abiding American citizens about matters that were none of the government's business to overhear. He also engaged in—or erroneously believed he was engaged in—a private life, which also was none of the government's business to monitor. His telephone contact with the New York lawyer was an extremely small and sporadic part of his activities (and there is no evidence that he met with *him* in the bugged hotel rooms). Yet the wiretap picked up and recorded *all* of the conversations on these phones. Even if the scenario suggested by the Marshall version is accurate, would it not have been more sensible to tap the New York lawyer's phones? (Indeed, since it is technically feasible to monitor and record only calls placed between two specified numbers, it would have been possible to tap and record only those calls placed between King and the suspected lawyer.)

It is significant that a former public official as respected and dedicated as Burke Marshall would argue that it would "not be responsible" for an attorney general to have declined, or even delayed, authorization for a warrantless national security wiretap on the basis of the evidence that he suggests existed. We only rarely have men in positions of power as sensitive and as committed to civil liberties as Marshall. If this is what we can expect of a Burke Marshall, what can we expect of the men who generally populate high office?

Another justification offered by some Kennedy intimates is that the tap was authorized, as former attorney general Katzenbach put it, "for the protection of Dr. King." Giving the FBI the power to protect King is like giving the cat the power to protect the canary. In fact, it is now widely acknowledged that no sooner did J. Edgar Hoover come up with some damaging information about King—relating to his sex life—than he leaked it to the press. Was this also done to protect King?

It is not difficult to understand what really motivated the King wiretap. The existence of the lawyer in New York provided a plausible—that is perhaps too strong a word—argument that some vague national security interest was involved. The FBI seized upon this excuse to request authorization to do what they wanted to do for other—completely illegitimate—reasons. It was difficult for the Justice Department to deny the request: what would it look like later on if it did turn out that King was indeed involved with Communists and if Hoover leaked to his congressional or newspaper cronies the fact that Kennedy had stood in the way of an investigation which would have disclosed this? So Kennedy took the least politically risky course. And J. Edgar Hoover got his wiretap.

The King episode does not stand alone in suggesting that the primary reason certain domestic national security taps are employed has little to do with the genuine needs of national security. The recent case involving Muhammad Ali, which revealed the previously unacknowledged King tap, also disclosed that pervasive taps had been authorized on the phones of Elijah Muhammad, the leader of the Black Muslim Church. Here, too, I would speculate that there may have been a plausible national security interest in a limited aspect of Elijah Muhammad's activity. But the warrantless tap was not limited, as one with a warrant would have to be. It extended to every call to and from Elijah Muhammad's various offices over a considerable period of time. And it picked up conversations relating to political and personal activities that were none of the government's legitimate business (for example, a disclosure that a well-known person's brother had been kicked out of the Muslim Church for being out with a girl all night).

The phrase "domestic national security wiretap" is not self-limiting or self-defining. It means what its history tells us it means. It means what this and previous administrations have defined it to mean. Only if we are given some idea of how it has been used can the people, and the courts, have any intelligent basis for judging whether the alleged need for a domestic national security exception outweighs its potential for abuse. On the basis of the evidence presently available, I would suggest that if we were to examine all the domestic national security wiretaps conducted by the FBI, a disturbing picture would emerge. We would find numerous cases where a plausible but narrow national security concern has been used as an excuse for an improper and pervasive wiretap whose real purpose is political surveillance. Unfortunately, however, there is no way for the citizenry—or even the courts—to examine the logs of all national security wiretaps. We are left instead with the assurances of people like former Attorney General Herbert Brownell that "Experience demonstrates that the Federal Bureau of Investigation has never abused the wiretap authority."

But what "experience" is Brownell referring to? To whom has this been "demonstrated"? Certainly not to the public. I, for one, do not feel that we can rely on the self-interested assurances of former Justice Department officials that all is in order. My surmise is that if the Justice Department were to turn over the records of domestic national security wiretaps in any given year for study to a nonpartisan group of scholars, many abuses of the kind suggested above would emerge. If I am wrong—if an impartial evaluation were to disclose that warrantless domestic national security taps have been narrowly employed only in cases of immediate, extreme, and irremediable danger to our survival—then there might be grounds for exempting this class of wiretaps from the usual constitutional requirements. But neither the people nor the courts can intelligently decide whether this is so until we are given some idea of how such wiretaps have in fact been used. In the meantime, on the basis of what we already know, we have good reason for supposing that "national security" is sometimes invoked as a pretext for political surveillance of an altogether illegitimate kind.

United States v. United States District Court

Mr. Justice Powell delivered the opinion of the Court.

The issue before us is an important one for the people of our country and their government. It involves the delicate question of the president's power, acting through the attorney general, to authorize elec-

From *United States* v. *United States District Court,* 32 Lawyers' Edition, 2nd, 752.

tronic surveillance in internal security matters without prior judicial approval. Successive presidents for more than one-quarter of a century have authorized such surveillance in varying degrees, without guidance from the Congress or a definitive decision of this Court. This case brings the issue here for the first time. Its resolution is a matter of national concern, requiring sensitivity both to the government's right to protect itself from unlawful subversion and attack and to the citizen's right to be secure in his privacy against unreasonable government intrusion.

This case arises from a criminal proceeding in the United States District Court for the Eastern District of Michigan, in which the United States charged three defendants with conspiracy to destroy government property in violation of 18 USC § 371. One of the defendants, Plamondon, was charged with the dynamite bombing of an office of the Central Intelligence Agency in Ann Arbor, Michigan.

During pretrial proceedings, the defendants moved to compel the United States to disclose certain electronic surveillance information and to conduct a hearing to determine whether this information "tainted" the evidence on which the indictment was based or which the Government intended to offer at trial. In response, the Government filed an affidavit of the attorney general, acknowledging that its agents had overheard conversations in which Plamondon had participated. The affidavit also stated that the attorney general approved the wiretaps "to gather intelligence information deemed necessary to protect the nation from attempts of domestic organizations to attack and subvert the existing structure of the Government."[1] The affidavit, together with

---

[1] The Attorney General's affidavit reads as follows:
"John N. Mitchell being duly sworn deposes and says:
"1. I am the Attorney General of the United States.
"2. This affidavit is submitted in connection with the Government's opposition to the disclosure to the defendant Plamondon of information concerning the overhearing of his conversations which occurred during the course of electronic surveillances which the Government contends were legal.
"3. The defendant Plamondon has participated in conversations which were overheard by Government agents who were monitoring wiretaps which were being employed to gather intelligence information deemed necessary to protect the nation from attempts of domestic organizations to attack and subvert the existing structure of the Government. The records of the Department reflect the installation of these wiretaps had been expressly approved by the Attorney General.
"4. Submitted with this affidavit is a sealed exhibit containing the records of the intercepted conversations, a description of the premises that were the subjects of the surveillances, and copies of the memoranda reflecting the Attorney General's express approval of the installation of the surveillances.
"5. I certify that it would prejudice the national interest to disclose the particular facts concerning these surveillances other than to the court in camera. Accordingly, the sealed exhibit referred to herein is being submitted solely for the court's in camera inspection and a copy of the sealed

the logs of the surveillance, were filed in a sealed exhibit for in camera inspection by the District Court.

On the basis of the attorney general's affidavit and the sealed exhibit, the government asserted that the surveillances were lawful, though conducted without prior judicial approval, as a reasonable exercise of the president's power (exercised through the attorney general) to protect the national security. The District Court held that the surveillance violated the Fourth Amendment, and ordered the government to make full disclosure to Plamondon of his overheard conversations.

The government then filed in the Court of Appeals for the Sixth Circuit a petition for a writ of mandamus to set aside the District Court order, which was stayed pending final disposition of the case. After concluding that it had jurisdiction, that court held that the surveillances were unlawful and that the District Court had properly required disclosure of the overheard conversations, 444 F2d 651 (1971)....

I

Title III of the Omnibus Crime Control and Safe Streets Act, 18 USC §§ 2510–2520, authorizes the use of electronic surveillance for classes of crimes carefully specified in 18 USC § 2516. Such surveillance is subject to prior court order. Section 2518 sets forth the detailed and particularized application necessary to obtain such an order as well as carefully circumscribed conditions for its use. The act represents a comprehensive attempt by Congress to promote more effective control of crime while protecting the privacy of individual thought and expression. Much of Title III was drawn to meet the constitutional requirements for electronic surveillance enunciated by this Court on *Berger* v. *New York*, 388 US 41, ... (1967), and *Katz* v. *United States*, 389 US 347, ... (1967).

Together with the elaborate surveillance requirements in Title III, there is the following proviso, 18 USC § 2511(3):

Nothing contained in this chapter or in section 605 of the Communications Act of 1934 (48 Stat 1103; 47 USC § 605) shall limit the constitutional power of the President to take such measures as he deems necessary to protect the Nation against actual or potential attack or other hostile acts of a foreign power, to obtain foreign intelligence information deemed essential

---

exhibit is not being furnished to the defendants. I would request the court, at the conclusion of its hearing on this matter, to place the sealed exhibit in a sealed envelope and return it to the Department of Justice where it will be retained under seal so that it may be submitted to any appellate court that may review this matter."

to the security of the United States, or to protect national security information against foreign intelligence activities. *Nor shall anything contained in
this chapter be deemed to limit the constitutional power of the President to
take such measures as he deems necessary to protect the United States
against the overthrow of the government by force or other unlawful means,
or against any other clear and present danger to the structure or existence
of the Government.* The contents of any wire or oral communication intercepted by authority of the President in the exercise of the foregoing powers
may be received in evidence in any trial, hearing or other proceeding only
where such interception was reasonable, and shall not be otherwise used or
disclosed except as is necessary to implement that power. [Emphasis
supplied.]

The government relies on § 2511(3). It argues that "in excepting
national security surveillances from the act's warrant requirement
Congress recognized the president's authority to conduct such surveillances without prior judicial approval." Government Brief, pp. 7, 28.
The section thus is viewed as a recognition or affirmance of a constitutional authority in the president to conduct warrantless domestic
security surveillance such as that involved in this case.

We think the language of § 2511(3), as well as the legislative history of the statute, refutes this interpretation. The relevant language
is that:

Nothing contained in this chapter . . . shall limit the constitutional power
of the President to take such measures as he deems necessary to protect . . .

against the dangers specified. At most, this is an implicit recognition
that the President does have certain powers in the specified areas. Few
would doubt this, as the section refers—among other things—to protection "against actual or potential attack or other hostile acts of a foreign
power." But so far as the use of the president's electronic surveillance
power is concerned, the language is essentially neutral.

Section 2511(3) certainly confers no power, as the language is
wholly inappropriate for such a purpose. It merely provides that the
act shall not be interpreted to limit or disturb such power as the
president may have under the Constitution. In short, Congress simply
left presidential powers where it found them. This view is reinforced
by the general context of Title III. Section 2511(1) broadly prohibits the
use of electronic surveillance "except as otherwise specifically provided in this chapter." Subsection (2) thereof contains four specific
exceptions. In each of the specified exceptions, the statutory language
is as follows:

"It shall not be unlawful . . . to intercept" the particular type of communication described.

The language of subsection (3), here involved, is to be contrasted with the language of the exceptions set forth in the preceding subsection. Rather than stating that warrantless presidential uses of electronic surveillance "shall not be unlawful" and thus employing the standard language of exception, subsection (3) merely disclaims "any intention to limit the constitutional power of the President."

The express grant of authority to conduct surveillances is found in § 2516, which authorizes the attorney general to make application to a federal judge when surveillance may provide evidence of certain offenses. These offenses are described with meticulous care and specificity.

Where the act authorizes surveillance, the procedure to be followed is specified in § 2518. Subsection (1) thereof requires application to a judge of competent jurisdiction for a prior order of approval, and states in detail the information required in such application. Subsection (3) prescribes the necessary elements of probable cause which the judge must find before issuing an order authorizing an interception. Subsection (4) sets forth the required contents of such an order. Subsection (5) sets strict time limits on an order. Provision is made in subsection (7) for "an emergency situation" found to exist by the attorney general (or by the principal prosecuting attorney of a state) "with respect to conspiratorial activities threatening the national security interest." In such a situation, emergency surveillance may be conducted "if an application for an order approving the interception is made . . . within forty-eight hours." If such an order is not obtained, or the application thereof is denied, the interception is deemed to be a violation of the act.

In view of these and other interrelated provisions delineating permissible interceptions of particular criminal activity upon carefully specified conditions, it would have been incongruous for Congress to have legislated with respect to the important and complex area of national security in a single brief and nebulous paragraph. This would not comport with the sensitivity of the problem involved or with the extraordinary care Congress exercised in drafting other sections of the act. We therefore think the conclusion inescapable that Congress only intended to make clear that the act simply did not legislate with respect to national security surveillances.

The legislative history of § 2511(3) supports this interpretation. Most relevant is the colloquy between Senators Hart, Holland, and McClellan on the Senate floor:

"Mr. Holland. . . . The section [2511(3)] from which the Senator [Hart] has read does not affirmatively give any power. . . . *We are not affirmatively conferring any power upon the President.* We are simply saying that nothing herein shall limit such power as the President has under the Constitution. We certainly do not grant him a thing.

"There is nothing affirmative in this statement.

"Mr. McClellan. Mr. President, *we make it understood that we are not trying to take anything away from him.*

"Mr. Holland. The Senator is correct.

"Mr. Hart. Mr. President, there is no intention here to expand by this language a constitutional power. Clearly we could not do so.

"Mr. McClellan. Even though we intended, we could not do so.

"Mr. Hart. . . . However, we are agreed that this language should not be regarded as intending to grant any authority, including authority to put a bug on, that the President does not have now.

"In addition, Mr. President, *as I think our exchange makes clear, nothing in Section 2511(3) even attempts to define the limits of the President's national security power under present law, which I have always found extremely vague. . . . Section 2511(3) merely says that if the President has such a power, then its exercise is in no way affected by title III.*" (Emphasis supplied.)

One could hardly expect a clearer expression of congressional neutrality. The debate above explicitly indicates that nothing in § 2511(3) was intended to *expand* or to *contract* or to *define* whatever presidential surveillance powers existed in matters affecting the national security. If we could accept the government's characterization of § 2511(3) as a congressionally prescribed exception to the general requirement of a warrant, it would be necessary to consider the question of whether the surveillance in this case came within the exception and, if so, whether the statutory exception was itself constitutionally valid. But viewing § 2511(3) as a congressional disclaimer and expression of neutrality, we hold that the statute is not the measure of the executive authority asserted in this case. Rather, we must look to the constitutional powers of the president.

II

It is important at the outset to emphasize the limited nature of the question before the Court. This case raises no constitutional challenge to electronic surveillance as specifically authorized by Title III of the Omnibus Crime Control and Safe Streets Act of 1968. Nor is there any question or doubt as to the necessity of obtaining a warrant in the surveillance of crimes unrelated to the national security interest. . . . Further, the instant case requires no judgment on the scope of the president's surveillance power with respect to the activities of foreign powers, within or without his country. The attorney general's affidavit in this case states that the surveillances were "deemed necessary to protect the nation from attempts of *domestic organizations* to attack and subvert the existing structure of Government" (emphasis supplied). There is no evidence of any involvement, directly or indirectly, of a foreign power.

Our present inquiry, though important, is therefore a narrow one. . . .

"Whether safeguards other than prior authorization by a magistrate would satisfy the Fourth Amendment in a situation involving the national security. . . ."

The determination of this question requires the essential Fourth Amendment inquiry into the "reasonableness" of the search and seizure in question, and the way in which that "reasonableness" derives content and meaning through reference to the warrant clause. . . .

We begin the inquiry by noting that the president of the United States has the fundamental duty, under Art II, § 1, of the Constitution, "to preserve, protect, and defend the Constitution of the United States." Implicit in that duty is the power to protect our government against those who would subvert or overthrow it by unlawful means. In the discharge of this duty, the president—through the attorney general—may find it necessary to employ electronic surveillance to obtain intelligence information on the plans of those who plot unlawful acts against the government. The use of such surveillance in internal security cases has been sanctioned more or less continuously by various presidents and attorneys general since July 1946. Herbert Brownell, Attorney General under President Eisenhower, urged the use of electronic surveillance both in internal and international security matters on the grounds that those acting against the government "turn to the telephone to carry on their intrigue. The success of their plans frequently rests upon piecing together shreds of information received from many sources and many nests. The participants in the conspiracy are often dispersed and stationed in various strategic positions in government and industry throughout the country."

Though the government and respondents debate their seriousness and magnitude, threats and acts of sabotage against the government exist in sufficient number to justify investigative powers with respect to them. The covertness and complexity of potential unlawful conduct against the government and the necessary dependency of many conspirators upon the telephone make electronic surveillance an effective investigatory instrument in certain circumstances. The marked acceleration in technological developments and sophistication in their use have resulted in new techniques for the planning, commission and concealment of criminal activities. It would be contrary to the public interest for government to deny to itself the prudent and lawful employment of those very techniques which are employed against the Government and its law abiding citizens.

. . .

There is, understandably, a deep-seated uneasiness and apprehension that this capability will be used to intrude upon cherished privacy of law-abiding citizens. We look to the Bill of Rights to safeguard this privacy. Though physical entry of the home is the chief evil against which the wording of the Fourth Amendment is directed, its broader spirit now shields private speech from unreasonable surveillance. . . . Our decision in *Katz* refused to lock the Fourth Amendment into instances of actual physical trespass. Rather, the Amendment governs "not only the seizure of tangible items, but extends as well to the recording of oral statements 'without any technical trespass under . . . local property law.' " That decision implicitly recognized that the broad and unsuspected governmental incursions into conversational privacy which electronic surveillance entails necessitate the application of Fourth Amendment safeguards.

National security cases, moreover, often reflect a convergence of First and Fourth Amendment values not present in cases of "ordinary" crime. Though the investigative duty of the executive may be stronger in such cases, so also is there greater jeopardy to constitutionally protected speech. . . . History abundantly documents the tendency of government—however benevolent and benign its motives—to view with suspicion those who most fervently dispute its policies. Fourth Amendment protections become the more necessary when the targets of official surveillance may be those suspected of unorthodoxy in their political beliefs. The danger to political dissent is acute where the government attempts to act under so vague a concept as the power to protect "domestic security." Given the difficulty of defining the domestic security interest, the danger of abuse in acting to protect that interest becomes apparent. Senator Hart addressed this dilemma in the floor debate on § 2511 (3):

> As I read it—and this is my fear—we are saying that the President, on his motion, could declare—name your favorite poison—draft dodgers, Black Muslims, the Ku Klux Klan, or civil rights activists to be a clear and present danger to the structure or existence of the Government.

The price of lawful public dissent must not be a dread of subjection to an unchecked surveillance power. Nor must the fear of unauthorized official eavesdropping deter vigorous citizen dissent and discussion of

Government action in private conversation. For private dissent, no less than open public discourse, is essential to our free society.

III

As the Fourth Amendment is not absolute in its terms, our task is to examine and balance the basic values at stake in this case: the duty of government to protect the domestic security, and the potential danger posed by unreasonable surveillance to individual privacy and free expression. If the legitimate need of government to safeguard domestic security requires the use of electronic surveillance, the question is whether the needs of citizens for privacy and free expression may not be better protected by requiring a warrant before such surveillance is undertaken. We must also ask whether a warrant requirement would unduly frustrate the efforts of Government to protect itself from acts of subversion and overthrow directed against it.

Though the Fourth Amendment speaks broadly of "unreasonable searches and seizures," the definition of "reasonableness" turns, at least in part, on the more specific commands of the warrant clause. Some have argued that "the relevant test is not whether it was reasonable to procure a search warrant, but whether the search was reasonable," *United States* v. *Rabinowitz,* 339 US 56 (1950). This view, however, overlooks the second clause of the Amendment. The warrant clause of the Fourth Amendment is not dead language. Rather it has been "a valued part of our constitutional law for decades, and it has determined the result in scores and scores of cases in the courts all over this country. It is not an inconvenience to be somehow 'weighed' against the claims of police efficiency. It is, or should be, an important working part of our machinery of government, operating as a matter of course to check the 'well-intentioned but mistakenly overzealous executive officers' who are a part of any system of law enforcement." . . .

Over two centuries ago, Lord Mansfield held that common law principles prohibited warrants that ordered the arrest of unnamed individuals whom the *officer* might conclude were guilty of seditious libel. "It is not fit," said Mansfield, "that the receiving or judging of the information ought to be left to the discretion of the officer. The magistrate ought to judge; and should give certain directions to the officer." *Leach* v. *Three of the King's Messengers,* (1765).

Lord Mansfield's formulation touches the very heart of the Fourth Amendment directive: that where practical, a governmental search and seizure should represent both the efforts of the officer to gather evidence of wrongful acts and the judgment of the magistrate that the collected evidence is sufficient to justify invasion of a citizen's private premises or conversation. Inherent in the concept of a warrant is its issuance by a "neutral and detached magistrate." . . . The further requirement of "probable cause" instructs the magistrate that baseless searches shall not proceed.

These Fourth Amendment freedoms cannot properly be guaranteed if domestic security surveillances may be conducted solely within the discretion of the executive branch. The Fourth Amendment does not contemplate the executive officers of Government as neutral and disinterested magistrates. Their duty and responsibility is to enforce the laws, to investigate and to prosecute. . . . But those charged with this investigative and prosecutorial duty should not be the sole judges of when to utilize constitutionally sensitive means in pursuing their tasks. The historical judgment, which the Fourth Amendment accepts, is that unreviewed executive discretion may yield too readily to pressures to obtain incriminating evidence and overlook potential invasions of privacy and protected speech.

It may well be that, in the instant case, the government's surveillance of Plamondon's conversations was a reasonable one which readily would have gained prior judicial approval. But this Court "has never sustained a search upon the sole ground that officers reasonably expected to find evidence of a particular crime and voluntarily confined their activities to the least intrusive means consistent with that end." . . . The Fourth Amendment contemplates a prior judicial judgment, not the risk that executive discretion may be reasonably exercised. This judicial role accords with our basic constitutional doctrine that individual freedoms will best be preserved through a separation of powers and division of functions among the different branches and levels of government. . . . The independent check upon executive discretion is not satisfied, as the government argues, by "extremely limited" post-surveillance judicial review. Indeed, post-surveillance review would never reach the surveillances which failed to result in prosecutions. Prior review by a neutral and detached magistrate is the time tested means of effectuating Fourth Amendment rights.

. . .

The government argues that the special circumstances applicable to domestic security surveillances necessitate a further exception to the warrant requirement. It is urged that the requirement of prior judicial review would obstruct the president in the discharge of his constitutional duty to protect domestic security. We are told further that these surveillances are directed primarily to the collecting and maintaining of intelligence with respect to subversive forces, and are not an attempt to gather evidence for specific criminal prosecutions. It is said that this type of surveillance should not be subject to traditional warrant require-ments which were established to govern investigation of criminal activity, not on-going intelligence gathering. Government Brief, pp. 15–16, 23–24. Government Reply Brief, pp. 2–3.

The government further insists that courts "as a practical matter would have neither the knowledge nor the techniques necessary to determine whether there was probable cause to believe that surveil-lance was necessary to protect national security." These security prob-lems, the government contends, involve "a large number of complex and subtle factors" beyond the competence of courts to evaluate. Gov-ernment Reply Brief, p. 4.

As a final reason for exemption from a warrant requirement, the Government believes that disclosure to a magistrate of all or even a significant portion of the information involved in domestic security surveillances "would create serious potential dangers to the national security and to the lives of informants and agents. . . . Secrecy is the essential ingredient in intelligence gathering; requiring prior judicial authorization would create a greater 'danger of leaks . . . , because in addition to the judge, you have the clerk, the stenographer and some other official like a law assistant or bailiff who may be apprised of the nature' of the surveillance." Government Brief, pp. 24–25.

These contentions in behalf of a complete exemption from the warrant requirement, when urged on behalf of the President and the national security in its domestic implications, merit the most careful considera-tion. We certainly do not reject them lightly, especially at a time of worldwide ferment and when civil disorders in this country are more prevalent than in the less turbulent periods of our history. There is, no doubt, pragmatic force to the government's position.

But we do not think a case has been made for the requested depar-ture from Fourth Amendment standards. The circumstances described do not justify complete exemption of domestic security surveillance from prior judicial scrutiny. Official surveillance, whether its purpose be criminal investigation or on-going intelligence gathering, risks in-fringement of constitutionally protected privacy of speech. Security surveillances are especially sensitive because of the inherent vague-ness of the domestic security concept, the necessarily broad and con-tinuing nature of intelligence gathering, and the temptation to utilize such surveillances to oversee political dissent. We recognize, as we have before, the constitutional basis of the president's domestic secu-rity role, but we think it must be exercised in a manner compatible with the Fourth Amendment. In this case we hold that this requires an appropriate prior warrant procedure.

We cannot accept the government's argument that internal security matters are too subtle and complex for judicial evaluation. Courts regularly deal with the most difficult issues of our society. There is no reason to believe that federal judges will be insensitive to or uncomprehending of the issues involved in domestic security cases. Certainly courts can recognize that domestic security surveillance involves different considerations from the surveillance of ordinary crime. If the threat is too subtle or complex for our senior law enforcement officers to convey its significance to a court, one may question whether there is probable cause for surveillance.

Nor do we believe prior judicial approval will fracture the secrecy essential to official intelligence gathering. The investigation of criminal activity has long involved imparting sensitive information to judicial officers who have respected the confidentialities involved. Judges may be counted upon to be especially conscious of security requirements in national security cases. Title III of the Omnibus Crime Control and Safe Streets Act already has imposed this responsibility on the judiciary in connection with such crimes as espionage, sabotage and treason, § 2516(1)(a)(c), each of which may involve domestic as well as foreign security threats. Moreover, a warrant application involves no public or adversary proceedings: it is an ex parte request before a magistrate or judge. Whatever security dangers clerical and secretarial personnel may pose can be minimized by proper administrative measures, possibly to the point of allowing the Government itself to provide the necessary clerical assistance.

Thus, we conclude that the government's concerns do not justify departure in this case from the customary Fourth Amendment requirement of judicial approval prior to initiation of a search or surveillance. Although some added burden will be imposed upon the attorney general, this inconvenience is justified in a free society to protect constitutional values. Nor do we think the government's domestic surveillance powers will be impaired to any significant degree. A prior warrant establishes presumptive validity of the surveillance and will minimize the burden of justification in post-surveillance judicial review. By no means of least importance will be the reassurance of the public generally that indiscriminate wiretapping and bugging of law-abiding citizens cannot occur.

IV

We emphasize, before concluding this opinion, the scope of our decision. As stated at the outset, this case involves only the domestic aspects of national security. We have not addressed, and express no opinion as to, the issues which may be involved with respect to activities of foreign powers or their agents. . . .

Moreover, we do not hold that the same type of standards and procedures prescribed by Title III are necessarily applicable to this case. We recognize that domestic security surveillance may involve different policy and practical considerations from the surveillance of "ordinary crime." The gathering of security intelligence is often long range and involves the interrelation of various sources and types of information. The exact targets of such surveillance may be more difficult to identify than in surveillance operations against many types of crime specified in Title III. Often, too, the emphasis of domestic intelligence gathering is on the prevention of unlawful activity or the enhancement of the Government's preparedness for some possible future crisis or emergency. Thus, the focus of domestic surveillance may be less precise than that directed against more conventional types of crime.

Given these potential distinctions between Title III criminal surveillances and those involving the domestic security, Congress may wish to consider protective standards for the latter which differ from those already prescribed for specified crimes in Title III. Different standards may be compatible with the Fourth Amendment if they are reasonable both in relation to the legitimate need of government for intelligence information and the protected rights of our citizens. For the warrant application may vary according to the governmental interest to be enforced and the nature of citizen rights deserving protection.

. . .

It may be that Congress, for example, would judge that the application and affidavit showing probable cause need not follow the exact requirements of § 2518 but should allege other circumstances more appropriate to domestic security cases; that the request for prior court authorization could, in sensitive cases, be made to any member of a specially designated court (e.g., the District Court or Court of Appeals for the District of Columbia); and that the time and reporting requirements need not be so strict as those in § 2518.

The above paragraph does not, of course, attempt to guide the congressional judgment but rather to delineate the present scope of our own opinion. We do not attempt to detail the precise standards for domestic security warrants any more than our decision in *Katz* sought to set the refined requirements for the specified criminal surveillances which now constitute Title III. We do hold, however, that prior judicial approval is required for the type of domestic security surveillance involved in this case and that such approval may be made in accordance with such reasonable standards as the Congress may prescribe.

. . .

The judgment of the Court of Appeals is hereby affirmed.

RESEARCH GUIDE

Important governmental actions are reported in serial sources, arranged by subject matter and indexed for reference. The law school or university librarian is trained to assist students in locating and using these sources.

THE EXECUTIVE BRANCH

Presidential speeches, news conferences, executive orders, proclamations, and other actions are contained in the *Weekly Compilation of Presidential Documents* and in the *Papers of the President* issued yearly in bound volumes. Regulations issued by executive agencies are reported daily (except Monday) in the *Federal Register* and are found in the bound volumes of the *Code of Federal Regulations.* The *National Journal* is a magazine which specializes in reporting on the actions of executive agencies. Annual reports and other publications of bureaucracies are listed in the *Monthly Catalog of United States Government Publications.* Especially useful are the *Reports* of the United States Commission on Civil Rights.

THE LEGISLATIVE BRANCH

Bills introduced by members of Congress are found in the *Digest of General Bills and Resolutions,* issued in five cumulative volumes for each session of Congress. Hearings held by committees on bills are usually listed in library card catalogs under the name of the committee. The *Cumulative Index of Congressional Committees* lists hearings held between 1935 and 1963. Hearings after 1963 are also listed in the *Monthly Catalog of United States Government Publications,* under the name of the committee.

Bills reported from committee for floor action in each house are accompanied by a committee report. These reports are listed, by the name of the committee, in the *Monthly Catalog of United States Government Publications.* Each report is accompanied by a report number. Using that number, one consults the *Numerical Lists of Reports and Documents* to find the bound volume in which the report is located.

Reports on some important bills are also found in a private publication, *United States Code Congressional and Administrative News,* appearing weekly.

233

Congressional debate, floor amendments, and votes are contained in the *Congressional Record,* published daily when either house is in session.

Laws passed by Congress and signed by the president are bound by date of passage in *United States Statutes at Large.* Some bills are also reported after passage in *United States Code Congressional and Administrative News.* Laws are arranged by subject matter in *United States Code Annotated* (the latter version adds cases and executive orders which bear on the legislation). The *United States Code* has a table that indicates the relationship of each section to the *Code of Federal Regulations.* By using the two codes, one can find the legislation, executive orders based on the legislation, and the effect of judicial decisions on the law.

Congressional activities are reported extensively in a private publication, *Congressional Quarterly Weekly Reports.* A bound volume, the *Congressional Quarterly Almanac,* is published annually. Two massive volumes containing summaries of government action since World War II are *Congress and the Nation,* Parts I and II.

THE JUDICIARY

The most recent cases decided by the United States Supreme Court appear in *United States Law Week,* a private publication. The United States Government Printing Office distributes *Preliminary Prints* of Supreme Court decisions, and monthly reports are issued by two private companies: Lawyers Cooperative Publishing Company and West Publishing Company. *Lawyers' Edition, Supreme Court Reports* are monthly and yearly volumes that contain decisions of the Supreme Court, summarizing "headnotes" of points of law in the decisions and materials from briefs in important cases. The work of the Supreme Court is reviewed annually in the *Harvard Law Review* and in the *Supreme Court Review* issued by the University of Chicago School of Law.

Cases decided by the federal courts of appeal, the intermediate level of the federal court system, are contained in *Federal Reporter, 2nd Series.* Selected cases decided by the federal district courts are contained in the *Federal Supplement.*

The *Index to Legal Periodicals* lists law review and bar journal articles by author and subject. There is also an *Index to Periodicals Related to Law.* The *Public Affairs Information Service* (PAIS) volumes index articles, government documents, and books on public policy. *Law Books in Print* (1965) and its supplements are arranged by author and subject.

A citator is a reference book that locates each case in which a prior decision is cited in a particular jurisdiction. There are Shepards Citators for each state jurisdiction and for the federal system. One determines whether a particular case is still controlling or whether it has been modified, reversed, or distinguished in part in subsequent decisions by using the citator.

STATE GOVERNMENT

State legislation is usually published in an annotated code by private publishers. The *Automated Statutory Reporter* lists current amendments and new legislation for all states. The *Martindale-Hubbell Law Directory* (Volume IV) gives the text of important state legislation. The *Monthly Checklist of State Publications* is a bibliography, arranged alphabetically by state names, of the state publications that have been received by the Library of Congress.

LOCAL GOVERNMENT

Large cities generally have municipal libraries that have volumes containing executive proclamations and orders and municipal ordinances.

STATE AND LOCAL JUDICIARY

Selected state court decisions are published by West Publishing Company in seven regional reporters: Atlantic, Northeast, Northwest, Southern, Southeast, Southwest, and Pacific. Most states also publish court decisions. Municipal court decisions are often not reported in bound volumes but may be obtained at the courthouse in the clerk's office.

READINGS AND INFORMATION SOURCES

CHAPTER 2. RACISM

GENERAL

Logan, Rayford. *The Betrayal of the Negro.* (New York: Collier Books, 1965). The classic account of Reconstruction politics which led to deprivation of black civil rights and political power.

Bailey, Harry, ed. *Negro Politics in America.* (Columbus, Ohio: Charles E. Merrill, 1967). Recent studies of black politics.

Storing, Herbert, ed. *What Country Have I?* (New York: St. Martins Press, 1965). Black political thought.

Rodgers, Harrell, and Bullock, Charles. *Law and Social Change.* (New York: McGraw-Hill, 1972). Enforcement of civil rights acts and court orders.

LEGAL

Miller, Loren. *The Petitioners.* (Cleveland: World Publishing Co., 1966). An account of civil rights litigation before the Supreme Court.

Vose, Clement. *Caucasians Only.* (Berkeley: University of California Press, 1959). Case study of one Supreme Court case which ended judicial enforcement of racially restrictive covenants.

Friedman, Leon, ed. *Southern Justice.* (New York: Meridian Books, 1967). Shortcomings in the Southern judiciary.

King, Donald, and Quick, Charles, eds. *Legal Aspects of the Civil Rights Movement.* (Detroit: Wayne State University Press, 1965). Essays by lawyers and law professors on civil rights litigation.

SERIAL SOURCES

The Black Law Journal

The Civil Rights Citator

Poverty Law Reporter

Southern School News

ORGANIZATIONS

National Association for the Advancement of Colored People
14 Columbus Circle
New York, New York
(state and local chapters in most states)

NAACP Legal Defense and Educational Fund, Inc.
10 Columbus Circle
New York, New York

Congress of Racial Equality
200 West 135th Street
New York, New York

Law Students Civil Rights Research Council
156 Fifth Avenue
New York, New York

National Conference of Black Lawyers
112 West 120th Street
New York, New York

American Civil Liberties Union
156 Fifth Avenue
New York, New York

Southern Poverty Law Center
Washington Building
Montgomery, Alabama

U.S. Commission on Civil Rights
1405 Eye Street, N.W.
Washington, D.C.

CHAPTER 3. POVERTY

GENERAL

Harrington, Michael. *The Other America.* (Baltimore: Penguin Edition, 1964). The
    book that publicized the plight of the poor and led to the War on Poverty.
Keith-Lucas, Alan. *Decisions About People in Need.* (Chapel Hill: University of
    North Carolina Press, 1957). Case study of welfare office manipulation of
    clientele.
Steiner, Gilbert. *Social Insecurity.* (Chicago: Rand McNally, 1966). Definitive
    account of the patchwork social security and welfare systems.
Levitan, Sar. *The Great Society's Poor Law.* (Baltimore: The Johns Hopkins
    Press, 1969). Study of the effectiveness of the War on Poverty in its first
    four years.

LEGAL

Wald, Patricia, ed. *Law on Poverty.* (Washington, D.C.: U.S. Government Printing
    Office, 1965). A survey of legal problems of the poor.
Dorsen, Norman, ed. *The Rights of Americans.* (New York: Pantheon, 1971).
    See chapter by Edward Sparer, "The Right to Welfare."

SERIAL SOURCES

Welfare Law Bulletin

Poverty Law Reporter

ORGANIZATIONS

National Office for Rights of Indigents
10 Columbus Circle
New York, New York

The American Civil Liberties Union
Roger Baldwin Foundation
156 Fifth Avenue
New York, New York

The Southern Poverty Law Center
Washington Building
Montgomery, Alabama

Center for Law and Social Welfare Policy
Columbia University
New York, New York

Project on Social Welfare Law
New York University
New York, New York

The National Legal Aid and Defender Association
The American Bar Center
1155 East 60th Street
Chicago, Illinois

The Legal Services Program
Office of Economic Opportunity
1200 Nineteenth Street, N.W.
Washington, D.C.

National Welfare Rights Organization
Poverty/Rights Action Center
1419 H Street N.W.
Washington, D.C.

CHAPTER 4. SEXISM

GENERAL

Flexner, Eleanor. *A Century of Struggle.* (Cambridge: Harvard University Press, 1959). History of the suffrage movement and the work of women's organizations.

Kraditor, Eileen. *Ideas of the Woman Suffrage Movement.* (New York: Columbia University Press, 1965). Intellectual foundations of suffrage movement and discussion of splits within it.

Morgan, Robin, ed. *Sisterhood Is Powerful.* (New York: Vintage Books, 1970).

Anthology of current and past programs and proposals put forth by women to end discrimination against them. An extensive bibliography is included.

Tanner, Leslie, ed. *Voices From Women's Liberation.* (New York: Signet Books, 1970). Another useful anthology.

LEGAL

Kanowitz, Leo. *Women and the Law.* (Albuquerque: University of New Mexico Press, 1969). A review of the legal disabilities of women.

Brown, Barbara A.; Emerson, Thomas I.; Falk, Gail; and Freedman, Ann E. "The Equal Rights Amendment." *Yale Law Journal,* 80 (April 1971), p. 871. An analysis of the need for the Equal Rights Amendment based on shortcomings of Fourteenth Amendment and statutory protection.

"Equal Rights for Women." *Harvard Civil Rights-Civil Liberties Law Review,* 6 (March 1971), p. 215. A symposium with articles for and against the Equal Rights Amendment. Contributors include Norman Dorsen, Susan D. Ross, Paul A. Freund, Philip D. Kurland, Pauli Murray, Barbara Cavanagh, and Thomas I. Emerson.

SERIAL SOURCES

Women's Rights Law Reporter

The Spokeswoman

ORGANIZATIONS

National Organization for Women
Box 114, Cathedral Station
New York, New York 10025

Women's Action Alliance, Inc.
200 Park Avenue (Room 1520)
New York, New York 10017

New Women Lawyers
36 West 44th Street, Room 509
New York, New York

National Women's Political Caucus
707 Warner Building, N.W.
Washington, D.C.

Women's Coalition for Equal Employment Opportunity
2301 Forty-First Street, N.W.
Washington, D.C.

Citizens Advisory Council on the Status of Women
4211 Main Labor Building
Washington, D.C.

National Women's Political Caucus
1120 Fifth Avenue
New York, New York

CHAPTER 5. GAY LIBERATION

GENERAL

Weinberg, George. *Society and the Healthy Homosexual.* (New York: St. Martins Press, 1971). A critical study of psychoanalytic theories about homosexual behavior.

Teal, Donn. *The Gay Militants.* (New York: Stein and Day, 1971). A history of gay liberation.

Miller, Merle. *On Being Different.* (New York: Random House, 1971). Author discusses his homosexuality.

LEGAL

Szasz, Thomas. "Legal and Moral Aspects of Homosexuality." In Marmor, J., ed. *Sexual Inversion.* (New York: Basic Books, 1965). Legal disabilities of homosexuals.

SERIAL SOURCES

Gay Activist

Vector

Gay

Los Angeles Advocate

ORGANIZATIONS

Gay Activists Alliance
P.O. Box 2 Village Station
New York, New York

Society for Individual Rights
83 Sixth Street
San Francisco, California

Homophile Action League
928 Chestnut Street
Philadelphia, Pennsylvania

Metropolitan Community Church
2201 South Union
Los Angeles, California
(nationwide chapters)

The Mattachine Society
243 West End Avenue
New York, New York

Note: For a more detailed listing of the hundreds of gay organizations in the United States see *The Gay Insider, U.S.A.* by John Francis Hunter (New York: Olympia Press, 1972).

CHAPTER 6. CORRECTIONS

GENERAL

Rothman, David. *The Discovery of the Asylum.* (Boston: Little, Brown, 1971). History of movement for reform in treatment of criminals and the insane.

Jackson, George. *Soledad Brother.* (New York: Coward-McCann, 1970). First-hand account of prison life.

Pell, Eve, ed. *Maximum Security.* (New York: E. P. Dutton, 1972). Letters from prisoners in California.

President's Commission on Law Enforcement and the Administration of Justice. *Corrections* (Task Force Report). Washington, D.C.: U.S. Government Printing Office, 1967.

LEGAL

Packer, Herbert. *The Limits of the Criminal Sanction.* (Stanford: Stanford University Press, 1968). Critical view of the use of law to influence social behavior.

Hirschkop, Philip, and Milleman, Michael. "The Unconstitutionality of Prison Life." *Virginia Law Review,* 55 (1969) p. 795.

Jacob, Bruce. "Prison Discipline and Inmate Rights." *Harvard Civil Rights-Civil Liberties Review,* 5 (1970) p. 22.

Turner, L. "Establishing the Rule of Law in Prisons." *Stanford Law Review,* 23 (1971) p. 473. These articles provide an overview of current case law dealing with prisoners rights.

SERIAL SOURCES

The Black Law Journal

The Black Scholar

Journal of Police Science, Criminal Law, and Criminology

American Journal of Corrections

Federal Probation

Journal of Crime and Delinquency

Criminal Law Bulletin

Criminal Law Reporter

Prisoners Rights Newsletter

Crime Control Digest

FBI Law Enforcement Bulletin

ORGANIZATIONS

The Fortune Society
29 East 22nd Street
New York, New York

NAACP Legal Defense and Educational Fund
Corrections Project
10 Columbus Circle
New York, New York

The American Civil Liberties Union
156 Fifth Avenue
New York, New York

National Lawyers Guild
1 Hudson Street
New York, New York

Black Law Journal Prisoner Fund
3107 Campbell Hall
University of California, Los Angeles
Los Angeles, California

National Legal Aid and Defender Association
American Bar Center
1155 East 60th Street
Chicago, Illinois

National Council on Crime and Delinquency
200 Park Avenue
New York, New York

Law Enforcement Assistance Administration
633 Indiana Avenue, N.W.
Washington, D.C.

CHAPTER 7. SURVEILLANCE

GENERAL

Westin, Alan. *Privacy and Freedom.* (New York: Atheneum, 1967). A compre-
hensive account of the danger to individual freedom posed by surveillance
technology.
Miller, Arthur. *The Assault on Privacy.* (Ann Arbor: The University of Michigan
Press, 1971). A more recent survey of surveillance activities by various
levels of government.
Donner, Frank. "The Theory and Practice of American Political Intelligence."
New York Review of Books, April 22, 1971. Results of a study of local, state,
and national intelligence activities.
Uncle Sam is Watching You. (Washington, D.C.: Public Affairs Press, 1971).
Testimony offered before the Subcommittee on Constitutional Rights, Senate
Judiciary Committee, in February 1971 on military surveillance of civilian
political organizations. Contains an extensive bibliography.

LEGAL

Schwartz, Herman. "The Legitimation of Electronic Eavesdropping." *Michigan
Law Review,* 67 (1969), p. 455. Supreme Court and congressional action
between 1967–1969 studied.

"Note: Police Undercover Agents." *George Washington University Law Review*, 37 (1969), p. 634. Cases in which agents have played a role.

"Police Infiltration of Dissident Groups." *Journal of Criminal Law, Criminology, and Police Science*, 61 (1970), p. 181. Description of infiltration and legal remedies.

Askin, Frank. "Police Dossiers and Emerging Principles of First Amendment Adjudication." *Stanford Law Review*, 22 (1970), p. 196. Legal remedies against police practices of compiling intelligence dossiers.

SERIAL SOURCES

Criminal Law Quarterly

Crime Control Digest

Journal of Criminal Law, Criminology, and Police Science

FBI Bulletin

FBI Law Enforcement Journal

Criminal Law Reporter

Occasional hearings held by the Senate Committee on the Judiciary, Subcommittee on Constitutional Rights.

ORGANIZATIONS

American Civil Liberties Union
156 Fifth Avenue
New York, New York

Committee for Public Justice
50 West 57th Street
New York, New York

Emergency Civil Liberties Committee
25 East 26th Street
New York, New York

National Lawyers Guild
1 Hudson Street
New York, New York